IAN BAKER-FINCH

TO HELL AND BACK

IAN BAKER-FINCH

TO HELL AND BACK

GEOFF SAUNDERS

Foreword by **ADAM SCOTT**

Hardie Grant
BOOKS

Published in 2025 by Hardie Grant Books, an imprint of Hardie Grant Publishing

Hardie Grant Books (Melbourne)
Wurundjeri Country
Level 11, 36 Wellington Street
Collingwood, Victoria 3066

Hardie Grant North America
2912 Telegraph Ave
Berkeley, California 94705

hardiegrant.com/books

Hardie Grant acknowledges the Traditional Owners of the Country on which we work, the Wurundjeri People of the Kulin Nation and the Gadigal People of the Eora Nation, and recognises their continuing connection to the land, waters and culture. We pay our respects to their Elders past and present.

All rights reserved. No part of this publication may be reproduced, stored in a retrieval system or transmitted in any form by any means, electronic, mechanical, photocopying, recording or otherwise, without the prior written permission of the publishers and copyright holders.

The moral rights of the author have been asserted.

Copyright text © Geoff Saunders 2025

 A catalogue record for this book is available from the National Library of Australia

Ian Baker-Finch: To Hell and Back
ISBN 978 1 76145 164 5
ISBN 978 1 76144 283 4 (ebook)

10 9 8 7 6 5 4 3 2 1

Publishing Director: Pam Brewster
Head of Editorial: Jasmin Chua
Project Editor: Claire Davis
Editor: Martin Blake
Creative Director: Kristin Thomas
Cover Designer: Luke Causby, Blue Cork
Typesetter: Cannon Typesetting
Head of Production: Todd Rechner
Production Controller: Jessica Harvie

Front cover image David Cannon / Getty Images
Photo page xiii courtesy The R&A, 1991. Unless specified otherwise, photos are courtesy the Baker-Finch family.
Printed in China by RRD Donnelley.

 The paper this book is printed on is from FSC®-certified forests and other controlled sources. FSC® promotes environmentally responsible, socially beneficial and economically viable management of the world's forests.

With thanks to Maree, Jennie and Anna –
the heart of this book

CONTENTS

Foreword	xi
Introduction: Blue skies, no money and 'crap courses'	xv
Prologue: Beerwah Golf Club	xix

Chapter 1: The boy from Beerwah — 1
Growing up in the shadow of the Glass House Mountains

Chapter 2: Turning pro — 15
A fortunate choice of bosses at Gympie and Caloundra golf clubs

Chapter 3: Tales from the Troppo Tour — 25
The boys on the bus follow the sun

Chapter 4: Grinding it out — 39
'Ian, you have done it again' – the accountant delivers a lecture

Chapter 5: At the feet of the master — 51
A timely intervention from Peter Thomson

Chapter 6: The New Zealand Open 1983 — 61
Breaking through in Auckland

Chapter 7: The road to the British Open   71
Steve Frazer's inspired talent-spotting

Chapter 8: The 1984 Open, St Andrews   87
A major lesson around the Old Course

Chapter 9: The European Tour 1984   105
Travels with Jennie – and Steve Williams

Chapter 10: The Japan and Australasian tours 1985 to 1987   113
A world player

Chapter 11: A breakthrough in Europe   121
And first steps on the PGA Tour 1985 to 1988

Chapter 12: Joining the PGA Tour   137
Instant success on the toughest tour

Chapter 13: A return to the Auld Grey Toon   147
Studying Faldo – at close range

Chapter 14: The 1991 Open, Royal Birkdale   157
Leading after three rounds – again

Chapter 15: The final round   165
'I wanted to get my hands on that jug.'

Chapter 16: After the Open   177
Equipment changes and a new ball

Chapter 17: Cause for optimism   189
Contending in the majors

Chapter 18: The nightmare begins … and ends   199
'It was not my swing anymore.'

Chapter 19: A career change   213
'That is where you sit; there is the microphone.'

Chapter 20: Broadcasting – the beginning   223
From playing golf to analysing it

Chapter 21: Broadcasting – the later years   237
Welcoming – and farewelling – Sir Nick

Chapter 22: The Presidents Cup and the Olympics   247
And a gold medal

Chapter 23: Reflections   259
A life in golf

Q&A: Finchy on the future of golf   269
Bibliography   277
Acknowledgements   279

FOREWORD

I was a junior golfer in Australia from the late 1980s through the 1990s, when Ian Baker-Finch was a golfing hero to many, particularly to aspiring young players like me.

I grew up in the same region as Ian, the Sunshine Coast in South East Queensland, a beautiful part of the world that we both still gravitate to. In hindsight, we had an early connection. I won the 1991 Ian Baker-Finch Junior Classic at Beerwah Golf Club, under-12 division. Beerwah Golf Club happened to be Ian's home club. That win was a highlight early in my junior career. I still have a photo of Ian handing me my trophy. It was a special year for Australian golf – the year Ian won the Open Championship.

Whenever I think of Ian, I have a vivid mental image: a Daiwa visor, glasses, and his white glove still on while putting. And, of course, the Claret Jug.

I remember many stories about the prowess and excellence of 'Finchy' putting. He did not need to mark the comeback putts; Finchy just tapped them in with his Ping Anser putter like they were 'gimmies'. What confidence. These are legendary, true stories.

The things you remember!

How lucky it is when a childhood hero becomes a great mate. I've shared time with Ian, his wife, Jennie, and their two daughters,

Hayley and Laura, at three Presidents Cups. Throughout my career, I have had countless discussions with him on the range at PGA Tour events, and importantly we have shared a passion for the game of golf.

My passion for golf is partly instilled in me by my association with Ian. He has been a great role model to me for many years. He is a calm, thoughtful man who always gives back to the game. His play and demeanour at the highest levels of the game were exemplary. His support of junior golfers and young professionals remains. He has a long career in commentary and now serves as chairman of the PGA Australia board. All of that shows his incredible commitment to the game of golf.

I'm proud to know this man – a genuine man, a gentleman, a champion golfer, and an Australian golf legend.

Enjoy this book, this story of Ian's life. Well played, Ian. This is a life to be admired.

Adam Scott AM

Ian Baker-Finch, Champion Golfer of the Year 1991, with daughter Hayley.

INTRODUCTION

BLUE SKIES, NO MONEY AND 'CRAP COURSES'

Queensland, Australia, 1980

Something extraordinary was brewing in Queensland in the winter of 1980.

Over the next four decades, one golfer after another emerged from the Sunshine State's rough little courses to make a name for themselves in world golf. Within six years, the state was a conveyor belt for major champions.

In August 1980 two young professionals clambered on board a ten-seater Nissan rental van in Brisbane. Ian Baker-Finch, aged 19, and Wayne Grady, 23, joined 20 of their fellow professionals to contest the Sunshine Tour, a tiny pro-am circuit. This tour was at the very bottom of the pecking order of professional golf tours.

Jack Newton, a player who turned to commentating after a career-ending encounter with an aeroplane propeller in 1983, expressed his blunt view on Queensland's major winners: 'They are so good because they grew up playing such crap courses.'

As Baker-Finch and Grady set off to play the Sunshine Tour in a perfect climate for golf, another Queensland golf career was in its formative stages in a small country town 1300 kilometres north of Brisbane.

By 1980 five-year-old Karrie Webb had been playing golf for a year at the Ayr Golf Club.

West of Ayr, a mere 900 kilometres inland, the Norman family had also started playing golf on country courses. Toini Norman was still playing on the sand greens of Mount Isa Golf Club when, seven months pregnant with Greg, she was forced to take a short break from the game for her son's birth.

At about the same time the rented van left Brisbane, Greg Norman became No 1 on the European Tour Order of Merit, celebrating the milestone by spending US$100,000 on two Ferraris. The young pros may not all have liked Norman much, but he was instrumental in raising their career sights.

Grady's and Baker-Finch's aspirations were more modest than Norman's; they hoped to make enough money to survive as playing pros.

Six years on from the 1980 Sunshine Tour, the run of wins in the majors by Queenslanders started. Norman kicked it all off by triumphing in the 1986 Open Championship at Turnberry, the first of two majors for the 'Great White Shark'.

Two of the 'boys on the bus' – Grady, the PGA Championship 1990, and Baker-Finch, the Open Championship 1991 – secured their own majors. The run continued in 1993 with Norman's second Open at Royal St George's in England.

In 1996, Karrie Webb emerged as the best woman golfer in the world, accumulating seven major titles from 1999 to 2006. Webb is one of only a handful of Australians inducted into the World Golf Hall of Fame.

On a rainy Sunday afternoon at Augusta in April 2013, the Queensland major title baton was passed to Adam Scott from the Gold Coast, with his landmark win in the Masters anointing him as the first Australian to don a green jacket. Jason Day (US PGA 2015) from Beaudesert, south of Brisbane, and Cameron Smith (Open Championship 2022) continued the line of Queensland major winners. Smith came straight out of the Queensland mould, learning his golf as a toddler at working-class Wantima Country Club, 40 minutes' drive north of Brisbane.

In the last four decades Queensland golfers have won 14 of Australia's 19 major championships and have finished runners-up 21 times in majors in the same period.

Beginning with Norman's Open win in 1986, tiny rural towns like Beerwah, Ayr, Beaudesert and Kooralbyn have produced a steady stream of major golf champions.

It is hard to argue with Queensland's successful three-part formula when it comes to success at the top level: blue skies, no money and rugged golf courses.

This book tells the story of one of Queensland's major champions. Ian Baker-Finch left school as early as he could, scratched out a living as a golfer for five years, somehow reaching the pinnacle of world golf in 1991 by winning the Open Championship. Mark H McCormack commented that Baker-Finch's Open win 'couldn't happen to a nicer guy'.

What followed was one of the swiftest and cruellest collapses the game has witnessed. Within three years of his Open win at Birkdale, Baker-Finch's playing career was in tatters. But why? What went wrong? He only blamed himself for the crash.

When I discussed the reasons for writing this book with Ian Baker-Finch, he offered this thought: 'I think golfers will want to know what the hell happened to me.' After a pause he added, '*I* want to know what the hell happened to me!'

I hope this book provides the answers.

Geoff Saunders, 2024

QUEENSLAND'S MAJOR WINS SINCE 1986

- Australian golfers have won a total of 19 majors since 1986.
- Australian women golfers have won ten of the 19 majors.
- Queenslander Karrie Webb has won seven of the ten.
- Australian male golfers have won nine majors.
- Queenslanders have won seven of the nine.

Queensland's final tally: 14 of 19 Australian majors since 1986.

PROLOGUE

BEERWAH GOLF CLUB

South East Queensland 1975

THE 14-YEAR-OLD BOY placed the new book carefully on the grass. He opened it to a page with illustrations and laid his two new Brosnan irons on either side of the book to act as makeshift paperweights. Then Ian Baker-Finch began to hit balls.

It was 1975 and the book, which he would later refer to as his golfing bible, was *Golf My Way* by Jack Nicklaus with Ken Bowden. Released the year before, it had been a birthday present from his parents. The colour images he was concentrating so hard on showed Nicklaus near the top of his backswing and then completing his high follow-through. They were accompanied by lavish illustrations of the Nicklaus swing and method. The book was a bestseller, easy to follow and full of coaching wisdom.

Nicklaus, the greatest golfer of all time, graced the cover. Immaculately clad, he wore red trousers, a yellow pullover, and a white shirt and shoes. His fresh look was topped off with a mane of stylishly cut, longish blond hair. Nicklaus had arrived on the golf scene a few years earlier as 'Ohio Fats' and 'Fat Jack', but by 1974 he had lost a significant amount of weight. He was now the talisman of his sport, the incomparable 'Golden Bear'.

When teenager Ian was given his book, Nicklaus was at the peak of his career and regularly played the finest courses in the world. By contrast, young Baker-Finch had only recently fallen in love with the game and could frequently be found on the makeshift practice area between the 3rd green and the 4th tee at Beerwah Golf Club in rural Queensland. The nine-hole country course in the Sunshine Coast hinterland was not groomed, but Ian Baker-Finch still hit his practice shots from the rough, carefully avoiding taking divots on what passed for fairways. He followed his routine every day until darkness fell, when his mother would drive down from their hillside home in tiny Peachester and pick him up for dinner.

Nicklaus's book went with Ian to every practice session. As he hit balls, the boy would periodically glance down at the pages between shots, trying to duplicate the Nicklaus swing. He longed to inhabit Nicklaus's glamorous world of professional golf, travelling the world like a movie star and competing in the new era of golf, with its colour television broadcasts and enticing prize purses.

He wasn't the only devotee of the Nicklaus method of playing golf.

Just an hour and a half's drive south in Brisbane, a young, very blond trainee had just started working in the pro shop at Royal Queensland Golf Club for Charlie Earp, the club professional. At 20, Greg Norman was earning $38 a week and was also practising hard. As a 15-year-old learning the game at the Virginia Golf Club in Brisbane, he too had been given a Nicklaus book: *My 55 Ways to Lower Your Golf Score*. Like Ian, Norman studied *Golf My Way* intently when it was released in 1974.

Norman would say in 2020 of the Nicklaus books: 'That is all I studied. I could relate to Jack; I didn't know him but after reading those books I felt like I knew him.'

Ian Baker-Finch recalls the effect the Nicklaus book had on him. 'Jack's book was my bible when I left home, and I used it to teach myself golf. His book must have kick-started numerous golf pros' careers.'

Improbable as it may have seemed in 1975, both young Queenslanders were not far away from their own first-hand encounters with the 18-time major champion – and with each other.

CHAPTER 1

THE BOY FROM BEERWAH

Growing up in the shadow of the Glass House Mountains

THE GLASS HOUSE MOUNTAINS area in the hinterland of South East Queensland is visually one of the most dramatic in Australia. Travelling north from Brisbane on the Bruce Highway to the lookout at Wild Horse Mountain, a panoramic view reveals the gnarly cluster of cores of the extinct volcanoes making up the range. The peaks tower above the surrounding landscape. Standing on the deck of Her Majesty's Bark *Endeavour* in 1770, Lieutenant James Cook described the range as 'mountains of mystery which rise abruptly from rich volcanic flatlands'. He chose the name because the 12 peaks of the area reminded him of the soaring glass-factory furnace cones dominating the skylines of Yorkshire, back home in his native England.

The tiny village of Peachester sits on a hillside above the town of Beerwah, with views of the Sunshine Coast and white sand beaches shimmering in the distance.

Despite the natural beauty of the area, it was a hard-scrabble life for the occupants of the logging town when Tony and Joan Baker-Finch and their young, growing family moved to Peachester in 1951.

Tony's paternal grandfather's name was Baker, but he was killed in the Boer War in 1899. His widow remarried a man named Finch, and Tony's father grew up as Anthony Finch. However, when Anthony emigrated to Australia, he added 'Baker' to his surname in memory of his birth father.

Tony and Joan Baker-Finch had both served in World War II, and after being posted to Singapore Tony worked on the firing mechanisms of warplanes. When Singapore fell to the Japanese in February 1942, Tony and a group of mates had already escaped on a 26-foot boat to avoid capture. Ian Baker-Finch's father did not talk about his exploits in the war often, but when Ian was older Tony would sometimes open up to his youngest child, and so Tony's story was pieced together.

Ian learned that his father's group left Singapore harbour, scuttling as many boats as they could on the way out. 'They had no real weapons to defend themselves. All Dad had with him was a large knife he subsequently mounted on the wall at home in its scabbard – presumably reminding him of his war experience. He showed me some photos of the boat in which he sailed across the Timor Sea before finally landing in Darwin. He did tell me about being close to a hospital ship the Japanese bombed, right next to them, as they left the harbour.'

Joan grew up in Brisbane and served in the Women's Auxiliary Australian Air Force (WAAAF), working in signals and operating the 24-hour radar, protecting Australia's coastline from the Japanese during the six years of global conflict. Tony and Joan married straight after the war and started raising their family. Jennifer was born in 1946, Leslie in January 1948 and Lawrie in October 1951.

It would not have been easy for Tony and Joan and their first three children to make the transition from comparatively civilised Brisbane to the sparsely populated rural area 90 minutes north at Peachester. But they exchanged their tidy city home in the suburb of Toowong, with an inside toilet and bathroom, for a tiny farmhouse with an outside toilet and no shower. Any hot water required for bathing had to be boiled first. The Baker-Finches paid £1600 for their 11-hectare farm and worked the land intensively.

Ian Baker-Finch reflects on lives that were not easy for his working-class family. 'Mum and Dad did not have a car when they moved to Peachester with only a horse-drawn sled for transport; it was not until 1960 they could afford to buy a car, an old World War II vintage Buick. To go shopping six miles away in Beerwah, Mum had to cadge a lift on the milk truck early in the morning and she worked long days on our land while raising six children – with no money in the system.'

Ian Elks, a childhood friend of Ian's, remembers Tony and Joan Baker-Finch well. 'Ian's parents were tall, broad-shouldered people. Tony was softly spoken unless he wanted to get his point across, and Joan was a commanding woman. They needed to work hard, and be hard themselves, to survive.'

Ian recalls, 'Dad was a tough man, and we were all raised realising we had to work long hours to succeed.'

Post-war, Tony Baker-Finch finished his electrical apprenticeship after moving to the Sunshine Coast and was working from 7 am to 4 pm each day in a local sawmill. 'Dad eventually left the sawmill in the late 1950s when his electrical business became more viable, becoming the electrician for the area at a time when all the local farms were converting to electricity – he was busy. Mum had to work the farm mainly by herself and embarked on the backbreaking task of planting ten acres of pineapple plants, with Dad helping in whatever little spare time was left.'

Ian was the youngest of six children and was born in nearby Nambour Hospital on 24 October 1960. The family was close, but there was a 14-year spread of ages between the children, and with each child leaving home on reaching the age of 17 there was only a short time span when they were all living together. However, the family would still get together for Sunday lunches and Christmas dinners.

'The eight of us would sit around our small dining table with our elbows tucked in, with me guarding my food from my two older brothers! It was a reasonably meagre existence for my family back in those days. No one had any money, and we would have only one pair of shoes. I was the youngest boy in the family, but eventually grew enormous feet and always seemed to have hand-me-down shoes far too small for me! Trying to squeeze my size-twelve feet into size-ten shoes did not do my feet much good, creating some real problems in later years. However, we had a farm, plenty of healthy food and all of us children grew up big and strong. I ended up as the shortest of the three boys at six feet four. It was a good upbringing, and Dad was an intelligent man who was heavily involved in the community and running his own business.

'Mum was also a hard worker; a good woman who would occasionally slap me around the ear if I gave her cheek. She also had to put up with Dad, who was busier than a one-armed paper hanger. He had been through a rugged war, and he and his mates had undoubtedly done it tough while battling the Japanese for five years. They probably arrived home after the war with PTSD, not that any such condition had been heard of at the time.'

Having started out growing pineapples, the Baker-Finch farm developed into a chicken operation with 10,000 laying hens, as well as 500 pigs and 40 cattle. Barter was common in the local community, and the family would exchange eggs for butter, tomatoes, bananas and avocados.

'We would give milk to our next-door neighbour, and she would make butter for us,' recalls Ian. 'We would swap eggs for pineapples with her.'

He remembers his father as being 'a bit rough around the edges – and as children, often in bare feet, we learned to swear at the cows from an early age'. When Ian was about six, Joan Baker-Finch's life became even tougher when she contracted skin cancer on her nose. She had to endure the 90-minute drive down to Brisbane and back three times a week for radiation treatment.

Recreation time was scarce for Ian's parents, but in 1967 Tony started to take an interest in the smattering of golf coverage on television. *The Big Three*, named after Arnold Palmer, Gary Player and Jack Nicklaus, was first broadcast in Australia in 1966. Venues for the original series, such as the Firestone Country Club in Ohio and Mauna Kea in Hawaii, must have seemed exotic to Tony Baker-Finch.

He became hooked on golf, passing on to his family just how much fun the sport appeared to be, encouraging them to watch golf whenever it came on television. *The Big Three* and television were made for each other. Golf's popularity snowballed, mainly due to Arnold Palmer's remarkable charisma.

To Ian's father and his friends, seven-time major winner 'Arnie' appeared to be one of them, with his working-class background and massive forearms.

By the late 1960s the number of courses in Queensland was unable to satisfy the demand, particularly from new golfers. Tony Baker-Finch was far from the only farmer in the Beerwah area whose interest had been aroused, but the nearest courses were Caboolture (22 miles) and Woodford (13 miles). Mostly, they went to Woodford, but a decision was brewing, and Ian recalls, 'Dad and his mates decided they needed a golf club closer to home.'

They dealt with the problem with typical pragmatism and built it themselves. Tony Baker-Finch approached the Forestry Department, and the community was allocated 100 acres of white clay land in

Beerwah. 'It was swampy ground surrounded by pine trees and required extensive drainage work if their new course was to be made playable.'

Tony Baker-Finch was president of both the local Lions Club and the Returned and Services League of Australia (RSL). At an RSL meeting on 17 October 1967, Tony and his neighbour, Alan Free, proposed a feasibility study for the new course, to be known rather grandly as the Beerwah and District Memorial Golf Club, in acknowledgement of the connection with the RSL. The project was approved, and the local farmers and their machinery were mobilised to build the course while the curious local kangaroo population looked on. Charlie Earp, the professional at Royal Queensland Golf Club, provided advice to the enthusiastic group of volunteers on the course layout.

Ian remembers growing up while the course was built. 'I was seven years old, and I often travelled the six miles down from the top of the ridge at Peachester with Dad on his tractor to help the other farmers who were building our new golf club. One of the farmers had a big scoop and a crane to drain the land and build a small dam. It was a true community effort. The volunteer group constructed nine small "push up" greens. A bunch of old guys were running around planting paspalum in white clay as they built their course. I was even allowed to drive the machinery.' The new club members succeeded in building their course on a virtual swamp, with an early member describing the conditions as 'sodden in summer, rock hard in winter'.

The course opened in April 1970 and, in a familiar scenario, Ian's introduction to golf came at the age of ten when he started caddying for his father, who was playing Beerwah as regularly as his work schedule permitted. At the end of the round, when Tony Baker-Finch and his friends went into the clubhouse for a beer, Ian started swinging his father's clubs. The original clubhouse was the RSL building, which was on the inland side of the Bruce Highway, the main connection between Sydney and Cairns.

The course had one slight quirk: eight of its nine holes were situated on the opposite side of the highway from the clubhouse. For the first year of play, golfers had to walk across both lanes of the Bruce Highway to access eight holes and then cross back to their makeshift clubhouse at the conclusion of play. A new clubhouse was built in 1971, the course modified slightly, and crossing the highway was no longer required.

Joan Baker-Finch may have been busy with her family and the farm, but she certainly did not lack community spirit, becoming involved in the RSL, the Country Women's Association and the golf club.

When he was old enough, Ian was able to earn $5 an hour picking pineapples and tobacco, but inevitably he joined in the family fascination with golf and started playing himself when he was 11. For his twelfth birthday in 1972 he was given his own little set of clubs comprising a two-wood, three-iron, five-iron, seven-iron and putter. He also had a small black buggy and a brown golf bag. He worked hard to upgrade to a full set of clubs and played with his father regularly, enjoying the contact. Ian had no problems mixing with his father's friends and was occasionally offered a beer. He would refuse and explain he was only 12. A common response was: 'You're not twelve – look at the size of you!'

Ian Elks and his brothers grew up playing cricket and golf with the Finch family, as they were known in those days. Elks recalls the adults at Beerwah would go out to play their round on a Saturday and leave the two Ians and their mates at the golf club largely unsupervised. They would chip and putt, hit balls and unsurprisingly get up to the usual boys' brand of mischief.

Growing up, Ian tried most of the available sports on offer in the area, and liked them all – tennis, soccer and cricket. Of these, cricket was his favourite. He tried to play rugby, but because he was so large for his age he found himself out of his age group – a 12-year-old playing against 17-year-olds. 'Boys regularly hammered me as they were older and tougher than me. I was a big soft kid and rugby was not for me.'

The two Ians played in the same cricket team in their early teens, and one of their teammates was Steve Irwin from nearby Landsborough, who went on to find fame as the Crocodile Hunter, becoming the driving force behind his family's expansion of Australia Zoo. Ian remembers, 'Growing up, Steve was a weird little kid who used to play with snakes. Later in life we worked together for ten years, and I started running my junior tournament from 1991 in Beerwah. With the help of John Mellish, the pro at Beerwah, I would co-sponsor the event with the Irwin family's thriving business, Australia Zoo.'

The Elks family, with their poultry company Woodlands, and the Irwin family, operating Australia Zoo, would grow their businesses to become two of the largest employers in the Landsborough–Beerwah district. Tragically, Steve Irwin died in an encounter with a stingray in 2006, but his family continues to run the business successfully on a considerable scale.

When the time came for Ian to leave Peachester's tiny 35-pupil primary school he started high school in Caboolture, which was a return journey of two and a half hours from home. There was no formal golf program at the school, but Ian was granted limited access to play at the Caboolture Golf Club on Wednesdays. He still had to put up with ribbing from his peers as he took his golf clubs with him on the school bus each day so he could practise golf after school in Beerwah, before going home back up the hill at dusk. 'The other kids didn't even know what golf was and they often gave me a bit of stick – especially the older ones.'

When he arrived at Beerwah, Ian practised on the side of a vacant fairway. On Wednesdays he could often get a ride home to Peachester in the dark with his father after Tony had played nine holes with friends. On the other days of the week, Ian would either get a lift home from the golf club if one were available, or his devoted mother would drive down and pick him up to bring him home after his practice sessions. Once Ian was home, there was no compulsion to complete homework or study.

He worked tirelessly to improve his game. Ian Elks observed that by 13 Ian was practising every day and turning himself 'from a good club player into an exceptional golfer'. He was also benefitting from lessons given by a group of dedicated teaching professionals who regularly visited country courses on the Sunshine Coast. The group of pros drove from their larger urban clubs near Brisbane to foster the game in country Queensland. Denis Brosnan, a PGA professional, was part of this group and Ian Baker-Finch's first coach.

Ian Elks remembers, 'Before the afternoon competition started, we would get out on the 4th fairway, and I still remember ten to fifteen kids being lined up along the fairway hitting golf balls as the pros walked up and down the line coaching us. Ian and I were both in the group.'

From the moment the pros saw the big kid swing a club they recognised his potential. He possessed a naturally fluent swing and was developing a deadly short game. Ian was studying the golf books he had been given and soaking up regular advice and instruction from Brosnan. The pro's catchphrase was to 'reach for the sky' at the top of the backswing, which fitted neatly in with the images from *Golf My Way* as Ian developed his high-handed, upright swing.

Jack Egan (left) with Ian (right) in 1972. Ian was the Under-13 Queensland Schoolboy Champion.

Ian's competitive career started early and developed rapidly. In 1972 he won the under-13 title at the Queensland Schoolboy Championship and repeated his win two years later in the under-15s. The star of junior golf in Queensland at the time was Peter Senior, who was a better player than Ian as a junior and later became a legendary Australian player. Fortunately for Ian, Senior's age always kept him one grade ahead. Also ahead of Ian in age, Wayne Grady and Ossie Moore (also a future pro) were following in Greg Norman's footsteps and turning into fine players and state representatives at the senior level, while Ian had started matching par around Beerwah. By 1974 his handicap was down to around five.

Denis Brosnan was the professional at Redcliffe Golf Club and also ran the pro shop at the Caboolture Golf Club. He was a regular visitor to the country courses along with other pros Charlie Earp and Paul King, the group of committed professionals taking it as their duty to grow the game as they travelled around South East Queensland on weekends coaching groups of juniors and other golfers – at the same time as juggling their club responsibilities.

Two assistant pros with high-level playing skills, Terry Adcock and Tony Trimms, became role models for Ian and other Queensland juniors. 'It was great to have players who were better than me to play with – even if it was only once a month,' Ian remembers.

Brosnan had a work ethic mirroring Tony Baker-Finch's, and by 1974 he had started his own golf club manufacturing company, Brosnan Golf. At 14 Ian saved hard to acquire a new set of golf clubs from his mentor, in a distinctive lime green Dunlop–Slazenger golf bag. Brosnan custom-made the set for Ian. 'They were my own brand – Brosnans. I made them longer than standard and built them with thicker grips.' The coach emphasised to his young pupils the importance of chipping and putting. 'I encouraged all my pupils to chip as close to the hole as possible, and then I always made them putt out. Perhaps I stressed this too much as the juniors started betting against each other in their own form of skins game; by his early teens Ian had turned himself into a brilliant chipper and putter.'

Ian was devoting an increasing amount of his energy to his golf game – and rather less energy to schoolwork. His father Tony's mantra was being drilled into him: 'If you want something enough, you need to work your arse off.' Ian was doing just that with his golf, with the full support of both his mother and father. By 13 he had developed into a skilful player, chipping in on the last for 71 to break par on his home course for the first time and winning his first Beerwah club championship in 1975.

By 1975 Ian was winning titles above club level. Brosnan recalls Ian winning his under-15 age group by a whopping 20 shots in one of Australia's most prestigious junior tournaments, the Gary Player Classic.

The win at Pacific Golf Club in Brisbane was impressive enough but the pro was just as impressed by Ian, and by Tony's loyalty to him. Tony drove his son to and from Brisbane to play in the event, but on the long drive home to Peachester they detoured to the pro shop in Redcliffe to proudly show the trophy to Ian's coach.

The cricket career and school life of Ian Baker-Finch were already starting to take a back seat.

THE CROCODILE HUNTER CATCHES TWO SNAKES AND A DUCK

On the day that Ian was in Brisbane capturing the Gary Player Classic, his friends Ian Elks and Steve Irwin were representing the Southern District Cricket Club under-15 team in the 1975 district cricket grand final.

Ian would usually have been a team member. In the final, Steve Irwin's contribution to the team win was modest. He scored an early 'duck' (no runs) and then found himself in a spot of bother after disappearing to hunt reptiles. Using the coach's Esky cooler as a makeshift cage, he captured two poisonous brown snakes for the Irwin family reptile park. He earned one hiding from his coach and another from his father when he arrived home.

There is a team photo of the victorious team proudly displaying the shield. Ian Elks sits cross-legged in the front row and Steve Irwin stands solemnly in the back row.

The team photo notes: *Absent – I. Finch.*

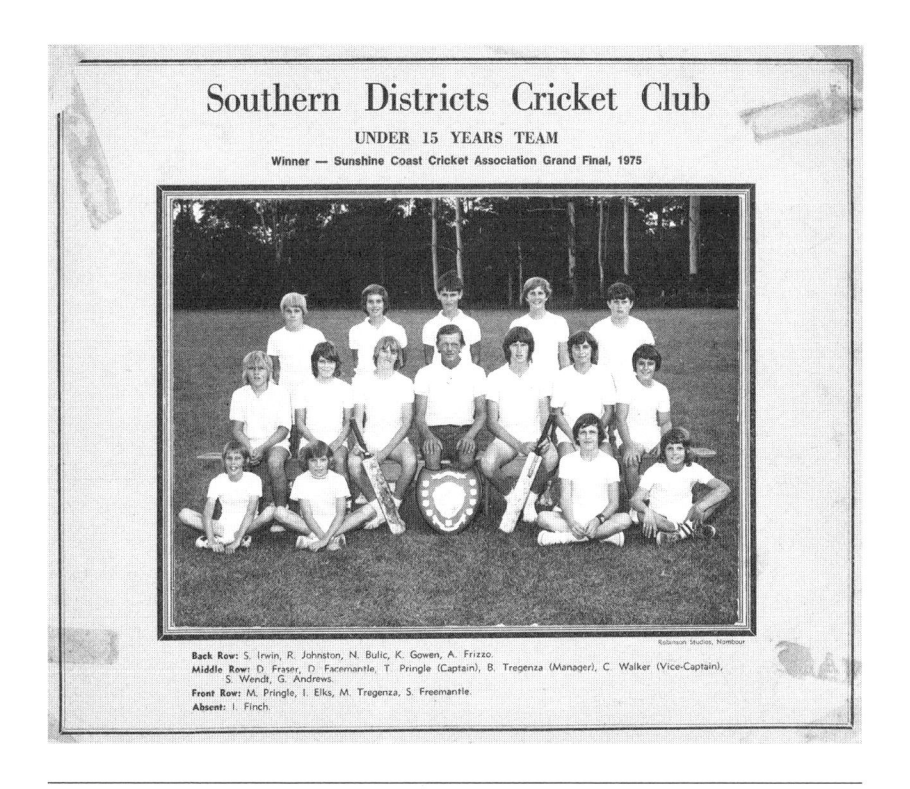

Southern Districts Cricket Club
UNDER 15 YEARS TEAM
Winner — Sunshine Coast Cricket Association Grand Final, 1975

Back Row: S. Irwin, R. Johnston, N. Bulic, K. Gowen, A. Frizzo.
Middle Row: D. Fraser, D. Facemantle, T. Pringle (Captain), B. Tregenza (Manager), C. Walker (Vice-Captain), S. Wendt, G. Andrews.
Front Row: M. Pringle, I. Elks, M. Tregenza, S. Freemantle.
Absent: I. Finch.

CHAPTER 2

TURNING PRO

*A fortunate choice of bosses at Gympie
and Caloundra golf clubs*

AT 15, IAN had given up any pretence of being interested in school or schoolwork. He had performed adequately enough at Caboolture High School to be in the A stream from grade eight and, with heart and mind elsewhere, still managed to remain in the top stream through grades nine and ten. In 1974 and 1975, the family home must suddenly have seemed very quiet and spacious: Robyn had left home at 17 for teachers' college, leaving Ian as the only remaining child.

Regular competition in tournaments was steadily improving Ian's golf. Ian may not have been a scratch golfer in 1975, but he was playing to a handicap of around five, which required him to average 70 around Beerwah's par-72 layout, which had a standard scratch rating of 65.

At the end of his junior year in high school (grade 10), Ian broached the subject of turning pro with his parents. He had occasionally been catching lifts to pro-ams with Gary Wright, the club pro at Gympie Golf Club, who helped advocate for Ian's new career in golf.

Plucking up his courage with Wright's support, Ian told Tony and Joan he wanted to leave school to pursue an unlikely career in golf.

'Gary took me home one night from a tournament on his way to Gympie – it was half an hour out of his way – drove up and told Mum and Dad, "Ian loves the game and could have a bit of potential. He can start working casually in the shop with me and, if he likes it, he can sign on as my assistant on either 1 January or 1 July next year."'

Tony replied, 'Well, he is starting young enough; I suppose he can always go back to school if it doesn't work out.'

Ian remembers, 'Mum and Dad were both so pleased to see me go they probably helped me pack! I was a pain in the backside at the time, but I knew what I wanted.'

The rules of the PGA of Australia at the time meant there were only two dates each year for an assistant to be indentured to their pro. There was only one problem: Wright already had an assistant. But in a happy twist of fate, shortly afterwards, the incumbent assistant's parents won the lottery and he resigned, clearing the way for Ian, who eagerly accepted the role in February. Wright hired Ian immediately but he could not start his traineeship until 1 July. He went to work at Gympie anyway, helping Wright while retaining his amateur status until the end of June, allowing him to win his second club championship at Beerwah.

Ian's new boss was a competent player who had previously tried his hand at playing golf for a living. A single season of mixed results on the Australian circuit was enough for the newly married Wright and his wife, and the struggling touring pro accepted her request to settle down and find a club job. At the time of first meeting Ian, Wright had only recently taken the club pro position at Gympie, a hilly 18-hole country course. The town, two hours' drive north of Peachester, had a population of 10,000 and was one of the larger regional centres in South East Queensland.

Wright had one child and another one on the way, and making a decent living at the club was hard – extremely hard. 'I needed to do plenty of extra coaching outside the club and visited another seven clubs in the area to give lessons,' he says. 'My work life involved getting up at three in the morning and going to wherever there was work. I used to go as far south as Noosa and west to Kingaroy and the other small clubs in the area.'

Wright was following this demanding pattern two to three days a week, travelling with a car full of clubs to sell to members. 'It was a hard life and I needed someone good back in the shop while I was away coaching. From the day Ian started he was a great assistant, responsible and terrific in the shop when I was away.'

Ian quickly learned the basics and excelled in what would now be called 'member services'. A range of mundane tasks was allocated to the new trainee, such as cleaning and buffing the members' clubs and learning basic club repairs. 'My job was to look after the members, and I liked looking after the shop; I could sell clubs and equipment to the members with Gary giving me a small percentage of each sale as a commission. It was only a couple of dollars, but it amused me how some of the members would hold off buying new clubs until Gary was away, knowing I would earn a commission.

'Gary was a great boss in every way. There was a metal roller door in the shop and when it was quiet at the club, he would let me roll it down and go over and practise my putting on the practice green nearby. In quiet times I used to putt for hours and hours. It probably did me no harm at all!

'I was a big, heavy kid when I first went to Gympie. Gary wanted me to be fitter and stronger and lose some weight. Gary was a runner and would get me up early in Gympie's bloody cold mornings. We would run on the course, and sometimes I would take a five-iron and hit a ball or two as far in front of me as I could and run after it. Great fun and very good for me.'

Later in life, Wright became an excellent speed golfer and could break 70 in under an hour.

Ian and his boss used every chance they had to practise their golf together, and Wright would give Ian some relatively basic coaching. 'The kid could play,' Wright recalls. 'I did a little bit of work on Ian's swing – he was always very upright as a young guy, not long off the tee, but very straight – and he always had a great short game.' They would practise near the 9th and 10th holes and aim at trees and other targets when their duties allowed. Wright made minor changes to Ian's game at Gympie.

Jack Nicklaus was still close at hand, recalls Ian. 'Gary taught me as best he could, but I still had my golfing bible with me, *Golf My Way*.'

Taking the lead from his boss, Ian worked hard at Gympie. He was paid $40 for a 60-hour week and was playing in as many tournaments as he could manage. Wright took him to a few of the local tournaments but, in the main, Ian needed to get up at 3 am each Monday to catch the bus for the six-hour $4 return trip to Brisbane to compete in 36-hole trainee matches.

'My mate Jeff Woodland was the assistant at Indooroopilly in Brisbane, and he would pick me up at the bus station in Brisbane and take me with him to each event. If I won, I might win ten or twenty dollars. Often, I would stay overnight at Jeff's place, and we might get up early to play eighteen holes the next morning. After the day's golf was done, we would share a pizza at Pizza Hut, have a few beers with one or two of the other trainees and then I would hop on the bus back to Gympie.'

Life for Ian as an apprentice pro in Gympie was a far cry from the cushioned comforts of young golfers playing college golf in the United States or even the aspiring amateurs and young pros competing in cities down south like Melbourne and Sydney. In 1976 Brisbane was a large country town with virtually no first-grade golf courses, but Ian was happily chasing the dream, aspiring 'to be a pro at a good club and hopefully become good enough to play in tournaments while holding down a club job'. He was aware of Australian club pros like Billy Dunk and Ted Ball, who were good-enough players to compete in professional tournaments.

Eighteen months into Ian's traineeship, Gary Wright's circumstances at Gympie changed and Ian was out of a job. No matter how hard Wright tried, the 500-member club at Gympie was not providing him with a sustainable living – despite the club's supportive membership. Wright had been coaching at the nine-hole Tewantin-Noosa Golf Club and when the course expanded to 18 holes in 1978, the club advertised for its first resident professional. Wright applied for the job and was successful, presenting an immediate problem for Ian: there was not enough work for Wright to take a full-time assistant with him to his new club. Wright recalls he also inherited 'an old bloke who would work in the bar, do some odd jobs and help in the pro shop when required, so I did not need a full-time assistant in the new position'.

After the first 18 months of his traineeship, Ian was stranded. He had to find a new club where he could complete the second half of his three-year traineeship to qualify for PGA membership.

Ian's inspired choice of bosses (or perhaps their choice of him) continued when he considered his next move. Gympie had been too far to travel to and from Peachester, but an opportunity as a trainee opened up at the Caloundra Golf Club in the southern Sunshine Coast, an hour east of Peachester and relatively close to Brisbane.

Much like Gary Wright, Tim Bell, the professional at Caloundra, epitomised the dedicated career club pro. He had worked in a pro shop at his golf club in Brisbane from the age of 13 and went on to complete his traineeship at the Pacific Golf Club. (In 1968 only a two-year term was required.) In 1971 he married Jenny, a top squash player, and the couple moved to New Guinea, where he was appointed the professional at the Rabaul Golf Club.

The Bells' two years in the area were happy enough until their concerns about security in Rabaul meant it was time to return to Queensland.

In 1974, still only in his mid-twenties, Tim Bell was appointed the professional at Caloundra Golf Club. Jenny Bell's brother was a member of Gympie Golf Club at the time of Gary Wright's departure, and Ian heard of the opportunity for an apprenticeship under Tim at Caloundra. Bell recalls, 'It all fell into place as Ian wanted to be closer to his parents, making it far easier for him to travel from Caloundra down to the tournaments around Brisbane.'

When Ian arrived in late 1977 to work at Caloundra, he sorted his own transport solution. 'Mum and Dad had been letting me drive from the age of fifteen – quite often to Gympie and back from Peachester. I could not get my first driver's licence until I was seventeen and I remember sitting on the steps of the police station in Gympie on my seventeenth birthday to pick up my licence. I was six foot four, one hundred and ninety pounds, and on the same day I went out and I bought my first car. It was a 1968 VE Valiant 273 V8 and it was an absolute beauty – dull sky blue with bucket seats. Here I was, living a Queensland boy's dream. What more could I want for – playing and working in golf for a living and owning my own car.'

From the outset Ian and the Bells formed a great working relationship at Caloundra.

Jenny Bell recalls with amusement how Ian sometimes asked for advice on sartorial matters. 'Ian was meticulous with his appearance,' she says. 'I put a mirror up in the shop for him and he would ask me questions like, "Do my socks match my shirt?" You just needed to look at his mother to see what she passed down to Ian. She was always immaculate and so was Ian.'

His daily duties had not changed too much from Gympie – cleaning the members' clubs, doing basic repairs and working long hours in the shop – but there were compensations for the young pro, such as the great social life at Caloundra.

Ian's living arrangements were about to change again. On his way home after work to his parents' new home in Morayfield, Ian was delivering a pair of golf shoes to a member when he had a serious car accident. The crash wrote off his treasured Valiant and Ian was thrown from the car, severely injuring his neck. Various hospital visits followed with one doctor gloomily predicting the teenager would never play golf again, but he did eventually recover.

While living with his parents at Morayfield, Ian received some good-natured ribbing from his father. Ian was a big teenager, 15 stone (95 kilograms) at age 15, and his father encouraged him to get fitter. Ian often awoke to Tony splashing cold water on his face and a wake-up call: 'How is the athlete this morning? Have you already been for your run?'

Jenny recalls, 'His mum naturally became concerned about Ian after the accident and asked us if Ian could stay at our home. Our kids were young at the time, and we had just moved into a house close to the golf course, but there was spare space under the house, so we built a bedroom and ensuite in there for Ian. We kept motorised carts at the house and he would start his working day by driving these over to the golf course early each morning. Ian became part of our family, happily babysitting our two young girls, Lisa and Jane, whenever requested.'

In the late 1970s the Caloundra Golf Club was a typical country course with about 650 members, but it was a step up from Gympie.

Ian worked hard on his golf in the club's triangular-shaped practice area and mixed easily with the members.

'They were great times. I learned to bet and play pool when I was back in Gympie with Gary, who was a keen gambler. I often bet five dollars with only one dollar in my pocket. Staying with the Bells I would stay on in the clubhouse for an hour after dark, playing pool with the members, before going back for dinner. As a fifteen- to nineteen-year-old I was in the company of adults most of the time, growing up quickly and learning how to play for money and gamble – you may not want a similar type of life for your kids now, but I don't think it did me any harm.'

While Ian was working at Caloundra, Tim Bell quickly realised Ian saw his future as a player. He remembers, 'Ian's father, Tony, was tough but supportive, a great man. However, it was clear he was genuinely concerned about Ian wanting to make his living as a player.'

Ian entered the 1979 Queensland Open, his first significant tournament. He made the cut after shooting 67 on the second day with his brother Laurie caddying for him. The Baker-Finch brothers were an imposing pair, with Laurie even taller than six-foot-four Ian, but Ian faded in the last round to finish tied in last place, winning the princely sum of $81.

As his trainee came to the end of his apprenticeship, Tim Bell gave the young pro the best advice he could by suggesting Ian expand his playing horizons. 'You need to get down to Melbourne and play the courses on the Sandbelt and the other great courses down there.'

After his performance in the Queensland Open, Ian took his boss's advice. Because he had made the cut at Indooroopilly in the Queensland Open, the young pro qualified to play in the next tournament, the 1979 Victorian PGA at Woodlands. Ian remembers the trip well. 'It was cold, rainy and miserable down south and I wasn't used to playing in those conditions. I didn't even own a jumper.'

Looking back on those early days at Gympie and Caloundra, Baker-Finch could not have found better mentors and bosses than Gary Wright and Tim and Jenny Bell. The two club pros stayed on in golf for the remainder of their working lives and, at 78 and 75 respectively in 2024, both look back fondly on Ian's time with them as their trainee. Their love of, and commitment to, the game has been passed on to the next generation. Gary Wright's son Michael became a playing professional with a 2024 PGA Champions Tour card. The Bells' daughter Jane Bell-Kent developed into a fine amateur player, turned professional and married another golf pro, Steve Kent.

By the end of June 1979 Ian had completed his three years as an apprentice at two unpretentious Queensland country clubs and was on his way as a player. At the same time, he was rubbing off some rough edges.

Looking back on Ian's development while away from Peachester, boyhood friend Ian Elks says, 'Ian had gone from Ian Finch, a bit of a smart alec and overweight, to working his arse off as a trainee. He came back as Ian Baker-Finch and was transformed. He arrived home in Beerwah a gentleman, polite and much improved as a player.

The masters and the apprentice. From left: Tim Bell, Gary Wright and Ian.

He walked into the room svelte, strong and confident, and everyone loved him. He had become what he is today.'

CALOUNDRA GOLF CLUB

In 2001, Ian contributed to the 50-year jubilee booklet for the Caloundra Golf Club.

> Caloundra Golf Club holds a very special place in my life and my golf career. As a seventeen-year-old assistant professional my lasting memories of the club and all its members, or family I should say, began. Memories of how the club sent me off on tour with $600 still burn deeply in my mind.
>
> Best wishes from one of the family.
> – Ian Baker-Finch

CHAPTER 3

TALES FROM THE TROPPO TOUR

The boys on the bus follow the sun

O<small>N 30 JUNE</small> 1979 Ian Baker-Finch's time as a trainee was over and his priority was to find tournaments to compete in, within the constraints of his meagre budget. He had no choice but to earn additional income outside golf. After leaving Caloundra, he returned home to work on farms in the surrounding area. His fitness and strength improved from hard physical labour, throwing tobacco bales around and picking pineapples. 'Somehow it always seemed to fall to me to load the trucks,' he says. 'The guys would be sitting down having smoko while I was running after the truck tossing the bales up on the back. I did this for two years and it did me a lot of good.'

He had shown that fleeting glimpse of form in the 1979 Queensland Open and played reasonably well in the few pro-ams he could find the time and money to compete in. Straight after qualifying as a professional, he entered the A$1500 Ipswich pro-am in July. The event brought him his first tournament victory and a first-prize cheque of A$285 – equivalent to three weeks' pay in the pro shop.

He was good at practising and a very straight hitter. Added to the mix were his great putting stroke and fine short game.

He played in whatever tournaments he could find, frequently topping up his bank account with work in the pro shop at Caloundra and whatever farm work was available. He remembers, 'I was now fully qualified, but still needed to come back and work for Tim from time to time. I could make a hundred dollars a week working for him, but I could earn one hundred and fifty dollars a week working for Jack Gowan on his farm picking pineapples and tobacco. It was hand-to-mouth stuff, but it kept me strong. It was a 5 am to 3 pm job with golf after work and on weekends.' After playing without distinction in pro-ams in Sydney, he took the opportunity to test his game on the two-month-long 1979 Sunshine Tour in Queensland. The tough, dead-end little tour, meandering haphazardly through his home state, beckoned Ian and 20 of his fellow professionals. Ian would play the tour for the next four years until 1982.

The Sunshine Tour had an interesting history. In 1959 at the age of 21, Charlie Earp was appointed professional at the Royal Queensland Golf Club, commonly called 'RQ'. Not far into what would end up a 40-year term, Earp was asked to attend a meeting of the Queensland PGA. One of the agenda items was the consideration of forming a subcommittee to establish a series of pro-am events on the east coast of Queensland. As 'the kid who had just started at RQ', Earp was appointed to a subcommittee whose aim was to find venues and prize money for the new circuit.

Earp had just seen the 1951 movie *Follow the Sun*, the Hollywood depiction of the life of Ben Hogan (played by Glenn Ford) on his climb to the top of American professional golf. In the movie, Hogan and his wife, Valerie (Anne Baxter), drove from tournament to tournament in the United States seeking fame and fortune. Earp was entranced by the concept of 'following the sun' and the glamorous life of a touring pro chasing prize money. He enlisted his friend and fellow professional Paul King to help him establish this new circuit, and the Sunshine Tour started modestly with three events in Mackay, where King was based, Townsville and Cairns.

Under the stewardship of Earp and King, the tour grew steadily. The events were held in Queensland's 'winter' months, which were generally sunny and, by most standards, warm. The events gave young professionals the chance to try their hand at tournament golf, and Earp and King played in several events themselves.

At its peak, the tour would start in South Australia, go to Alice Springs, up to Darwin, down to Mount Isa and then cross over to New Guinea, and head back to Cairns and down the east coast.

Even the prize money was improving. 'We were playing for about two to three thousand pounds in Alice Springs and Darwin but, without knocking the courses in Queensland, they did not compare with the courses down south. Players had to manufacture a broad range of shots to get results, which did not do us or the other players any harm.'

The mid-1960s saw a struggling young professional, David Graham, playing the Sunshine Tour after failing as a club pro in Tasmania. The teenager fled the nine-hole Seabrook Golf Club in debt, finding menial work in Sydney with golf manufacturer PGF. He reflected later that his 'life had hit rock bottom' around this time as had his self-confidence, and that he considered he possessed 'less natural ability than anyone on the circuit and was reminded of this often by the other players'. Graham's career only turned around after he met his future wife, Maureen, at the Cairns Open on the Sunshine Tour, as she went on to help the dour young golfer face his demons. Graham's fierce work ethic and his wife's support would lead to him winning both the US PGA Championship and US Open, two of the four men's major championships. He is one of three of his countrymen (with Peter Thomson and Greg Norman) to have won more than one major.

The tour attracted players from as far away as New Zealand. In 1969 22-year-old Kiwi professional John Lister had run out of the funding provided by his sponsors. He travelled to Queensland to play the Sunshine Tour with fellow New Zealand pros Walter Godfrey, Terry Kendall and Brian Boys. Their aim was to gain experience, play in decent weather and hopefully cover their expenses. The rugged condition of the courses was not a factor for the young pros. Lister won his first tournament at Alice Springs in 1969 with three identical rounds of 64. The event was played on sand greens and, before putting, players were permitted to rake the green down the line of the putt to the hole.

Lister remembers, 'We were allowed to take a one-club-length place on the fairways and a two-club-length placing was allowed in the rough, which consisted mainly of rocks and sand. Our accommodation on tour was often basic, with up to four of us young professionals sharing a motel room together. None of us complained and we had a lot of fun.' Lister would eventually graduate to play on the US PGA Tour.

Charlie Earp recalls a promising young amateur by the name of Norman showing up to play in a few Sunshine Tour events in the mid-1970s before turning pro. He eventually entered into an apprenticeship with him at Royal Queensland in 1975.

Growing coaching and club duties led both Earp and King to take a step back from organising and playing on the tour. In their absence during the early 1970s the number of pros entering the events dwindled as interest waned. In 1978 the Queensland PGA employed a young professional, John Downs, to reinvigorate and promote the tour. Downs had completed his apprenticeship at the Nudgee Golf Club in Brisbane under his father, Jack.

As Downs travelled throughout South East Queensland, coaching and selling clubs for Denis Brosnan, he recognised the potential for growing the pro-am circuit and how keen the smaller clubs were to host events. Downs successfully revived the Sunshine Tour, increasing the number of events from 20 to 50 by the time Ian's 1980 tour was underway. The 1980 schedule of 50 pro-ams was demanding and included venues like Gayndah, Maryborough, Rockhampton and Yeppoon. The circuit moved north as far as Cairns and then west to finish at Mount Isa. This final four-round event at Mount Isa was played for A$15,000.

Downs initiated an Order of Merit on the tour with a first prize of a return trip to the British Open Championship donated by Singapore Airlines. Entry into the Open was not guaranteed and the series winner would still be required to pre-qualify for the major. Downs ran the tour for seven years from 1978 and by 1985 the prize money at stake had increased from A$50,000 to approximately A$1 million.

One of the most memorable Sunshine tours was played in 1980 when Downs hired a Nissan ten-seater van, in which Ian and nine other young pros travelled in a bid to reduce their expenses. They set off in their basic rig, towing a U-Haul trailer for their luggage, chasing slim prize purses of between A$1000 and A$5000. The standard of the courses was variable, and about half of the venues were nine-hole courses rather than the full 18 holes and the pros were often billeted by the members of host golf clubs.

One of Ian's contemporaries on the van in 1980 was Wayne Grady. Ian and Wayne knew each other from junior golf and had both been coached earlier in their careers by Denis Brosnan, the professional based at Redcliffe Golf Club.

Grady immediately renamed the circuit the Troppo Tour: 'If you have to play on it, you go troppo!' The name aptly repurposed Aussie slang, where to 'go troppo' is to exhibit the signs of tropical madness.

Grady's place on the bus was hard-earned. The hierarchy of the Queensland PGA had been unconvinced of his ability and initially blocked his application for status as a playing pro. He was finally granted PGA membership after his father threatened legal action and forced a vote by members at the AGM.

Mirroring Norman's path to success, Grady had won two club championships in a row at the Virginia Golf Club near Brisbane before turning pro, and in 1978, two years after Norman, Grady duplicated Norman's win in the West Lakes Classic in Adelaide. Grady's early win in a full Australian Tour event was ample proof the Queensland PGA had underestimated his ability. But after his West Lakes victory, success proved to be elusive for Grady and, in the winter of 1980, he had nowhere else to play other than the Sunshine Tour.

Looking at photos taken at the time, it would be easy to mistake the group standing in front of the Nissan for a 1970s rock band, or perhaps a group of young Aussies having their first taste of Europe on a budget bus tour. With their fashionably long hair, bell-bottoms and lush moustaches – on those who could manage to grow them – the only indications these were professional athletes were the golf bags stowed none too carefully on the roof rack.

In the Australian way, Grady nicknamed Ian 'Bluebeard'. At 19 Ian was still not shaving every day and was trying – unsuccessfully – to cultivate a moustache.

When the Sunshine Tour pulled into town it was natural the group of fashionably dressed, single young golfers would attract a high degree of attention from women. John Downs remembers with amusement Ian's unique approach to meeting local girls who were generally the golf club members' daughters. Downs recalls how every year before 1983, the group of pros would pay return visits to the towns on the circuit, and he and his friends would be amazed when Ian immediately seemed to have a girl with him. 'IBF was a ladies' man before he met Jennie,' Downs says. 'And we all wondered how he did it in every town. We discovered his secret. After meeting a girl in one of the towns on the circuit, he would always send her a Christmas card – every year. He would also write letters to them and explained to me, "You have to keep in touch, mate."'

In 1980 Celeste Kutek was a newly minted teenager of 13 and living with her parents, Bill and Jan Pilcher, at 18 King Street, Ayr. The Pilcher family's life revolved around Ayr Golf Club and Celeste remembers Karrie Webb playing there as a young junior. When the Troppo Tour rolled into town it was party time. 'Ian was billeted with my family at our home for three or four years,' says Celeste. 'My sister Timmone and I happily shared a bedroom while Ian stayed, so he had a room to himself. He loved Mum's old-fashioned home-cooked meals and I vividly remember Ian wearing long white pants. All of the pros were broke, living from win to win; if one of them won a tournament they would compulsorily share their winnings within the group and shout everyone a meal and drinks. There was nowhere for a winner to hide, and they sure enjoyed the afterparties. I have to say King Street was golf mad. Mum was the associate president; she joined in and loved a beer as much as they did. For Ayr, the pro-am was an entire week of partying.'

A hierarchy quickly developed on the bus as it pulled out of Brisbane for the first pro-am at the tiny town of Gayndah, population 1200, four hours' drive north. John Downs drove and Ian sat next to him up the front. The remaining eight passengers filled the rest of the bus. The two occupants of the front seats swiftly acquired titles. Ian was 'Dad', the navigator and support driver when Downs needed a beer, and Downs, the driver, was 'Mum'. Grady contributed to the atmosphere by installing a large black rubbish bin filled and refilled with bottles of the beer of choice in Queensland at the time: XXXX lager.

Ian remembers, 'Grady was the ringleader. He had already been overseas to play and for him the Troppo Tour was probably more about fun. Most of us had to try and make a living out there. Wayne sat one row behind John and me, and he used his sand wedge to open the stubbies and as a baton to conduct the rabble throughout the day. There was a metal cage behind John and me. If Grady thought there was any bad behaviour, he would bang the rubber grip on the cage and call the bus to order.'

The songs of the 1970s blasted out at full volume on the van radio as the tour began. Music from the Beatles played, along with favourites like the Eagles, Black Sabbath and Creedence Clearwater Revival. 'I still know all the words of these songs,' Ian says. 'Even today when I hear them, I see Grades conducting us with his sand wedge. We were travelling around the tour happily in our bus, being billeted along the way by lovely families who seemed to enjoy having us to stay every year. We created many great relationships over the years and would also have far too many beers at night with the members of the host clubs.'

Not every player was lining up to secure a seat on the bus. At 21, Peter Senior was 18 months older than Ian. He had been an outstanding amateur and was – and still is – an exceptionally talented player. Looking back at the players he grew up with, Ian readily concedes Senior 'had more talent than the rest of us put together'. Senior had turned pro in 1978. Like Grady, he possessed a good-enough playing record to turn pro without having to serve the usual mandatory three-year apprenticeship at a club.

Senior says emphatically, 'I was never going to go on that bus and, as a non-drinker, did not ever want to be on that bus!'

Senior remembers the Troppo Tour 'as a training ground for us because there was nothing else on in the winter months for the pros.

Winter in northern Queensland is not winter in the usual sense and all the mining towns were just fantastic. We often used the mines' own accommodation, and they would put on barbecues for us most nights. The tournaments were usually eighteen-hole pro-ams, but there was the odd thirty-six-hole event. I am sure the courses we played on helped make better players of us. There was so much rubbish to play out of around the greens we quickly learned to play off anything.'

Ian has similar memories of the playing conditions on tour. 'The condition of some of the courses was pretty horrible,' he says. 'Many of them were municipal country courses on which stock was grazed to keep the grass down. When we played in Mount Isa, which was probably a thirty-thousand-dollar tournament, it was easy for us to damage our clubs. I remember being given a lovely set of Honma irons by Peter Thomson in 1981. They were mild steel irons and I was always scared on those courses in Queensland that I would ruin them, so I took the Honma seven-iron out and replaced it with an expendable "rock iron" to use from the rough.'

The touring group was mainly made up of Queenslanders and the occasional visitor from New Zealand, with a few players from the southern states gradually joining the tour. Two of these players, Mike Harwood and Peter Fowler, initially struggled with the courses and conditions on tour but were good-enough players to adapt. Despite John Downs's wry comment 'We didn't like the southerners too much', the non-Queenslanders were readily accepted as part of the group. Harwood retains vivid memories of his time on the Troppo Tour and its playing conditions. 'I would say in general the courses were disgusting. The best course we got to play all year was probably Townsville. It was a breath of fresh air to get to a place where there was grass, rather than having to play off stones.'

Not all the hazards on tour were confined to the golf courses and touring life was not for the faint-hearted. Senior recalls the young pros generally travelled in a convoy of about seven vehicles including the notorious van. He travelled with Peter McWhinney, who had a CB radio, and Gary Burmester. Senior's car with its radio would generally bring up the rear just in case any of the other vehicles got into trouble.

Travelling from town to town could be perilous on the Troppo Tour. There would often be high-speed warfare between the vehicles as eggs and other missiles were thrown from car to car. Ian proved to be a particular menace after an event at Dysart, near Rockhampton, in 1982 when travelling with Mike Harwood in his little General Motors Holden. He scored direct hits on most of the other cars and the van with eggs hurled from the open sunroof.

Revenge was sweet. The rest of the tourists lay in wait for the Holden in a ditch down the bottom of a hill and, when it slowed down, Jeff Woodland jumped out and landed a large, very moist cowpat in the middle of the Holden's windscreen.

The tourists regrouped in Mackay, cleaned their vehicles and played a game of cricket.

Further north of Mackay, near the Whitsunday Islands, lies South Molle Island, one of the more unusual stops on the Troppo Tour. Journeyman pro Tim Ireland, known affectionately as 'the Groover', played the tour in the late 1960s and remembers the venue well. 'We went over to South Molle to play for five hundred dollars. It was a six-hole course, and we had to play it three times to complete the eighteen. It was party time over there and after drinking all night some of us could barely tee it up. Ted Ball played the six first holes and sat down under a palm tree for a break. He fell asleep and we could not wake him, so six holes was it for Ted.'

Looking back, Senior recalls how much fun the tour was but, he says, 'It was also extremely competitive. We were young and we all wanted to be good. The main circuit would come along near the end of the year after the Troppo Tour and continue into early February the next year. The Troppo Tour was a wonderful place to prepare.'

Downs has his own take on this, believing the long days of travel, frequent hangovers and competing on poor courses hardened the players. 'On the rough courses we played we had no choice but to learn to hit all these different shots. It was good for the golfers' mental toughness. After every pro-am the players were the last to leave the clubhouse. Because so many of us were playing with horrendous hangovers, you had to concentrate hard to hit the ball, let alone post a number.'

Downs had his hands full maintaining decorum on the bus. 'We were getting close to Innisfail on tour in 1980 when I noticed all those in the back of the bus had decided to get naked. We had just pulled into the motel to check in, so I locked them in the bus and would not let them out until they put their clothes back on.'

Downs's nickname was amended from 'Mum' to 'Mother Superior'.

PETER SENIOR TAKES A DIVE – BUT SURVIVES

Despite the teetotal Peter Senior avoiding alcohol on tour, he almost suffered harm on one occasion in a bar in Gladstone, south of Rockhampton. He had been persuaded to step out of character by his fellow tourists and drank a large quantity of Kahlua, an innocuous-looking liquid that tasted like coffee to Senior. Sandbagged by his mates, he escaped back to his room worse for wear, where he decided to have a bath to sober up.

Downs recalls, 'The bath filled right up, and semi-conscious Peter slipped under the surface. Luckily Peter McWhinney returned to the room and managed to save Peter from drowning.'

Wayne Grady only toured twice – in 1980 and again in 1982. He recalls an alternative nickname for the Troppo Tour. 'At times we used to call it WAFWOTAM for "What a Fucking Waste of Time and Money". It was fantastic, but no one made any real money. I remember practising hard after playing one day, when one of my mates, Richard Lee, came out and said, "What are you practising for, Grades? We are not playing for any real money." I answered, "I am practising so that I never have to play on this bloody tour again!"'

Downs remembers scores of 'seven or eight under on some of these little country courses were common'. Part of his role was to arrange the prize-giving presentations and allocate the purse for each event. There was an unwritten rule the winner would have to wear a jacket at the presentation to maintain some decorum. Celeste Kutek from Ayr recalls, 'It became clear the boys only carried one jacket between them on the bus, which they rotated around the winners, much in the same way as they shared prize money. The winner would wear the jacket at the prize-giving, big or small. It was an amazing era.'

Ian did not help Downs to maintain standards when he won a pro-am event at Weipa in Cape York and promptly went missing just before the formalities started. 'Ian had tried a small amount of the Bob Hope [marijuana] given to him by one of the members after golf at Weipa,' says Downs. 'The presentation was due, and we could not find him anywhere. I looked around the back of the clubhouse and there he was, throwing his heart out behind a tree.'

Ian was consistently one of the better players and generally placed near the top on tour, without winning the Order of Merit or the Singapore Airlines prize trip to the Open. He remembers, 'Peter Senior certainly won the Order of Merit and possibly Peter McWhinney, Paul Foley and Gerry Taylor. This group on tour contained the best players and perhaps it was no coincidence that Senior, McWhinney and Foley did not really drink.'

By 1986, the tour Downs had helped to build had become so successful the Queensland PGA was able to employ a full-time staff member to run it.

In a 1980 photograph taken near Walkabout Creek, the boys on the bus are standing in front of the Nissan van, Ian Baker-Finch draping his right arm in relaxed fashion over his friend Wayne Grady's shoulder. A pair of young professional golfers having the time of their lives as they traversed the country courses in Queensland – two major champions in waiting.

The boys on the bus. From left: John Downs, Wayne Grady, Ian, Barty Hamers, Jeff Woodland, Gerry Taylor, Richard Parkin, Keith Ewald and Paul Foley. (Bob Hunt is not photographed.)

CHAPTER 4

GRINDING IT OUT

'Ian, you have done it again' – the accountant delivers a lecture

IAN BAKER-FINCH PLAYED on the Troppo Tour occasionally in 1979 and then full-time for four years from 1980 to 1983. The tour may have been great fun but was never going to provide the young pro and his mates with a living. They were cementing lifelong friendships while taking the opportunity to sharpen their games in winter on a tour of last resort.

He recalls, 'Wayne Grady and I were part of a group of the better players, and we would generally finish in the top few by the end of the tour but there was no real money in it. If one of us won a first prize of around two hundred and fifty dollars in a pro-am, we would invariably end up shouting our mates a few beers or a meal out from the winner's cheque.'

Ian was surviving hand to mouth on whatever meagre returns were available from tournament golf and he would still return occasionally to work part-time for Tim Bell.

At the end of each tax year from 1979 to 1982, he would take his paperwork, bank statements and receipts to his accountant, his brother Laurie, who was working for the tax department at the time.

His tax returns in those early years as a playing pro told a depressingly consistent story, with his brother delivering the same annual lecture: 'Ian, you have done it again. You are earning ten thousand dollars each year from golf and your expenses are about fifteen thousand dollars – how the hell are you surviving?'

Ian remained optimistic. It may not have appeared on any balance sheet, but Ian's putting stroke was his major asset. Mike Clayton, a playing contemporary of Ian's and now a renowned golf course architect, commented on Ian's putting in his insightful 2003 book, *Golf from the Inside*:

> When he first came out on the tour at the very end of the 1970s, he had a putting stroke to die for, and it never left him. He always looked perfect with the putter in his hand – beautiful grip, wonderful posture that somehow held him still in the wind and a rhythm to it that gave such a beautiful pace to the ball. More importantly, not only did it look good, but he made an uncommon number of putts.

Those early days of studying Nicklaus and his book *Golf My Way* had left their mark on the Baker-Finch swing – and on Greg Norman's. Ian's long, flowing swing with its high hand action was, according to Clayton, 'typical of a generation that grew up revering the greatest champion, Jack Nicklaus. Players and teachers alike decided this method was the way of the future.'

Clayton was well qualified to observe and analyse the players of his era and their swing trends. He was the Australian amateur champion in 1978 and Rookie of the Year after turning pro in 1982.

Clayton's 2003 observations on Baker-Finch are interesting: 'Ian swung his arms and the club way above his head at the top of the swing, then arched his back on the way down to fly the ball high into the air, as Nicklaus did.' Ian was playing for a high fade but was short off the tee. Clayton continues, 'It fell to the ground about two hundred and thirty yards from the tee. His game consisted of a method that moved the ball forward and got him into a place where he could take advantage of his short shots.'

From the late 1970s through to the early 1990s, there was nothing unusual in Ian's method. Coaches like Denis Brosnan were teaching pupils to position their hands as high as possible at the top of the backswing, arching the back in a 'reverse C' shape and then moving into impact was the norm. An entire generation may have played this way, but to progress his career, Ian had to deal with his lack of length with the driver.

By late 1980 Ian was making small change with a few minor placings in the occasional Australasian Tour event. He banked modest cheques in the Traralgon Classic, New South Wales PGA, Tweed Classic and the West Lakes Classic. His fellow Troppo tourist, Wayne Grady, was having a far better time of it, placing in the top three on two occasions and regularly collecting worthwhile cheques.

Ian pushed on, working hard on his game. At last, promising signs emerged for him in 1981 when he played in the New South Wales Open at the Lakes Golf Club in Sydney starting on 29 October. He equalled the low score in the event with his 68 in the second round, climbing from nowhere to seventh place. Ian's round included six birdies in a row, demonstrating his ability to hit it close to the pin and hole putts. His streak was one shy of Billy Dunk's Australian record of seven birdies in a row, set 11 years earlier.

In the third round he played with the event's eventual winner, 1981 Open Champion Bill Rogers from the United States. Ian unexpectedly became exposed to world-class players for the first time. He remembers playing with Rogers while observing him closely. 'I was thinking, "If he can win the British Open, so can I. I hit it as far as he does." He was a low-ball player and I was a high-ball player, but our games were similar and we were both good around and on the greens.' Ian's A$2156 cheque for finishing tied sixth was the largest of his career to date.

The 1981 season was becoming a milestone year in his career. The next week, at the Australian PGA Championship at Royal Melbourne, he was drawn with the legendary Spaniard Seve Ballesteros, who by this point had already won the Masters and an Open Championship. Again, Ian ran hot, scoring 30 on the front nine and attracting the attention of the media for the first time. For Ian, playing with Seve was memorable as he scored a par round that included six birdies. Seve commented, 'That young man – he is very good putter.' Ian more than held his own in the tournament and a final-round 70 left him in tied ninth place, earning a cheque for A$3190.

This was better for the fledgling pro – much better.

The spectre hanging over him – a lifetime cleaning members' clubs, selling tees and Mars Bars in the pro shop – was gradually fading. Not only had his performances brought him to the notice of the press, but unwittingly Ian had ignited the interest of five-time Open Champion Peter Thomson.

In the early 1980s, the Australasian Tour Ian was finally making a mark on was flourishing. The tour attracted high-quality fields, bolstered by regular participation from some of the stars of world golf. Gary Player arrived the week after the PGA in mid-November to capture the 1981 Tooth Classic in Coolangatta by four shots. Bill Rogers returned home to the United States for a short break of two weeks to shoot quail, and then arrived back to win the Australian Open starting on 19 November at the Victoria Golf Club.

Underlining the quality of the field, Norman was runner-up with Player taking third place.

Recognising Ian's promise, Thomson approached him during the PGA at Royal Melbourne. Ian was quoted in Thomson's biography, *The Complete Golfer*, on their first meeting:

> Peter thought I showed potential and introduced himself to me around that time. He saw me as a fresh young guy coming through who did not have anybody helping him, or any major tutor, and he helped me with the odd comment here and there.

Thomson suggested to Ian that, rather than returning to Queensland for the pro-am circuit in his home state, he would be better served by flying to New Zealand to finish his year off there. The season-ending visit to New Zealand had been on Thomson's schedule for many years, as well as that of his friend and Centenary Open Champion Kel Nagle. Ian followed the elder statesman's advice by playing in the brief three-week series of events in New Zealand, finishing tied tenth at the NZ PGA Championship, and collected decent cheques from the final two events of the 1981 year: the Air New Zealand event and the New Zealand Open.

So, 1981 had been a year of progress for Ian with a handful of low rounds in noteworthy events on the circuit. He had demonstrated on his good days that he could hold his own when competing against strong fields.

Then his game took a turn for the worse in early 1982, and there were times when it seemed Ian's goal of playing golf for a living was turning into a pipe dream.

'Early 1982 was a tough time for me,' says Ian. The young pro was struggling with his golf and starting to harbour serious doubts about his prospects of continuing to play for a living. The annual lecture from his accountant brother about his lack of financial success must only have increased his doubts.

Ian's friend Mike Harwood recalls travelling with Ian to play in the Gympie pro-am in 1982. 'This story has probably haunted me all my life,' says Harwood. 'Ian and I were travelling together on the pro-am tour. I was having a lot of success, but Ian was playing terribly. We had both played in the pro-am event at Gympie, where Ian had completed part of his apprenticeship, and he told me the president and captain had offered him the club professional's job there. I had just won the pro-am and, as we were driving away from the course, he told me they had given him a couple of weeks to think about their offer. He was interested, but over the next two weeks I convinced him he should just keep playing. I should have told Finchy to take the club job he had just been offered, and I might have won the British Open!'

After serious consideration, a struggling Ian turned down the security of the club job at Gympie. His prospects of earning a living as a player gradually improved as the year wore on. 'I knew I could play after having some success at the end of 1981, but at the start of 1982 I was not very good at all. It was troubling me, and I did not think I was getting any better, but a couple of low rounds in the north of Queensland gradually altered my mindset.'

The Australian PGA Tour enveloped the three-event New Zealand Circuit in 1982 to form a combined Australasian Tour. Playing in the later Australian events, Ian finally started to pick up regular pay cheques. He placed in the top 20 in ten of the events played before the 1982 Australian Open.

Then came another landmark event for Ian in November 1982. He met Jennie Stanway in Melbourne.

'I had noticed Jennie working at events behind the tournament desk – she was a great-looking girl and impossible to miss. But I was still pretty shy then, just a young pro trying to make my way in golf. I had to lean on my friend and fellow pro Steve Bann to make the first introduction to Jennie at the 1982 PGA Championship in Melbourne.'

JENNIE AVOIDS DATING A GOLFER – ALMOST

Jennie's introduction to Ian by Steve Bann came with an obstacle or two. Jennie remembers, 'I was working at the tournament … and Ian noticed me. He knew my mum and was one of the golfers, among hundreds of others, and I thought, "Oh yeah, he's kind of cute." But I wanted nothing to do with golfers. I only knew the golfers who were starting out and thought, "That is not the life I want for myself." I had a good job and did not need all of that. So, he may have been very good-looking – but he was also a golfer.'

Some of Ian's qualities partly mitigated Jennie's prejudices against golfers. Jennie explains, 'Apart from the fact he was quite handsome, he was always very polite. He seemed to have time for everybody, not just me. Ian did not seem to be like a typical Aussie.

'He was also tall, nicely built and a clothes hanger.'

Jennie was born in the eastern Melbourne suburb of Bulleen and had been brought up in Melbourne with her older sister, Julie, and her twin, Jacquie. It was a happy, sporty early childhood, but Jennie's parents split up when she was six. Unusually for the time, Jennie's father was awarded custody of the three girls by a judge, but they would still see their mother for a day or two most weeks. Her mother then met a club professional, Viv Billings, and married him.

Her father also remarried. Jennie's stepmother, Eva Stanway, would become like a second mother to Jennie and her two sisters.

When Jennie was 13 her father and stepmother added to their blended family with a boy, Bill, and later a girl, Karen. Jennie remembers a happy childhood with plenty of sport in Melbourne – little athletics, netball and basketball.

Like Ian, Jennie left school in year ten but was two years older than Ian. Growing up, Jennie became fiercely independent. When she was 16 her father moved to Hong Kong and as a result Jennie and her twin moved to England to live with their mother and stepfather who had found a position there, eventually working for the respected English coach John Jacobs.

Jennie worked for a dentist while training at night to be a dental assistant, and also worked in the bar at the John Jacobs Golf Centre in Newcastle. She eventually returned to Australia via Singapore at the age of 20 and found a position working at golf tournaments for promoters Tony Charlton and Peter Williams.

She loved the new position, remembering, 'It was a great job. Only a few of us were in the office and we helped run the tournament. The director was Tony and Peter did the brochures and the publicity. It was a job where if I had nothing to do in the middle of the year before the season came, I would go home at one o'clock. During the golf tournament itself, when required, it could be a twenty-one-hour day for me.'

Ian remembers, 'Steve went into bat for me, telling Jennie, "You will like Ian. He is a mate of mine, and you should go out with him." Steve arranged a blind date for us.' The couple went out to dinner as part of a group of ten. Ian must have been keen, recounting, 'It was Friday night of the Australian PGA in Melbourne and Jennie arrived at the restaurant two hours late at around 9 pm. She had been required to stay behind to finish the draw for the tournament. We ate at a little place in Glen Iris, and after the dinner I drove her home to her aunt's place where she was staying.'

Jennie says, 'Everything really stemmed from our first dinner together … with both of us fighting it a bit.'

The 1982 Australian Open started in Sydney on 18 November at the Australian Golf Club. The event had attracted such strong fields in the past it was often referred to as 'the fifth major'. The strength of the fields on tour was demonstrated by the quality of the players finishing behind the winner of the event, Bob Shearer, who was the only player to break par. Payne Stewart finished runner-up, closely followed by Nicklaus and Rogers. Nicklaus had the last word on the appearance-money issue that had caused a media storm in Sydney. He insisted on forfeiting his A$50,000 appearance fee for attending the event, adding it instead to the event's total prize purse. Ian finished at the tail of the field after barely making the cut.

But Ian did see Jennie again during the Australian Open week. He was staying with the Hohnen family during the tournament, and she was invited to their house for a barbecue. Ian and Jennie chatted happily, but Jennie still did not seem very interested in going out with a golfer. The couple may have struck up a friendship during the two final Australian events of 1982, but Ian flew to New Zealand the morning after the Australian Open for the final three tournaments to wind up the Australasian circuit.

Ian arrived in New Zealand in late November to contest the New Zealand PGA, the New Zealand BP Open and finally the Air New Zealand–Shell Open in mid-December of 1982. On the first day of the New Zealand Open in Christchurch, Ian had not given up on Jennie. 'The twenty-fifth of November was Jennie's birthday, so I sent her flowers from New Zealand.'

His cheque for fourteenth place at the New Zealand Open, held at Christchurch Golf Club at Shirley Links, could have been healthier had he not hit shots out of bounds on the par-five 4th hole in each of his four rounds.

AN ACCOMMODATION UPGRADE

Ian and his fellow touring pros became conditioned to rudimentary shared accommodation, and even dormitories, on tour. Ian and his roommate Steve Bann were practising at Shirley Links before the New Zealand Open when Ian's 'impressively high and rather beautiful follow-through' caught the eye of Andrew Hopkins, the local manager of sponsor BP. He chatted to the young pros and asked them where they were staying. Ian said he had booked a low-cost motel near the course. Hopkins offered Ian the keys to his parents' substantial family home in Fendalton, one of Christchurch's wealthiest suburbs.

Steve and Ian promptly cancelled the motel near the course.

The house had a swimming pool, a large lawn tennis court and even a car. The two young pros made themselves at home, but Hopkins did receive an alarmed call from his parents' neighbour, who told him there were two trespassers pitching golf balls all around the immaculate lawn.

Peter Thomson, 53 years old and in the twilight of his playing career in 1982, appeared in New Zealand for his swansong. A member of the New Zealand press asked Thomson about the prospects of the next generation of Australian golfers, and Thomson responded, 'Young Baker-Finch is a fine prospect but perhaps worries too much about the look of his swing.'

Thomson's suggestion to Ian that he should consider contesting the tour, including the New Zealand Open, was based on his personal experience. As a 20-year-old, Thomson had won the same event at the same club 32 years earlier in 1950 – his first professional win. Thomson's suggestion to Ian to finish his season over the Tasman Sea proved its worth as he collected respectable cheques in all three of the New Zealand events.

At the end of 1982, the players looked back at an Australasian Tour with 17 events that was well placed to attract high-quality fields of Australian and New Zealand players, supplemented by regular visits from US PGA and European Tour players. Top European players such as Seve Ballesteros, Sandy Lyle, Bernhard Langer and Nick Faldo competed Down Under, where they were joined by Ryder Cup players such as Eamonn Darcy, Maurice Bembridge and Sam Torrance. The legion of golf fans in Australasia in the 1980s did not care about the appearance-money debate in the media. The fans were only interested in flocking to tournaments featuring the stars of world golf such as South African Gary Player, and many top American players including Arnold Palmer, Jack Nicklaus, Payne Stewart, Lee Trevino, Mark O'Meara and Bill Rogers.

Ian had made significant progress in his career during his 1982 season as he contended regularly against strong fields on the home circuit. By the early 1980s Ian and Wayne Grady were being joined further afield on various world golf tours by promising young Australian golfers such as Mike Clayton, Peter Fowler, Mike Harwood, Peter Senior, Rodger Davis, Jeff Woodland and Brian Jones. The players from a decade before also remained competitive: Terry Gale, Graham Marsh, Bob Shearer, Stewart Ginn and Jack Newton led the way, and they were inspired as a group by the feats of the ultimate Australian trailblazer of his era, love him or dislike him, Greg Norman.

Ian and Jennie were keeping their long-distance relationship alive by writing to each other. Jennie recalls, 'I used to leave these little cards you could get saying "I love you" and I would hide them in his suitcase.'

Ian also remembers the challenges at the incubation stage of the new relationship. 'Jennie kept me at arm's length until February–March the next year and then we started to see each other again.

In 1983 I went off on the Troppo Tour for the final time and was travelling a great deal, so the opportunities to see each other that year were very limited. Finally, by the beginning of 1984 we started to see each other full-time.'

Ian would also avoid the annual lecture from his accountant brother, as he placed thirty-eighth on the Australasian Tour money list to move for the first time into a positive cashflow from golf. Grady and Clayton had taken their own careers one step further than Ian in 1982, both placing in the top 200 money winners in world golf. Grady finished one hundred and eighty-ninth with US$42,494 and Clayton one hundred and ninety-seventh with US$40,629.

By the end of 1982 Charlie Earp had been proven correct: his beloved Sunshine Tour, with its nine-hole courses and quirky little greens, had done its graduates no harm at all.

CHAPTER 5

AT THE FEET OF THE MASTER

A timely intervention from Peter Thomson

THE BEGINNING OF Ian Baker-Finch's long-term friendship with fellow Australian and five-time Open Champion Peter Thomson was a milestone in his career. Thomson's interest in the young Queenslander was sparked by Ian's ability to run hot in streaks, and the all-time great's suggestion that Ian should go to New Zealand at the end of the 1981 season was perfectly timed. Over the next three or four years a series of low-key interventions from Thomson were important factors in the development of Ian's career.

It was an unlikely friendship in many ways. There was a 31-year difference in age between the two men, and in 1981 they were at quite different stages of their careers. Peter Thomson was 52, with five Open championships to his name, secure in his position as Australia's greatest golfer. Ian was a 21-year-old tyro, showing the odd fleeting sign of promise. Their clothing tastes were very different, but each had a distinctive style. Thomson dressed in muted greys and whites, favouring the button-up cardigan, paired with his preferred plain-white Dunlop shoes. It was his own look, not unlike his idol Hogan's – understated and classy. The young Baker-Finch's preference was for bright colours, often pink, and chequered, flared trousers. New Zealand *Sunday Times* writer Peter Williams described Ian as follows: 'tall, suntanned, with dark hair flowing to shoulder length, Baker-Finch has all the physical attributes needed to become a sporting pop star'.

There was little or nothing of the pop star in Thomson. The two men may have been from different sartorial planets, but this presented no barrier to the bond developing between them from 1981 – they had become master and pupil.

Thomson was a remarkable man and there was far more to him than his unquestioned ability as a player. The veteran champion had reached an interesting stage in his own golf career. For decades he had pursued his many and varied interests outside tournament golf. He had been a long-time columnist for *The Age* newspaper in his hometown Melbourne, a television commentator and president of the Australian PGA from 1962 to 1994.

In early 1982 Thomson even became embroiled in the rough and tumble of politics. However, he was badly mauled in his first and only attempt to enter the political arena. A dramatic swing against the Liberal Party on polling day thwarted his bid for a seat in parliament.

The end of Thomson's political aspirations presented him with the opportunity to pursue a short but extraordinarily successful senior golf career in America from 1984, on what is now the PGA Champions Tour.

At the time of meeting Ian, the multi-talented Thomson was also involved in his thriving golf course design practice with friend and partner Michael Wolveridge. The business started in 1965 in conjunction with Commander John Harris, a prolific English architect who had designed 250 courses, mainly outside the UK. South Pacific Golf Pty Ltd had developed from there into the international practice of Thomson Wolveridge and Associates. Thomson did not retire until the age of 86, after 50 years in the golf course design business.

Despite his other interests, Thomson still found time to mentor a few young golfers who were making their way through the ranks. His advice to the young hopefuls was frequently delivered in his typically dry style. One young pro sought out Thomson's counsel, expecting detailed advice from the great man. Thomson cryptically advised the crestfallen young player his way forward was to 'shoot lower scores'.

The senior pro observed 21-year-old Ian had talent coupled with a good work ethic but required some guidance with his swing. However, Thomson never assumed the role of a full-time coach with his interest being mainly paternal. Ian described Thomson's role as being like a father figure, noting, 'Peter was always there when I needed him.'

Thomson's method and approach to the game was quite different from Ian's and that of Ian's boyhood idol, Jack Nicklaus. Thomson played golf in America at an early stage of his career – and did not enjoy it. The courses he encountered in the States were, in the main, heavily watered and in poor condition. Golf in America was also played mainly in the air.

Thomson preferred the fine turf and classic courses of Britain – bouncy, firm, with the wind adding another dimension. Most of the famous Open venues were seaside or 'links' courses. His game suited such conditions as he quickly developed into the finest links player in the world. Strategising his way around the course, Thomson focused on where the ball should land and, equally importantly, where it would roll upon landing.

He made the United Kingdom his domain for 22 years from 1951 to 1973, during which time he never missed a cut in an Open. He won the Claret Jug three times in a row from 1954 to 1956, again in 1958, and then a fifth and final time in 1965, silencing the critics who had suggested his first four Open wins had been played against less than world-class opposition. In his 1965 Open win at Royal Birkdale, he overcame a new generation of players – including Nicklaus and the two other members of the 'big three', Palmer and Player.

The Melburnian's overall record in the Open is barely believable: five wins – bettered only by Harry Vardon's six and equalled by three others, James Braid, J H Taylor and Tom Watson – three times a runner-up and 18 times in the top ten in his 30 appearances.

Thomson's swing was characterised by its simplicity and effectiveness. He learned the game in Melbourne playing on quick greens and fast courses with their abundance of run, especially in summer. He set himself up beautifully to the ball, an area in which he exercised particular care. No excess movement was evident in his method, and seemingly little effort expended in his delivery of a flat swing appearing to be remarkably similar to his idol Ben Hogan's. While Hogan may have been an enigma to many of his fellow golfers on tour, Thomson became close to him in the 1950s, discovering they shared a similar dry sense of humour. He believed the dour little champion from Texas was the finest golfer he had seen and ranked Sam Snead not too far behind Hogan.

But by 1982 Ian's early devotion to the Jack Nicklaus method was causing problems for him, resulting in a high, weak fade off the tee and a lack of length. The 53-year-old Thomson was there and ready to help, quietly and understatedly stepping in to help the struggling young pro. In 1991 Ian looked back on his problems of the time, telling Peter Mitchell, author of *The Complete Golfer*, 'At the end of 1982 I was having a lot of trouble because I'd always tried to play like Nicklaus by hitting the ball high with fade, but I was never powerful enough.'

Ian reflects on his problems with his ball striking during this period. 'I was in New Zealand for the airline's tournament [the Air

New Zealand–Shell Open], and we had to practise down at a narrow park not far from Titirangi Golf Club. I was over to one side, hitting these pathetic, weak fades. Peter just happened to be walking past and watched me hit some dreadful shots to the right and on to the road. He stepped forward and said, "Okay, now is the time. I think you should do this." It was the first time he changed my swing around.'

The cure was to turn further and swing flatter. The impromptu lesson took place at Shadbolt Park, home of local rugby club Bay Lynn and walking distance from Titirangi's 16th and 17th holes. Peter Headland was an Australian touring pro at the time and happened to walk down to the practice fairway, observing the lesson in progress with interest. 'Ian was a lovely guy then but was certainly no world-beater. He stood open at address and had a big lateral movement off the ball with his arms and the club very high at the top of his backswing. I was quite taken aback to see Peter patiently teaching Ian to stand squarer, even slightly closed. The next step involved Peter telling Ian to swing around himself more and to lower his arms and the club. He was being taught a method exactly the opposite of his existing way of swinging. Right from that moment he started to play well, and his high weak cut disappeared.'

Ian's feet had been repositioned, and he immediately started hitting lower draws down the middle of the makeshift practice area. The lesson from Thomson was timely and effective, the tuition at the unlikely venue bringing Ian's 1982 season to a close.

Decades later Ian still recalls Thomson's intervention. 'The lesson from Peter in New Zealand was the start of it for me. I can still visualise everything he did for me at the time.'

Mike Clayton also remembers Thomson's advice to Ian. 'Peter was not a teacher at all, but he had a technically great swing. He knew the opposite of a high cut was a low draw and Ian told me Peter told him to "put the ball back in my stance and swing around my arse".

It made perfect sense. It completely changed Ian's swing and it was so much better.'

Early in his career Thomson had himself benefited from mentoring by the trailblazing Norman Von Nida, one of Australia's greatest players, and one of the first to travel abroad to earn his living as far back as the late 1940s. The mentorship went to the extent of the pair agreeing to pool their prize money and share expenses during Thomson's first visit to the UK in 1951.

When Ian travelled to Melbourne for tournaments he would often stay with Peter and Mary Thomson, but with the end of the 1982 season came the unexpected invitation for him to spend a few weeks with the Thomson family at their holiday home in Sorrento on Victoria's Mornington Peninsula, an hour or so south of Melbourne. Ian accepted with delight and spent a relaxed four weeks with the family over the Christmas holidays, playing golf each day with Thomson on the courses nearby.

He recalls, 'Peter and I would walk out the back of the Thomson holiday house, cross the road, jump on to the Portsea course and play together. We would also play at Sorrento – I cannot recall how many rounds we played together in the area, but it was a lot of golf.'

Ian reflects on why Thomson took so much interest in him. 'I think he could see how much I wanted to succeed at golf. We played a lot of golf and spent a great deal of time together.'

THOMSON AND WILLIAMS: IAN'S POWERFUL ALLIES

Steve Williams, the most successful caddie in golf, started his career with Peter Thomson in 1976 and believes he knows why Thomson showed so much interest in Ian. 'Even as a young pro, Ian was the consummate professional. His temperament was outstanding, his etiquette was perfect, and he had a great work ethic. Peter liked

Ian because he was the complete gentleman. In a way, Ian was "old school" and dressed immaculately. Peter never liked the way Tiger [Woods] would arrive at the course in jeans and leave in jeans, nor was Ian part of the "drinking mob", a major element in Australian golf at the time.'

Ian recalls some advice delivered to him in Thomson's dry style. 'I asked Peter what he did to exercise for golf, and he said, "I walk – what else would I do?" So, we would walk the beach together. After playing golf with him I would want to go and hit balls, but he would say, "Take four balls and go and play seventeen and eighteen – practise making four fours to win." He would tell me to think more deeply about what I was doing. He was not a big beater of practice balls.'

Thomson had a long association with the Portsea Golf Club, and the Sorrento Golf Club was nearby, as was Flinders Golf Club, on the eastern seaward side of the peninsula. Thomson enjoyed the cluster of courses around his holiday home and once labelled Flinders 'a distant cousin to Pebble Beach and a relative of Muirfield'.

Ian felt understandably honoured by the invitation and the intensive coaching he received from Australia's most famous golfer. The new concept of rotating his shoulders further was working for him, and the swaying and tilting in his swing gradually disappeared. He had previously formed a friendship with Peter and Mary Thomson's daughter Peta-Ann, known as Pan. Several of Ian's contemporaries were convinced, wrongly as it turned out, the main motivation for Thomson's interest in coaching the young Queenslander came from the existence of the friendship between Ian and Pan, and they gave Ian a tough time as a result.

Ian took maximum benefit from the time spent with Thomson at the end of 1982 and beginning of 1983. He says, 'I could fill a whole chapter with what Peter taught me. He passed on to me these pearls of wisdom about scoring and winning – quite simple things I still remember today. It was just what I needed at this stage of my career. I needed to get away from the circuit for a time and look at how I played golf. It was not as though I was getting lessons from Peter for hours. It was a far more subtle kind of support. He would say to me, "You can't play in the wind like that, my boy. You don't want to hit a high fade; you need to learn to hit a low draw." Another example is how he taught me to flight the ball better. Instead of trying to hit a hard wedge, he taught me to put the ball back in my stance and play an easy nine-iron. I became very good at the half shot with a hold-off finish. I used that technique a lot, as Thommo taught me.'

Peter Thomson and Ian meet for the first time at the 1981 Australian PGA Championship at the Royal Melbourne Golf Club.

Then there was the wisdom of Thomson's bank of course-management knowledge. He told Ian, 'Look carefully at the pin position and find the best place to land, but also bear in mind you are rarely in a bad position in the middle of a green, and on windy days always play to the middle of the green.'

Ian's technique was improving but he was also assimilating skills from Thomson on learning how to score, how to think his way around the golf course and, most importantly, how to win. It was the Peter Thomson way.

In 2023, Mary Thomson, having just celebrated her ninetieth birthday, recalled the unique relationship between her late husband and Ian. 'Ian stayed with us regularly in Melbourne in his early days as a touring professional. I know Peter was very fond of him and saw great potential in him. He saw Ian as a future champion.'

CHAPTER 6

THE NEW ZEALAND OPEN 1983

Breaking through in Auckland

After his summer holiday with the Thomson family, Ian Baker-Finch focused on the Australasian Tour. There was no other affordable option for the young touring professional without a sponsor. The circuit had peaks and troughs over the decades and sports agent, lawyer and writer Mark McCormack was well qualified to gauge the health of the tour each season. He found the 1983 tour disappointing.

McCormack had warned the previous year that the withdrawal of support by one of the Australian PGA Tour's biggest sponsors, Mayne Nickless, was not a good sign. The prize money for the flagship event decreased in 1983 from A$175,000 to A$40,000. Several other events on tour offered total purses of A$35,000 or A$40,000, meaning that only the top ten players were paid out more than A$1000. For context, the winner of a pro tournament generally receives 17 or 18 per cent of the prize pool, depending on the tour.

Ian had to make the most of the opportunities on his home circuit. After his break on the Mornington Peninsula and one-on-one mentoring from Thomson, his game was in reasonable shape coming into 1983 although his new technique was still evolving.

He started the South Australian Open, his first tournament of the year, with a 68 that equalled the best round of the day. It was downhill from there, and he finished with a total of 298 and a cheque for A$287.60. He was at the tail end in the Tasmanian Open with an even smaller cheque for A$210, and in the Victorian Open at Metropolitan he picked up A$310. At the Australian Masters at Huntingdale in Melbourne in February, Ian at least moved to the middle of the field with a score of 300, winning A$940, but it was hard work.

Ian was barely making expenses and particularly struggling in his final rounds.

After a break of three months, the circuit moved to Western Australia in May and the depressing trend in Ian's tournament play continued in the Western Australian Open at the Lake Karrinyup Country Club outside Perth, where a final round of 77 saw him drop down to the bottom half of the field. He won A$301.

The Western Australian section of the circuit concluded on 29 May at the Nedlands Masters held at the Nedlands Golf Club. Ian finally reversed his scoring trend with rounds of 69-68-72-68 for fourth position at 277 and A$1750. At last, he was on the credit side of the ledger in a tournament, with income exceeding expenditure.

At Lake Karrinyup, Jack Newton had played well, unluckily losing the tournament in near darkness in a sudden-death play-off to Terry Gale. Tragically, Newton would never play on the Australasian Tour again. He suffered a near-fatal accident on 24 July 1983, an event that shook the golf world – particularly in Australia.

Newton and five of his friends had decided to fly from Newcastle to Sydney to watch the Sydney Swans play Melbourne in an Australian Football League (AFL) match. The six Swans supporters had a few beers after the game and then caught separate taxis to the poorly lit side entrance at Sydney Airport's light aircraft terminal to board a Cessna 210 for the flight back home to Newcastle.

After experiencing difficulty calling a taxi, Newton and one friend were late arriving and, when they finally reached the edge of the tarmac, they could see the lights on their single-engine Cessna about 35 metres away. The aircraft, with four of their friends aboard, was taxiing slowly away. Newton's decision to run and try to catch the plane almost proved fatal. He was on the right-hand side of the plane and the pilot on the left. Trying to catch the pilot's attention, he ran towards the left-hand side and straight into the propeller.

His right arm was severed on impact as his entire right side suffered major damage from the rotating propeller through his hip, shoulder and eye. The accident happened shortly after 7.30 pm and Newton was in the operating theatre by 8.30 pm. *The Age* would report the next day that surgeons tried to reattach the severed arm but the team were forced to abandon any hope of the procedure succeeding.

At the time of the accident, Ian and his friend Jeff Woodland were on the Troppo Tour in North Queensland together. 'We were in my red Holden Commodore driving when we heard the news of Jack's accident on the car radio. We pulled the car off the road and cried.'

Newton fought hard in hospital just to survive. He had played well enough to narrowly lose the Open Championship in 1975 in a play-off against Tom Watson, he'd tied for second in the Masters in 1980, and he'd won the Australian Open in 1979, but he would never play competitive golf again. His horrific abdominal injuries almost ended his life.

Newton was fortunate that Professor Fred Hollows was on his surgical team. The renowned eye specialist operated on the area around Newton's right eye and, although the eye was lost, Hollows's skill was such that his patient required no further plastic surgery in that area. After six weeks in intensive care and further time in hospital, Newton recovered sufficiently by October to start a new career in golf as a commentator at the New South Wales Open.

There was a postscript to Newton's unlucky play-off loss in the Western Australian Open to Gale back in May. In near darkness on the fourth extra hole, Newton had driven well from the 18th tee, unluckily striking a spectator on the leg to finish 'dead' under a bush. He tells the story in his book *Out of the Rough*: a few months later, in pursuit of his new broadcasting career, he found himself sharing a flight to Perth with Terry Gale, his conqueror at Karrinyup. In mid-flight Gale discreetly handed Newton a cheque for A$1225. The cheque was calculated to even up the difference between first and second prize money in the 1983 Western Australian Open. Gale had been carrying the cheque with him waiting for the opportunity to square his private ledger with Newton.

Back on the Troppo Tour in the winter for a fourth and final time, the swing changes Thomson had suggested to Ian seemed to be paying off, evidenced by the larger prize cheques he was collecting. His friends on tour were noticing a difference in both his ball flight and the length he was achieving off the tee. He was also gaining extra strength by working out with Jennie in the off-season at a new Nautilus gym in Melbourne.

John Downs played a great deal of golf with Ian in their time together on the Troppo Tour. He remembers Ian's strengths and weaknesses as a golfer and recalls the change to Ian's ball striking that occurred in 1983, which became obvious when the Australasian Tour resumed at Belmont in New South Wales in October.

'When I first met Ian in 1980, he was a great putter but he never hit the ball far enough. Late in 1982 Ian and I were playing a practice round before a pro-am in Dysart against Paul Foley and Peter McWhinney and they were both knocking their drives thirty yards past us off the tee. We had finished golf and were having a few drinks and Ian said to me, "Mate, I am wasting my time out here – I must learn to hit it further." Thommo was about to take Ian under his wing, and I did not see him for another six months. The next time I saw him was when we were playing together in 1983 at Belmont. I was drawn with Ian and Peter Fowler, and it was noticeable that in six months Ian had gained forty yards off the tee from nowhere.'

The Belmont tournament was co-branded ABE Jack Newton Classic–New South Wales PGA Championship with Newton's hard-case friends Ian Stanley and Bob Shearer providing the driving force behind the event. They wanted to provide financial and moral support for their severely injured friend, and Newton made his first appearance on the golf course at Belmont not long after being discharged from hospital. Shearer won the event and Ian finished tenth for A$910.

The A$100,000 New South Wales Open coincided with Ian's best career performance of tied fifth and his largest cheque to date: A$3990. Ian competed well against a quality field as Norman won again, beating David Graham in a sudden-death play-off. Jack Newton made his commentary debut at the event and Ian remembers, 'Jack did it well. We all loved him because he saw it from a player's perspective immediately.'

Ian was in the top ten at Tweed Heads, steady in the Australian PGA and then fourth in the Victorian PGA, taking away healthy cheques in each of the three events, before heading to the Australian Open at Kingston Heath in November, which was the finale of the Australian leg of the tour. The prize pool was A$150,000 and the field included the Zimbabwean star Nick Price and the Englishman Maurice Bembridge.

The players struggled around a course in magnificent condition, but the majority found the hard and fast greens extremely difficult.

The tournament committee had decided to emulate the green speeds of Augusta National – around 13 feet on the stimpmeter. The committee nearly achieved its target, leaving most of the players unimpressed. Not only were the greens cut extremely short, but the superintendent's staff followed it up by rolling the putting surfaces until they were rock hard and glassy.

Rain helped to soften the greens for the first round, but even par was still a good score. The first-round leader, Ossie Moore, disappeared in the second round with an 82. The defending champion, Bob Shearer, had predicted a par total of 288 would be a winning score. He was close to the mark in his prediction – but then failed to make the cut himself with 77 and 83 as he retired to the commentary box for the final two rounds. The 36-hole cut was unusually high at 156.

No player broke 70 in the first round, but Ian had been close with 71 – the same score as David Graham and Bob Charles. Both the Australian and the New Zealander were previous major champions, with Graham winning the 1979 US PGA and 1981 US Open and Charles triumphing in the 1963 British Open. Ian was steady on the second day with 73 to be at even par, handily placed one shot behind Graham. The third round saw another young player, Peter Fowler, just 24, race up the leaderboard with a 68, as Ian faltered with 77. Normally a five-over-par round at that stage would have proved fatal, but on a day where the average score for the field was worse than 77, Ian and David Graham, on 78, somehow remained in contention.

After the carnage of the third round, the Australian Golf Union's tournament committee relented, and belatedly ordered limited watering of the greens by the superintendent's staff. Until that final round, the event had been a dour struggle for survival, with those professionals who made the cut complaining loud and long about the fiery condition of the course.

The final day changed all that. David Graham told the press he thought he still had a chance if he could shoot 67. He failed to achieve that target by a single shot, finishing with a final round of 68 for a total of 289 – one over par. Nick Price dropped away with a final round of 76, leaving the stage clear for the two youngsters, Ian and Fowler. Ian threw in one of his characteristic birdie bursts through the 7th, 8th and 9th holes. Instead of dropping away he was moving steadily up the leaderboard.

Ian knew by the time he reached the 18th green he needed to hole a 15-foot putt to beat David Graham for sole possession of second place. Withstanding the pressure, he stroked the ball firmly into the back of the cup for a magnificent closing round of 67. Peter Fowler arrived on the 18th still holding a two-shot lead, knowing that the Australian Open title was his for the taking. He finished out for 69, compiling the only sub-par total for the tournament of 285, three shots ahead of runner-up Ian on an even par total of 288.

Neither of the two youngsters had let the lightning-fast greens intimidate them and, with putters in hand, they mastered the conditions at Kingston Heath. Ian and Fowler shone in the event, fulfilling their promise and leaving much more established players in their wake.

Fowler's first-place cheque was A$27,000 and Ian earned A$16,200 for second place.

The players flew to Auckland for the New Zealand Open at Auckland Golf Club (now Royal Auckland and Grange Golf Club) and many of the golfers, their confidence shaken by the greens at Kingston Heath, found the putting surfaces in Auckland far friendlier. Terry Gale, speaking after his 70 in the first round, did not hold back, telling the press, 'The Australian Golf Union should send their greenkeeper over here to see hard, firm, fast greens – with some grass on them.'

A pair of visitors, American Bobby Clampett and Scotsman Sam Torrance, added glamour to the field, and a young 20-year-old from Fiji, Vijay Singh, had recently turned pro and would make the cut at the beginning of his remarkable career. Ian was still travelling on a tight budget and he and Wayne Grady stayed in the high-school dormitory at King's College next to the course. The two friends were no strangers to this type of accommodation after their time together on the Troppo Tour.

Ian was tied in the first round with Grady and New Zealand's Stuart Reese. His opening-round 71 was in the shadow of Grady's 65, but he moved up the leaderboard to third place after his second-round 66. Meanwhile Grady posted a steady par round of 70 to stay in the 36-hole lead. In 2023 he reflected on the tournament and especially

Breakthrough. Ian becomes the 1983 New Zealand Open Champion at Auckland Golf Club.

remembered his roommate's putting. 'If Finchy hadn't become the best putter in the world by the mid-1980s, I would like someone to tell me who was. I played with Ian in all four rounds in Auckland in 1983 … and if Ian actually did miss a putt, it would usually go four feet past. He was so confident and so pissed off when he missed a putt, even from a good distance out, that he only bothered putting one foot down on the ground for his return putt and would casually knock it in – all of them, every time, straight in the middle. He was such a brilliant putter.'

CONTINUOUS PUTTING – FINCHY STYLE

Stuart Reese remembers the tournament well and Ian made a strong impression on him during the event. 'I was in awe of both Finchy's attitude and his putting. In the first round on the 11th hole, he knocked his first putt six feet past and barely looked at it as he knocked that one straight in the hole. In general, his attitude was amazing, and he was right into the power of positive thinking at the time. It was almost as though he knew he was going to the top and he had the mental aptitude to do that.

'He also had absolutely no fear on the course.'

There was another aspect to Ian's mental attitude. He was working hard on self-improvement in this area, following the mantra of Brian Tracy, a Canadian-American self-help and motivational speaker and writer. 'All through the 1980s I read everything I could get my hands on about the subject of positive thinking and goal setting. I had a series of tapes by Brian Tracy that I listened to all the time on the power of positive thinking. I collected a library of these types of books in my search for success on the course.'

In the last two rounds Ian outlasted the field with steady rounds of 72 and 71, matching par over the four rounds for 280 to secure the win. Reese was second, three shots back, and Grady followed in third place, dropping nine shots to par in the last two rounds. Near the end of his round, Ian was playing steadily but left himself with a tricky 4-foot par putt on the 17th. Of course, he holed it, and knew then that the New Zealand Open was his. He had duplicated his mentor Thomson's 1950 feat in claiming the New Zealand Open title as his first tournament victory.

His last two tournaments – a runner-up placing and a win in two national Opens – changed Ian's career, as he banked A$33,000 in two weeks. The local press had a field day, citing his current nickname in the headline 'Sparrow Aims High'. Ian was quoted as saying, 'My long-term dream is to become the best golfer in Australia.'

He had moved up to fifth place on the Order of Merit behind Norman, Shearer, Gale and Fowler. New Zealand journalist Peter Williams partly credited the win to the four weeks spent with Thomson on the Mornington Peninsula, saying, 'Through coaching and playing every day with Thomson, Baker-Finch learnt first-hand more of the skill and mental attitude required for tournament success.' Williams tipped Ian for 'a major breakthrough in the tough, cut-throat world of pro golf'.

The 1983 circuit wound down with two final events: the Air New Zealand–Shell Open where Ian finished midfield, and the NZ PGA Championship at Titirangi where he finished strongly with 67 for fifth place. This had been a breakthrough season for the country boy from Beerwah – seven years after abandoning his schoolwork for an uncertain career in golf.

CHAPTER 7

THE ROAD TO THE BRITISH OPEN

Steve Frazer's inspired talent-spotting

IAN BAKER-FINCH'S PERFORMANCE by the end of 1983 left him in an altered state of mind as he headed into the 1984 season. At 23 years of age, having turned pro almost eight years earlier, his late-blooming success had been hard earned, but the sudden change in his financial position was dramatic. Ian says, 'I had gone from being broke, not having fifty dollars in the bank and having to pay off a car, to where I could now even think about putting down a deposit on a house.'

He wanted to test his game further afield. After winning the New Zealand Open in Auckland in November, he outlined to the assembled press his forthcoming trip to Europe, where he would be accompanied by Wayne Grady and Mike Clayton. He would play the early part of the Australasian Tour before embarking upon what journalist Peter Williams described as 'a great golfing adventure designed to establish him internationally'. There was talk of the trio of young pros playing in Asia and Europe, and hopefully playing on the secondary tour in the United States. He was asked by the press,

'Will you have to return home to Australia if you run out of cash?' Ian replied confidently, 'The money won't run out.' His prediction proved to be correct.

It was reported that his plans were ambitious for a youngster with no major sponsorship. In fact, he, Grady and Clayton had been approached in February 1983 by the promoter Glenn Wheatley and his partner Steve Frazer, both part of a Washington DC–based management group called Wheatley Sport.

Founded in 1970, the firm would grow to become part of Sportsco Advantage and would finally morph into the global sports and entertainment giant Octagon. Wheatley's background was interesting: from 1968 he had been a bass player in the rock group Masters Apprentices. Tiring of that life, he transitioned into sports and entertainment management. Within two years of assisting Ian and his friends in 1984, Wheatley would play a key role in the phenomenally successful career relaunch of the Australian singer John Farnham. Wheatley mortgaged his family home to finance the 1986 album *Whispering Jack*, which went on to be No 1 on the Australian charts for 25 weeks and the third bestselling album ever in Australia.

Frazer's background was as a tour manager for international artists and bands touring Australia. He was interested in golf, but more heavily involved in the promotion of tennis in Australia, particularly the Davis Cup. He took a lead role in providing support for the three young pros by obtaining entry for them into golf tournaments outside Australia – initially two events in the United States followed by ten additional tournaments on the European Tour.

Frazer recalled in 2023 his inspired piece of talent-spotting of the three young players. 'Mike Clayton had won the Victorian Open the year before, Wayne had won in Adelaide in 1978, and Ian was a player who could shoot sixty-four one day and eighty the next, but he looked to me like the best putter in the world. They were very talented young guys who attracted my attention so I approached the three of them and they all knew Glenn Wheatley. It was not a difficult recruiting process, to be honest. No one had asked to manage them before, and I made a good choice. Two out of three of them ended up as major champions. Mine was a very personal style of management, and we all became good friends.'

Ian remembers the trio's surprise at being approached by Wheatley and Frazer. 'I was a nobody. I had not done anything but thought I could do something. Glenn was "the name" and John Farnham's manager at the time, but he was not really into sport. Steve became our main connection, and they certainly opened doors for us. The three of us may not have made any money directly from the association but seeking invitations on their letterhead gave us a degree of credibility.'

Ian would retain Frazer as his manager until 1989.

One bonus from the association with Frazer came in the form of Melbourne-based accountant Drew Robinson. He became part of Ian's management 'package' and, more than that, a trusted advisor to the young golfer. Robinson had close connections with Wheatley Sport through his strong entertainment industry and sports network. His now late brother Brad was an Australian rock musician and lead guitarist for the 1980s band Australian Crawl.

He shared Frazer's interest in tennis and golf. 'I was extremely fortunate to meet Ian, Wayne and Mike in 1982 at the Victorian Open and to become involved with Wheatley Sport and Advantage,' he says.

Robinson was also on the boards of the PGA and Australasian PGA Tour at the time and his accounting firm, Duesburys, provided direct and innovative sponsorship to Ian. He recalls, 'We paid Ian ten thousand dollars to have our firm name on his bag and received Australia-wide publicity for the sponsorship, together with exposure in the *Financial Review*, as the first accounting firm to sponsor a golfer.' There was even a cartoon published depicting a suit-clad accountant carrying the golf bag of a pro golfer. Ian played his part and, when requested, would happily attend any cocktail functions arranged for Robinson's accounting clients.

Due to their year-end rankings on the Australasian tour, Ian, Grady and Clayton gained automatic entry into the Open Championship at St Andrews from 19 to 22 July.

Frazer worked hard on getting starts in Europe for his three new clients. 'We used telex machines in those days. I would put together a profile on my players and then present them as if they were the future of the sport. The organisers of the Dutch Open were supportive and helpful, and the tournaments in Ireland were also receptive to entry applications from young Australians.'

By 1984 the world of golf had entered an interesting phase. Greg Norman was climbing into the top three in the rankings that McCormack called at the time 'the top 25 golfers in the world'. Ballesteros and Watson eventually finished the season ahead of him on the world money list, but Norman won twice on the PGA Tour, losing a further three tour events in play-offs.

Norman topped the Australian Order of Merit, but his fellow Queenslander Ian had been hot on his heels. Norman remained the role model for any young Australian pros aspiring to successful playing careers and he was one of the main reasons Ian, Grady and Clayton were taking their chances on tours outside Australasia.

Ian reflects, 'Greg was the number-one player but he did not give any of us much help. I never thought I would be Greg Norman, but when I started my apprenticeship, he won the West Lakes Classic, inspiring me to try harder. We were never close, but when he came back to Australia we played with him and measured ourselves against him – and would try to beat him. He attracted huge crowds, and he *was* Australian golf. All of my group became better players because of Greg.'

Clayton agrees with this sentiment. 'This was the golden era of Australian golf and Greg was its brightest star. Golf crowds were largely golfers, but Greg even brought non-golfers along to watch. In my view, he could have won ten majors.'

Steve Williams had his own perspective, after caddying for several Australians, including Norman and Ian. 'That younger Australian group of players in the mid-1980s was exceptionally talented. There was Ian, Grady, Senior, Moore, Clayton – an abundance of exceptionally good players, all playing at the same time. Greg did not mix with that group of players, preferring to do his own thing and living the high life, enjoying success straight after turning pro. With Greg, everything was first class. He was a remarkable player, and when he played in Australia it was carnival time; he was an iconic player with charisma to burn and he loved beating his contemporaries.'

The economic health of the Australasian Tour improved marginally at the beginning of the 1984 season. The New South Wales Open and the Australian PGA Championship sourced increased sponsorship to take their purse totals up to A$250,000 per tournament. Panasonic and Toshiba were responsible for the uplift. Despite those increases, IMG founder Mark McCormack maintained there was still 'so little money' on the circuit that resident Australian touring pros should look overseas to make a decent living, which was Ian's focus in 1984.

The Tasmanian Open started the Australasian Tour's calendar year at Kingston Beach Golf Club in Hobart, where Ian played steadily for seventh behind his friend Clayton, for whom the winner's cheque of A$6300 was a valuable wedding gift. Clayton's marriage to Debbie took place on the Monday after the event.

On to Melbourne, where the stars of the tour, with the addition of American Craig Stadler, arrived for the Victorian Open at Metropolitan Golf Club, only to be greeted with the unwelcome news that several sponsors had withdrawn. The prize money had been cut from A$100,000 to A$60,000 and the entire field was unhappy with the last-minute reduction. Norman, benefiting from a week's coaching at Royal Queensland from his old boss and coach, Charlie Earp, won by two shots from Bob Shearer. Ian played with Stadler in the event, driving the ball with his newly acquired draw as far as the American in Sandbelt conditions. The Australian Masters field at Huntingdale was further bolstered by Bernhard Langer and Nick Faldo, with Norman winning again by three shots from Langer. Norman had just notched up an impressive seven wins in ten events – in four countries.

Ian finished better with 71 in fourteenth place for A$2100. By the end of the first section of three tournaments in February he had earned three respectable cheques but had not exactly starred.

The week after Huntingdale Ian travelled to Hong Kong, dipping his toe into the waters of the Asian and Japan tours for the first time. He finished well down the field in the Hong Kong Open but came fourth the following week in the Malaysian Open in Kuala Lumpur, winning US$6930. The fields varied in quality from week to week, with a number of top Americans putting in the odd appearance, Jack Nicklaus and Jeff Sluman among them. A smattering of Europeans such as Sam Torrance and Eamonn Darcy also turned up to single events. Ian battled on during his golfing odyssey through Thailand, India, Singapore, Indonesia and on to Japan, where in early April he was fourth in the Hakuryuko Open near Hiroshima, winning the equivalent of US$5200.

When Ian returned home for the Western Australian Open at Royal Perth in May, a new chapter in his career opened. His season would be transformational, and the change was triggered by something else besides the Thomson swing: Jennie.

'The thing that saved my life occurred when I returned from Japan, where I had been working my arse off,' says Ian. 'I contracted food poisoning in Asia, developed gastric problems and was not enjoying what I was doing. I said to Jennie, "I do not want to do this by myself anymore."'

Jennie remembers a similar theme. 'In Asia Ian was not feeling well, and he came home and told me he wanted me to give up work and travel with him. He was never one to travel cheaply or to go out to pubs and drink with the boys. He would rather be with me.' She recalls her first answer to Ian was negative. 'Initially I said, "No, I have a great job." In my mind, I was thinking, "He is a golfer, and golfers make no money," but it was not entirely about money. It was about travelling together, giving up my career. I was thinking, "I don't believe this is the right thing for me to do."'

Ian had an unexpected ally in the form of Kathie Shearer, Bob Shearer's wife. Shearer was a decade further advanced in his playing career, but Ian had played frequently with him in the early 1980s, regarding him almost as a big brother. Jennie felt she could confide in Kathie. 'I was having lunch with Kathie, who was deeply involved in golf, working in media centres at the tournaments – as she still does – and I had come to know her quite well.'

Jennie had chosen her confidante wisely. At the time, Kathie Shearer was fashioning a lengthy, distinguished career in golf media. In 1998, she would famously prevail in a heated battle with a truculent Tiger Woods over his refusal to appear in her media centre at the Johnnie Walker Classic in Thailand. She replied to Woods's dismissive 'I don't fucking have to' with her own 'But you fucking *do*'. Woods duly fronted up to the media centre.

Jennie explained her dilemma to Kathie over lunch. 'Ian has told me I have to give up work and travel with him to Europe. And Kathie said, "Really?" When I told her what the plan was, she said, "Do you want your relationship to work?" I said, "Well, yes, I do want it to work." And she said, "Well, give up your job and go." I was a little taken aback but we talked further, and I opened up to her, saying,

"It has been tough this year, with us kind of being together, but Ian is never around, and we aren't dating anyone else."'

Jennie still remembers Kathie Shearer's final words: 'Well, it may be tough, but if you want it to work you had better go.'

In a sizeable leap of faith, Jennie took Kathie's advice, quit both her jobs and travelled with Ian to Western Australia, the United States and on to Europe. Once the decision was made, Jennie acted with characteristic strength and decisiveness. She started saving by working in another job as front of house at a nightclub, collecting cash and dispensing tickets to the patrons. 'Often, I wouldn't be home until 5 am. So, I would go to work Friday, sleep Saturday, work Saturday night, sleep Sunday and then go back to work on Monday … just to save some money. During this period, I lived in a self-contained unit at the back of Mum's house and Ian would stay with me when he was in Melbourne.'

Jennie knew she was committing to becoming financially dependent on Ian. But Ian had another powerful ally – Jennie's mother. 'My mother loved him,' says Jennie. 'She loved golf and thought he was just so nice because of the way he respected our parents.' But Jennie still recalls her doubts. 'It was hard. Although I had said yes and was going to go, in the back of my mind I was still thinking, "Is this the right thing for me?" And Ian was probably also thinking, "I cannot get too close because I've got to think only about my golf."'

There was a lot at stake for Ian and Jennie – both personally and financially. Ian estimated that the cost to cover the expenses of the trip would be approximately $50,000. He also told Jennie, 'If we are going to do this, we will do it right. We are going to travel business class and stay in nice hotels. If I cannot make it work by the end of the year, I will get a club job.'

Ian and Jennie travelled to Perth on the first leg of their 1984 sojourn together. Their high-stakes trip could hardly have had a better start. The opening event in Perth became the scene of Ian's first major Australian title win. His victory in the Western Australian Open came with a surprisingly easy four-shot margin over Terry Gale and Graham Marsh against a field containing many of the top Australian players. His rounds of 70-67-67-68 left him at ten under par 272, earning him A$7200 in prize money.

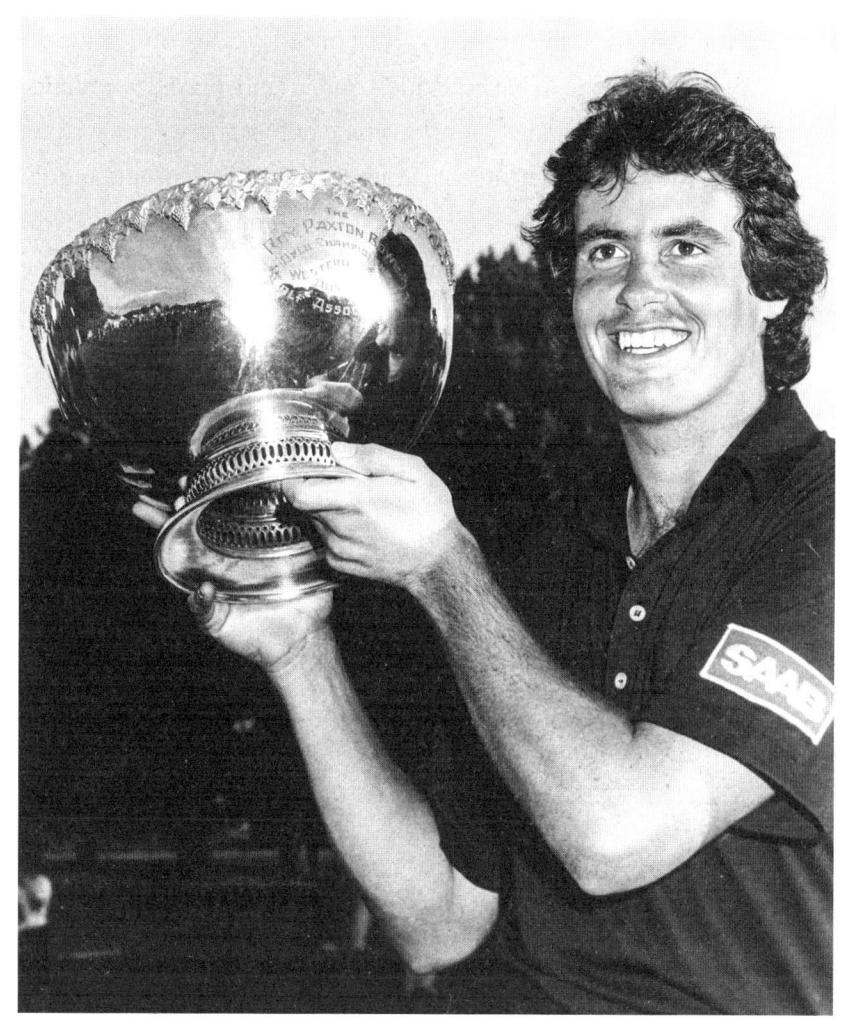

Australian breakthrough. Ian becomes the 1984 Western Australian Open Champion at Royal Perth Golf Club.

Ian was quoted as saying, 'It has not really sunk in yet. It is my first big win in Australia and was achieved against good company.'

At the Nedlands Masters in May at Nedlands Golf Club, Ian lost a play-off to Ossie Moore, having shot a stunning 63 in the second round, including nine birdies in an 11-hole stretch and seven in a row at one point. After banking approximately A$15,000 in Western Australia, the final events of the Australasian tour were excellent preparation for the adventure to the United States and Europe. Ian played well in the Charlie Pride Classic and played a practice round with Greg Norman at Congressional before the Kemper Open but missed the cut, which meant an early arrival in Europe and an unscheduled weekend in Paris for the couple. 'Jennie and I had a lovely time in Paris, meeting the Advantage representative and enjoying the sights and sounds of the city for the first time.'

Steve Frazer's management company had arranged the use of a car for Frazer's three clients and Ian picked up a Citroen to drive to the Timex Open starting on 14 June. 'Leaving for Biarritz from Paris in the left-hand-drive Citroen was quite an experience, and one that Jennie and I still laugh about.'

Wayne Grady, who had been playing in Europe intermittently since 1979, would not join the group until the week of the Open Championship.

At this stage of their tour, it was intended that 21-year-old Steve Williams would start caddying for Mike Clayton, but few of the group's arrangements with caddies were set in stone. Williams remembers his time on Clayton's bag. 'Mike was an extremely talented player. Even at that stage of his touring career he was regularly sourcing information about the design of the courses we played, and who the architects had been. To me, he already seemed to be a golf historian, and he was also a perfectionist, which may have hindered his career. Mike was a very good player but was also a tentative putter. He did tend to get down on himself from time to time.'

Williams recalls the fluidity of his caddying assignments from 1984 onwards. 'There was even a time where three weeks in a row I caddied for Ian one week, Mike the next week and then for Ossie Moore. They were all such good mates and back then the European Tour was not nearly as serious as it is today. I am not sure you will ever see three players rotating through three different caddies in three weeks again. We had such great times travelling as a group of close friends and talented golfers. But even back then I sensed Mike was different from the others in his fascination with all things golf. All his different interests in the game would serve him so well later in his career.'

Williams had his first caddying assignment for Mike Clayton at the Timex Open at Biarritz. Clayton was having a good year. He had won in Tasmania in February and followed that with a win in Korea in the Maekyung Open in April.

'The Timex Open was an unusual start to our caddie–player relationship,' recalls Williams. 'Mike was constantly moaning and groaning in the practice rounds. Finally, I couldn't stand it anymore and my exact words to him were: "For fuck's sake, Mike, pull your head in. Listen to what I say and get on with it." He shot sixty-one in the third round and broke the course record. My speech to him worked. It was the one and only tournament he won on the European Tour.'

Ian finished tied twentieth to cover his expenses in his first tournament in Europe and then he and Jennie caught the train from Biarritz to Monte Carlo in the company of European players Sam Torrance and David Feherty, playing cards along the way. Ian played well in the Monaco Open, finishing tied fourth in an event drastically shortened to 36 holes because of persistent low cloud cover plaguing the Mont Agel course. To Jennie the trip had an element of the fairytale about it. 'Biarritz was beautiful and at Monte Carlo we went to the palace and went parasailing there. It was just spectacular, and it remains one of our favourite places in the world.'

The adventure continued. Ian recalls, 'The car Advantage had arranged for us was a big old slopey Citroen. It was fine driving down to Biarritz. Then one of the caddies had to drive it via a Channel crossing to Scotland, but being left-hand drive, the Citroen was not all that great in the UK.'

Ian played well again in the Glasgow Open for tied fourth but missed the cut at the Lawrence Batley Tournament at the Belfry in Sutton Coldfield near Birmingham. 'Missing the cut at the Belfry did me no harm because it meant I could fit another practice round in on the Old Course, and back then the Belfry was a goat track, even though the PGA planned to hold the Ryder Cup there the following year.'

So they were off, two days early, to the Auld Grey Toon in the Kingdom of Fife on the Saturday before Open Championship week. Steve Frazer had arranged the rental of a farm cottage in the village of Wormit, about 20 minutes' drive from the Old Course. Across the week, Ian and Jennie were joined in the cottage by Frazer, Grady, Clayton and Steve Williams – who slept on the couch. There was only one bath and no shower, which was no real problem for the youthful group of six, and nearby there was a cosy, friendly pub overlooking the river. They all set out to enjoy the atmosphere at the Open; steak and kidney pie, a couple of pints and a game of darts helped them to relax after long days of practice and competition.

For the young Australian golfers this was the stuff of dreams. As youngsters their goal had been to play in the Open – the game's oldest major championship. Frazer called it 'a special time in all of our lives'.

Steve Williams was the first to arrive – one day before the others. He did his washing in an old washing machine with a manual wringer. Unfortunately for the Baker-Finches, he left behind, undetected, a pair of red undershorts in the ancient machine. After arriving at the cottage, Ian and Jennie put on a load of their own washing, only to discover that every item came out of the wash in different shades of pink. All Ian's branded clothing provided by his sponsor, Lacoste, had been ruined in the wash. Jennie picked all the Lacoste labels off the clothing and laboriously sewed them on a replacement wardrobe. There would be a sequel to the Lacoste saga two weeks after the Open finished.

Laundry challenges aside, the group were looking forward to their first glimpse of the Old Course. A pair of veteran Australians, at quite different stages of their careers, had made the trip to St Andrews to compete in the 113th Open. In May 1982, Peter Thomson and Kel Nagle had both been delighted at their election as honorary members of the Royal and Ancient Golf Club, and in 1983 Thomson was granted the honour by the venerable club of becoming both the first professional and first Australian to speak at the club's annual dinner.

The two old friends decided to make their final appearance in the 1984 Open at St Andrews. With six Open wins between them, the event was the perfect opportunity for a ceremonial farewell lap of honour in front of the knowledgeable and appreciative galleries. At 55 Thomson had at least been playing some golf on America's Senior Tour and his form was reasonable. He had 'retired' from the Open five years before but came out of his self-imposed retirement to compete in his 30th Open. At 63, Nagle was happy enough to play, envisaging that he and Thomson would be paired together.

Neither old champion wished to make a fool of himself, and both took their practice rounds seriously. For Ian, the benefits from his relationship with Thomson continued to accrue: Thomson arranged for Arnold Palmer's UK-based caddie James 'Tip' Anderson to carry Ian's bag on Sunday and Monday for two of his practice rounds, as he knew Palmer was not arriving in St Andrews until Tuesday.

Ian joined Thomson, along with Nagle and Graham Marsh, for four practice rounds, receiving a personal Old Course masterclass from the two senior statesmen. 'Here I was with Tip Anderson on my bag playing with Peter, Kel and Graham Marsh on the Old Course. I learned where to go on the course, where to aim and where to land. It was surreal, and a huge bonus for me to have two past champions from St Andrews showing me around. Graham was another of my role models.'

The course was a unique experience for Ian with its variable bounce and run. The best lines into many of the greens are often concealed from the newcomer. Thomson and Nagle unravelled the mysteries, passing on directions to Ian: where to aim in different conditions, how to manage wind and bounce, how to avoid the bunkers that are the Old Course's main defence to low scoring. There is a marvellous photo of Thomson, wearing a flat tweed cap and pointing at a distant spire in the town. Beside him, Ian, in pink trousers, hangs on every word. They may have been from different golf generations, but the two men clearly shared a bond.

Thomson was encouraged by how Ian assimilated his crash course on the intricacies of the Old Course. In *The Complete Golfer,* Thomson summed it up for author Peter Mitchell: 'At St Andrews, a player doesn't need particular power or length, and Ian doesn't possess them anyway.' Vintage Thomson: blunt but accurate. He continued, 'I could see he had the game to win there. He was a beautiful putter then, and I reckoned that if he followed the lines that I showed him, he would get to the green all right.'

Ian remembers the experience clearly. 'I still have so many great memories of Peter showing me around the Old Course with Kel.'

He would prove to be a good pupil. 'I learned as much as I possibly could in those few days before the event – specifically which horrendous bunkers to avoid and which church spires to aim at. One of the best strategies I adopted was to always play left off the tee, where it was much wider and safer, and my long hard draw worked well. When faced with difficult pin positions, I used my wedge game to spin the ball in the firm conditions, generally coming in from the left side.

'My preparation for the Open gave me a sense of self-belief and I could not have been better prepared for my first major.'

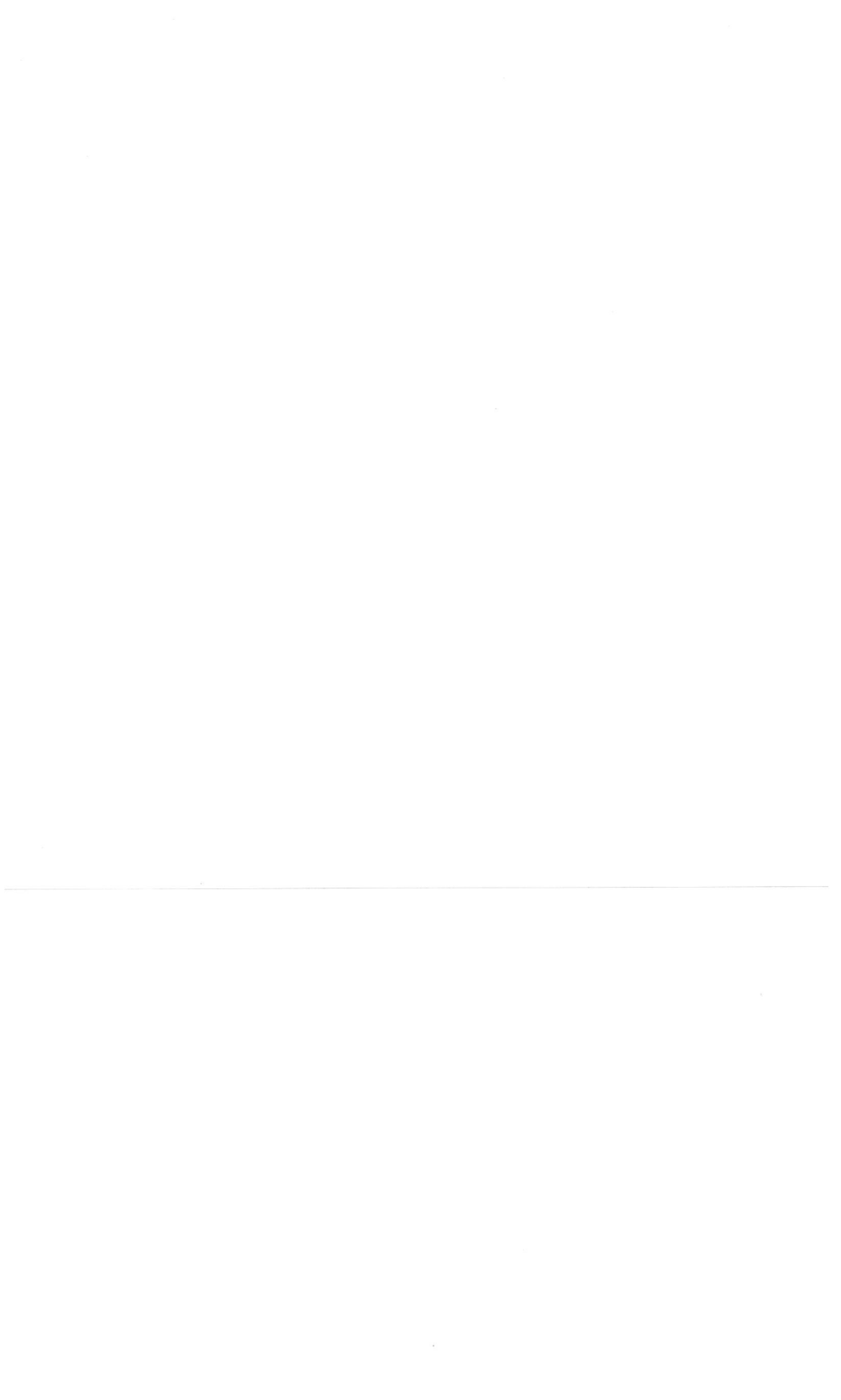

CHAPTER 8

THE 1984 OPEN, ST ANDREWS

A major lesson around the Old Course

On 19 July 1984 the stage was set for the first round of what would develop into one of the great post-war Open championships. At the time, the Open was often referred to as the British Open, especially in the United States and Australia.

In near-perfect weather for Scotland, record crowds of more than 190,000 gathered over four days to witness the twenty-third playing of the Open on the Old Course at St Andrews. At the direction of the R&A, water had been applied only sparingly to the hallowed turf, and the course was fast and firm. The field was strong, and the favourites were in good form.

American Tom Watson, with a peerless pedigree in links golf, was the clear favourite to take the title. He had won five Opens in the preceding nine years, including the last two. Peter Thomson had been the most recent golfer to capture the Claret Jug three times in a row; Watson's objective was to equal the feat. If successful, he would also tie Harry Vardon's record total of six Open Championship wins. At 44, Nicklaus was still in the picture, sharing Watson's affinity for links golf and golf's oldest major. Lee Trevino was there, also 44 and still capable of winning a major – especially one played on a links course. Trevino arrived with a new driver and a new wife, Claudia, who had the same name as his previous wife. He brought his usual repertoire of shots and quips, telling the press corps that marrying a second wife with the same name as his first was convenient because he 'didn't even have to change the names on the towels'. Despite their age, Nicklaus and Trevino were no jokes – the champions both had one more in them after St Andrews.

Greg Norman ranked high on the list of Open favourites. He had recently lost the US Open, with Charlie Earp on his bag, in a play-off to Fuzzy Zoeller. Then there was Severiano Ballesteros. The moody, sometimes fiery 27-year-old Spaniard had captured his first Open in 1979, followed by two Masters victories in 1980 and 1983. The press corps focused on Seve's current lack of form and relatively lacklustre recent showings, but he had finished tied sixth in 1983.

One player completely escaped the notice of the assembled press: 23-year-old Ian Baker-Finch, with a modest two-win golfing curriculum vitae comprising a recent New Zealand Open and a win in the 1984 Western Australian Open. Now contesting his first major, he had learned to play the game on the rough diamond courses of country Queensland, literally a world away. After all, his home course was 14 years old and 'the Old' was over 600 years old.

But Ian was not overawed by history and liked the condition of the course. 'It was dry, which suited me perfectly. Thanks to Peter I was now hitting the ball low with a draw.' He had a promising but inexperienced caddie for the tournament proper in 20-year-old Phil Morbey, known universally as 'Wobbly'. He would caddie for Ian through to the end of 1985. Morbey later graduated to caddie for the Spanish player Jose Maria Olazabal and then for Welshman Ian Woosnam in his 1991 Masters victory.

The vicissitudes of the draw often play a part in the first two rounds of the Open, and 1984 was no exception. Because of the large field of 156 players, the wide spread of starting times could have a dramatic effect on a player's score and his chances of making the cut. Ian's tee time for the opening round was relatively favourable, as he had been drawn with the sometimes-dour American Hale Irwin and the Japanese star Isao Aoki at 12.40 pm. He would also enjoy perfect scoring conditions for the second round on Friday morning.

Ian's former housemate Wayne Grady still recalls being none too thrilled with his draw in the 1984 Open. 'For me, I thought the tournament was over before it started as we were the last group in the first round to tee off at 4.25 pm. I played with Wayne Riley and the US player John Jacobs. We finally came down the 18th fairway at 9.45 pm that night. It was terrible. Any marshals had gone home, people were wandering across the course wherever they liked, and we had to finish our round in near darkness.'

Two other Australians were surprised by their allocation of playing partners in the draw compiled by the R&A Championship Committee. Any romantic notions Peter Thomson and Kel Nagle had of a relaxed game together were dashed when Thomson was drawn with long-hitting American Andy Bean and Nagle was rather cruelly paired with Ballesteros for the first two rounds. In the first round Thomson held his own, shooting 72, while the unfortunate Nagle must have been dispirited by his 84 in the company of Ballesteros who, almost four decades his junior, posted 69. Overall, their draw was an insensitive piece of work by the committee.

Heading to the first tee for the opening round, Ian's nervousness was greatly reduced by his depth of preparation and the tutoring he had received from Thomson. After driving down the left side of the 1st fairway, as directed, he was on his way, playing in a tournament that had been his Holy Grail growing up – and not only his but also that of his peer group of fellow Queenslanders.

He birdied the 4th, dropped a shot on the 6th and then astonishingly holed his wedge for an eagle two on the par-four 7th hole to be out in 33. He did not put a foot wrong on the back nine. He birdied the 14th hole, and navigated the famous 17th hole, known as 'Road', safely with a four-wood to the centre of the green, and two-putting for par. His opening-round 68 was well above his expectations, placing him just a single shot behind the leading trio of Norman, American Peter Jacobsen, and Scotland's Bill Longmuir.

It was not raised by the press until the following day, but there had been an incident involving Ian on the 10th hole during the first round. His drive landed in heather to the right of the fairway and could not be found. He was about to take the long walk back to the tee to replay his drive, when a spectator intervened and told Ian he had witnessed two boys making off with his ball, which they'd found lying near a cluster of television cables beside the heather. The spectator mentioned he had heard the youthful thieves specify the brand and number of the ball – a Dunlop DDH with the number 1.

A rules official listened carefully to the evidence and duly granted Ian a free drop, one club length from the cables. Ian hit it on to the green and two-putted for a par. The ruling apparently upset Ian's playing partner, Hale Irwin, who labelled it 'a bad decision' and called Ian 'a very lucky guy'. Unperturbed by all this, Ian was content he had been treated according to the rules, and simply played on. 'Hale was at a stage in his career where he was in his forties and a bit of a hard arse. He found himself drawn with a twenty-three-year-old Australian who got lucky with a drop and shot sixty-eight to beat him.'

Having to deal with a packed press gallery at an event on the scale of the Open was a new, potentially daunting, experience for Ian, although help was at hand in the form of the R&A press officer

David Begg. Steve Frazer observed, 'David Begg was really special in managing the press tent. He was an enormous help to Ian over the week, in an environment that Ian was completely unfamiliar with.'

In 2024 Begg remembered very clearly his interaction with Ian in the press tent after his first round. 'Ian was a natural with the press and I remember how relaxed he was. He completed a very measured interview for about twenty minutes and then moved on.'

After another relaxing night at the Wormit pub, Ian started early on the second day, taking full advantage of perfect scoring conditions. Clad smartly in yellow and black, he drove the ball beautifully, still adhering to the playing lines given to him by Thomson: 'Keep mainly left off the tee.' He birdied three of the first five holes and added another birdie at the par-three 8th after magnificently holing the 50-footer he had been left with after a poor tee shot. On the 13th he holed a 20-footer for another birdie.

Standing on the 14th he was six under par and threatening the course record of 65. He fought hard for par on the Road Hole, escaping the fearsome greenside bunker and holing an 8-foot par putt on indisputably the most challenging hole on the course. He saved a fine par on the 18th after a long-distance two-putt from deep in the Valley of Sin, the swale in front of the green. His ten under par total led the Open.

Looking back, Ian says, 'The whole week was surreal and at the halfway stage everyone seemed shocked that this Aussie kid with long black hair had shot sixty-eight and sixty-six.' The press corps had a field day, with headlines like 'Baker Who?' and 'Hyphen Who?'.

He also remembers walking down the 18th fairway as Grady was teeing off the adjacent 1st in the second round. Ian's score of ten under was leading. 'As we crossed, Wayne was clapping at me and clearly happy for me in the position I was in.' Not all the Australians present were as supportive as Grady. Ian remembers going into the players' tent near the putting green. 'Everyone was clapping and the head of the Australian Golf Union said, "You'd better go and get a photograph of that because you won't ever see yourself up there again." Clayton wanted to punch him for saying that to me!'

After the second round Irwin had recovered his composure somewhat and graciously told the press that Ian's performance with the putter over the first two days was among the finest he had witnessed.

After 36 holes the leaderboard was:

	R1	R2	TOTAL
Baker-Finch	68	66	134
Ballesteros	69	68	137
Trevino	70	67	137
Faldo	69	68	137

Tom Watson lurked five shots further back on 139. Norman had dropped well back with a second round of 74. Although not in contention, Thomson acquitted himself well enough, adding a 73 to his first round of 72 to make the 36-hole cut. Nagle returned to a form of respectability with 75 to farewell the Open for the final time, finishing at the end of the field on a total of 159. He tied for last place with the 1981 Open Champion, Bill Rogers, who had not helped his cause by running up a 12 on the 14th hole in his first round.

It was astonishing. Ian found himself leading his first Open – by three shots. He told the press at the halfway stage that he had originally been aiming for a top 20 finish and sounded quietly confident as he said, 'I knew I was capable of playing well because I like the course, but I did not expect to be leading.' Thomson's hand was still clearly guiding him when he added, 'I will not think of winning until the last nine holes – or maybe the last four.'

In an unconventional move the R&A reviewed the prize money for the event in light of the unexpectedly large galleries, increasing it by 10 per cent at the halfway stage. They had last taken a similar step at Muirfield back in 1966. More than 110,000 spectators had passed through the turnstiles in the first two days, and the total amount at stake for the players was increased to £451,000.

Ian's income from the event was also about to increase. Steve Frazer was approached by the American bank Manufacturers Hanover Trust, who proposed Ian wear a cap with their logo on it for the final two rounds for a payment of £5000. Ian was not keen, telling Frazer, 'I have never worn a hat. I have a chance of winning the Open, and I am not going to wear a hat this time.' A compromise was reached, and the bank paid £2500 for Ian to wear a logoed patch on the sleeves of his shirts and pullovers, which Jennie sewed on in time for the final 36 holes. 'It was a funny little deal and was an early form of ambush marketing that often occurred during the majors,' says Ian.

Ian's housemates Grady and Clayton were disappointed and gave themselves an enforced weekend off. They exited the Open with identical totals of 150, missing the cut by two shots.

The third round started early for Thomson as he set off on what would be the closing chapter of his 30 Open Championships. He finished with a respectable 76 in front of a small and appreciative gallery, mostly comprised of locals. He narrowly missed the 54-hole cut of 219 – by two shots. It was a typically quiet and understated end to a brilliant Open career. He doffed his cap, acknowledging the muted cheers and heartfelt applause of the gallery gathered around the green of 'Tom Morris', his final hole. The gathering of the mainly Scottish faithful appreciated the historic round they had just witnessed, and Thomson left his beloved Old Course for the final time as a competitor. At 55 he had not disgraced himself by any means, finishing on a similar score to several players of the contemporary era, including Ray Floyd, Larry Nelson, Payne Stewart and Ian Woosnam.

But Thomson was not quite finished influencing this Open.

Ian slept well on his lead and was relaxed as he walked through the crowds to the 1st tee on the afternoon of the third round, clad in black trousers and a pale pink pullover. The friendly atmosphere in the company of friends in the Wormit pub the night before had helped him maintain his sense of calm. Peter Thomson quietly eased his way through the spectators and somehow materialised next to Ian, shaking his hand. He touched the younger man's shoulder and told him, 'You can't win this on the third day, but you can lose it.'

Englishman Nick Faldo, who had been in the top ten in the previous two years, was Ian's playing partner for round three. Reassured by the wise counsel of his mentor, Ian holed a long putt from behind the pin for a birdie on the 1st green. The incomparable Peter Alliss exclaimed in his unique style, 'I say, good morning, Doctor, what a lovely afternoon!' as Ian's birdie putt disappeared into the hole.

Ian's impression: 'Faldo didn't know who I was and didn't really care – but I kicked his arse that day!'

Completely in command and seemingly immune to pressure, Ian played brilliantly as he went out in three under par 33 to move to 13 under par overall. The back nine started well as he drove the green on the 10th, but then he uncharacteristically three-putted for a par. Playing into a stiff breeze coming home, Ian dropped a shot on the 14th and again found trouble on the 17th. This time he could not save par from one of the worst positions on the course, well left of the green. His back nine may have been completed in a poor total of 38, two over par, but he had finished the round with a creditable one under par 71 against Faldo's lacklustre 76.

At 11 under par 205, Ian had taken Thomson's advice on board, withstood the pressure and had certainly not lost the tournament in the third round. He was quoted in the press as saying, 'I felt like there was no pressure on me at all today.'

In the meantime, Tom Watson had found a vein of ominous form, hitting the ball superbly in his round, making seven birdies and a single bogey in his 66. Watson complained he could have holed more putts. He shared his initially unfavourable impressions of links golf with the press, admitting that he 'did not particularly like the Old Course at first, as a hard, bouncing type of course'. He admitted the layouts back in the States may have conditioned him negatively to links golf and referenced US design trends of placing hazards and bunkers in front of the greens. But latterly he had become a links convert and he professed his new love for the traditional style of golf. His conclusion: 'Golf over here was how it was meant to be played.'

Watson had come from five shots behind to tie Ian for the 54-hole lead at 11 under par.

Ballesteros played steadily in the third round for 70 without any of his characteristic fireworks. Germany's Bernhard Langer completed the quartet from within which the winner seemed most likely to emerge. Langer had arrived at the Open in a poor state with a sinus infection, a high temperature and aches and pains. But his more serious ailment in golfing terms was his recurring bouts of the 'yips', hardly helped by his ever-changing array of putters. However, he was long off the tee and his third round of 68 had put him firmly in contention.

With a round to play, the leaderboard featured a rookie tied in the lead with a legend of the game.

Baker-Finch	205
Watson	205
Langer	207
Ballesteros	207

Trevino, Lanny Wadkins and Hugh Baiocchi were a distant five shots back on 212 and Norman had disappeared out of contention with a second straight 74.

Surely the winner had to come from the top four.

As well as attracting plenty of media attention, Ian's golf and dramatic arrival as a contender at the Open had attracted the interest of IMG, and particularly its founder Mark McCormack. Steve Frazer became aware of this interest. 'Ian was in rare air. I remember during that Open, McCormack was making it clear to anybody who would listen that Ian would become part of his empire very soon. There was a lot of arrogance involved in his attitude. In the meantime, I just continued with my own style of management of Ian.'

Saturday night of the Open followed the pattern of the previous week, with Ian and his friends relaxing in the pub down in Wormit. 'The town and the community we were staying in were wonderful,' says Frazer. 'Everyone in this little country pub after three days of the Open was so engaged and excited that Ian was leading and that he may be the winner after the final day.'

Jennie Baker-Finch recalls, 'Ian was just trying to remain calm. He tried to set to one side in his own mind that this was the British Open. I had no control over the outcome and my only role was to be there as his support.'

On Sunday morning the atmosphere in St Andrews was electric. This had been one of the finest Opens in memory in terms of weather, crowds, and the quality and variety of the players at the top of the leaderboard. Ian's presence as a young, good-looking, charismatic 'unknown' provided further interest. He was drawn for the last-round finale with his co-leader Tom Watson, the dominant Open player of the previous decade. Watson walked over to Ian on the 1st tee to shake hands. Ian remembers, 'He said to me, "This is the 1st tee of the last round of the Open and you are not human if you are not nervous."'

Ian momentarily wondered whether this was an act of 1st tee gamesmanship by the senior pro, but concluded this was not the case. In Ian's view, Watson was most likely just trying to calm the younger man's nerves.

Steve Frazer did not hold such a charitable view of Watson's discussion with Ian. 'The thing about Ian is that he always thinks the best of people. There is no doubt in my mind that Watson was playing a game with Ian, but at the time I am sure it did not bother him. Nevertheless, after that incident if anyone other than Ian was going to win, I was hoping it would be Seve, not Watson.'

Seemingly untroubled, Ian turned to his caddie, Wobbly, and held out his rock-steady hand, saying, 'I am not nervous. How about you?'

Ian opened his final round with a perfect three-wood off the tee down the left centre of the 1st fairway of the innocuous-looking par four. For his second shot to the green he faced his first choice of the round, as the hole was cut in its customary final-round position, just over the Swilcan Burn, the stream running in front of the 18th tee and crossing in front of the 1st green on the Old Course.

Peter Thomson was interviewed by Andrew Crockett in 2015 for *Inside Golf* and gave his view on the opening hole on the Old Course:

> The fairway is about 150 yards wide, and it is a beautiful piece of turf, but when you play the championship there, it is a frightening hole. The wind is blowing, and the cup is perhaps four yards from the burn in front of it … If you attempt to get close to the flag, you get caught.

Ian and his caddie selected a nine-iron for the treacherous approach shot. Ian was sure they had made the correct club selection. 'I went with a little nine-iron when I was only wedge distance away. I did not want to get caught by spinning it.' In the air it looked to be the perfect choice of club as the shot pitched just over the burn, landing in a small depression, seemingly ready to nestle close to the hole for an opening birdie. The dry turf had been yielding minimal backspin during the week, but Ian's shot inexplicably spun back into the burn. Shocked as he was with the result, he recovered as best he could, hitting a delicate pitch close to the hole and limiting the damage to a bogey five.

Before his eyes, two shots had disappeared. Just like that. Ian was stunned. 'That was really weird,' he says.

In 2015 Thomson recalled the advice he had given Ian. 'I told him to ignore the flag on the 1st hole and hit his second to the back of the green.'

Watson did not start particularly well either, dropping a shot on the 2nd hole to fall back to ten under. From the 4th hole, Ian slowly started to unravel, dropping another shot there and following it with bunker trouble and a double bogey on the 6th hole. His worst front nine of the Open to this point had been 33, but now in the final round he had amassed a tournament-wrecking 41. He commented later, 'Nothing specific put me off on the front nine, but I knew that I suddenly couldn't do what I had been doing in the first three rounds of the tournament.'

After nine holes, the tournament appeared to have turned into a two-person matchplay contest between Watson and Ballesteros. Ian's chances of winning had all but disappeared. Watson finished the front nine in an uninspired 37 as Ballesteros went out in 34 to lead by one shot at 11 under. Watson then birdied the 10th and a seesaw battle ensued over the back nine.

Ian played marginally better on the way home, but a double-bogey seven on the par-five 14th hole reduced his final round to the point where he was facing the embarrassment of a score of more than 80. But he steadied himself on the 15th with a face-saving birdie.

In one of the tournament's great finishes, the Open had come down to the last two holes, with the formidable Road hole taking centre stage. Playing in the group in front of Ian and Watson, Ballesteros stood on the 17th tee in the knowledge he had dropped a shot on the hole in each of his first three rounds. He drove conservatively, well to the left, leaving himself 200 yards to the pin. The Old Course's most storied and feared bunker (also named 'Road') lay almost directly on his line to the pin. The Spaniard played a magnificent six-iron to the green, stopping his ball 30 feet away and two-putting safely for par to remain tied for the lead.

Ballesteros drove safely off the 18th tee as Tom Watson, with Ian looking on, stood in perfect position in the centre of the 17th fairway. Watson had initially feared he had cut his drive out of bounds into the Old Course Hotel on the right. After fortunately remaining in play, he found himself on the perfect line for his crucial second shot to the narrow green, but with his ball resting on the side of a small mound, leaving him with a sloping lie.

He grappled with indecisive club selection and, apparently encouraged by his caddie, Alfie Fyles, finally chose too much club (a two-iron) for the shot into the narrow green. He lost the Open then and there. Ian says, 'He tried to hit it high, straight at the pin and hold the green, rather than trying to draw it in low.' Watson would tell CNN in 2022, 'Now I had to be a hero. I was going to take a risk and hit that perfect shot to win the Open.'

Watson's far from perfect iron flew well past the pin, landed hard, rolled off the green and bounced over the road to the right of the green, finishing hard up against a stone wall, an integral feature of the hole. From an impossible position, Watson's seven-iron chip with a restricted backswing stopped 30 feet from the pin; in the circumstances, it was a reasonable effort. At the same time, Ballesteros was wedging to 13 feet on the final green, his shot sending up a cloud of dust from the bone-dry fairway. He had no idea what shape Watson was in on the 17th hole but knew he had to hole his right-to-left putt to ensure victory. His putt started on the perfect line, broke towards the hole, momentarily hanging on the lip, before toppling in.

Ballesteros raised a fist into the sky, pumping it repeatedly in a gesture of unbridled exhilaration. The Spaniard had finished with 276, 12 under par. Watson heard the roar from the 18th green, missing his 30-footer for par to slip two shots behind Ballesteros.

Watson now required an unlikely eagle two to tie Ballesteros on the par-four 18th hole, 'Tom Morris' – named after four-time Open champion Old Tom Morris. He drove well, leaving himself approximately 90 yards to the pin. As they walked up the final fairway, Watson and Ian received a magnificent ovation. Watson paced off the shot to the green, hitting his approach too far onto the back edge as the crowd invaded the 18th fairway to circle the green. Ian and Watson faced their respective putts with Watson missing his long birdie putt for sole possession of the runner-up position. A sixth Open had escaped him as he finished with a disappointing 73 for a total of 278, in a tie for second with Langer.

Ian holed a face-saving 15-foot birdie putt to finish with 79 and a four under par total of 284 in a tie for ninth place. His putt was the last shot of a memorable Open as he walked off the final green with Watson to the loud applause of a sympathetic crowd.

Jennie was there at the end of a long day. 'He was sad coming off the final green. He had not played that poorly and had bad luck that escalated. He seemed embarrassed, possibly at letting people down.'

For Ian, it had been a traumatic day, and in the locker room he cried. He confesses, 'The crying was more from the relief that it was all over. Unfortunately, I had messed up.'

Frazer was also on hand at the end of the round to console his distraught client. 'For me it was an extraordinary experience to be there with Ian after the round. He was completely and utterly broken. I remember sitting with him in the locker room down in the bowels of the clubhouse. He was weeping and it was unbelievably hard for him. I found it very difficult to find the right words and I am sure he took some time to get over that last round.'

David Begg from the R&A sought out Ian in the locker room after he had interviewed Ballesteros. 'I did go down into the locker room to see if I could commiserate with Ian and get a word or two out of him. I saw him lying there in the locker room, and thought, "No, I will just leave you."'

Several of the other players consoled Ian, among them Zimbabwean Nick Price. Ian recalls Price's words: '"You should be in the States. You have the game for it; do not stay here in Europe." I did not know Nick at the time, but I really appreciated his words.'

Jennie gave Ian a big hug when he finally emerged from the locker room, and there was some consolation when the R&A presented him with a silver-engraved card for being the first player to post 66, the lowest round of the Open that week.

Ian had arranged to meet Jennie in the players' marquee after the presentation. Paul Smith was there, an Australian touring pro who had failed to pre-qualify for the Open at nearby Ladybank Golf Club. Smith was friendly with Ian and kept Jennie company in the middle of the packed marquee. He remembers, 'There must have been a thousand people in there and we were in a group of Aussies in the middle of the crowd. After waiting for half an hour, we heard a huge ruckus and wondered what was causing it. People around us were suddenly standing and clapping. Ian had arrived and the ovation for him must have lasted for five minutes; it was unbelievable. I had a tear in my eye, and Jennie was crying. It was a very moving experience and a thank you to Ian for how he had handled himself during that harrowing last round.'

That night, Jennie remembers, 'We sat in the house at Wormit and reflected on the past week over a wine and beer. We were just so young and had never experienced anything like that Open before. We talked about the good that had come out of the experience and how much great golf Ian had played under extreme pressure.'

For head-to-head drama, the 1984 Open had matched two other great post-war Opens: the Doug Sanders–Jack Nicklaus contest in 1970 at St Andrews, and the Watson–Nicklaus 'duel in the sun' at Turnberry in 1977. Ballesteros's win also marked the end of the US domination of the Open from 1970 to 1983, during which 12 out of 14 Opens were captured by Americans, interrupted only by Gary Player in 1974 and Seve himself back in 1979.

Kenny Reid, author of *Seve Ballesteros's Touch of Class*, points to the tournament's significance:

> The 1984 Open was a pivot point, a moment in time when global golf wobbled on its axis. Ballesteros's victory at the Old confirmed the modern era Americans were flesh-and-bones defeatable. Greg Norman was fulfilling the Seve role by dint of his power game and self-confidence and encouraging the next wave of Aussie talent.

Seve had turned the Open tide in 1984. Eight of the next ten events would be captured by European and Australian players, and one by the Zimbabwean Nick Price. In the majors after 1984, players like Langer, Scotland's Sandy Lyle and Norman came into prominence and the next American-dominant era was not ushered in until 1995.

This trend was mirrored in Ryder Cup results from 1985 when 25 years of US dominance also came to an end. The vision of Ballesteros raising his arm triumphantly to the crowd in 1984 is one that became frozen in time. The Spaniard died prematurely at 54, and the victorious European Ryder Cup team of 2012 carried a silhouette of the famous Seve pose for inspiration on their blue-and-white uniforms – the same colours worn by Ballesteros in 1984 in the final round of the Open.

It had been a memorable major debut for Ian in this landmark Open. His goal as a teenager had been just to play in the tournament. Now, after leading the best in the world for three rounds, he believed he could win it one day. 'It made me realise, "I can do this." This was the start of my thinking, "I can really play; I am not just one of the boys anymore. Golf is my career, and I can win the Open." Thommo had been telling me this for two years, but I hadn't been listening.'

POSTSCRIPTS TO THE 1984 OPEN AT ST ANDREWS

There are two postscripts to Ian Baker-Finch's 1984 Open. One is light-hearted and was revealed shortly after the event. The other is more serious and took several decades to emerge.

The first involved Ian's Open wardrobe, provided courtesy of French company Lacoste. Two weeks after the Open finished, Ian was playing in the French Open with Catherine Lacoste, a great player and member of his sponsor company's family. Ian recalls, 'She congratulated me on my play in the Open and mentioned how proud she was of me but asked, "And where did you get that beautiful pink Lacoste sweater you wore in the third round of the Open?" She mentioned that she and her staff could not find it anywhere in the Lacoste inventory.'

Ian had purchased the white woollen pullover for A$20 at the airport when departing on his overseas odyssey. Thanks to Steve Williams and his red underpants, Lacoste had been given an addition to their colour range.

The second and more serious postscript took longer to emerge – decades longer.

On the 1st hole of the final round, Ian and his caddie were shocked and mystified by his seemingly perfect nine-iron shot to the 1st green inexplicably spinning back into the Swilcan Burn. Ian uncovered the explanation in the late 1990s. 'Brian Twite, the head pro at Metropolitan Golf Club in the Melbourne Sandbelt, approached me and said, "I think it has been long enough now. I can tell you this story." Twite's good friend had been the greenkeeper at St Andrews in 1984. He told me his friend had been lightly watering the front of the 1st green the evening before the final round. The greenkeeper became distracted by another member of the green staff asking him to come over and check something on the 17th hole. He went over, laid his hose down in front of the 1st green, and when he finally came back a puddle had formed in a depression on the front edge of the green.

'The greenkeeper had mistakenly flooded the area. He nervously watched the entire field go through on the final day and no one landed in the damp area where the puddle had formed — until I came along. He was horrified when my shot landed in the depression and spun back into the water. Had I started with the birdie three that the nine-iron should have produced, it could have been a different story.'

Looking back with little regret and no rancour, Ian wryly concludes, 'I could have been the Open Champion at St Andrews in 1984.'

CHAPTER 9

THE EUROPEAN TOUR 1984

Travels with Jennie – and Steve Williams

Despite the traumatic experience of that final round on the Old Course, Ian Baker-Finch had achieved his long-held dream of playing in the Open Championship. His last-round collapse may have been the stuff of nightmares, but his first major was an experience from which much had been learned, and ninth place had earned him £11,264. There was a living to be made and his and Jennie's expenses to be covered on the remaining Steve Frazer–arranged program of ten post-Open tournaments in Europe.

The fields the three young Australians were competing against were consistently strong, but the trio continued to perform with distinction in Europe. Major winners made regular appearances, such as Sandy Lyle, Seve Ballesteros, Greg Norman, Nick Faldo, Bernhard Langer and even Johnny Miller. In 1984 the European Tour was not a 'feeder tour' for the PGA Tour as it is today, and marquee players or future major champions often featured.

Ian and his two friends Wayne Grady and Mike Clayton were proving themselves more than capable of holding their own.

In 1984 21-year-old Steve Williams also stayed on in Europe after the Open, plying his caddying trade there with different players. The top present-day players usually take their full-time caddies as part of their team, but that was not the norm in the 1980s. Williams found himself carrying bags for multiple players on multiple tours during the early to late 1980s until he finally obtained his work permit in the United States to caddie full-time for Greg Norman from 1988. Had the young New Zealander been caddying for a player with a lower profile than Norman's, his lack of a work permit may not have presented such a problem.

Williams recalls, 'When I first started working for Greg, I never envisaged caddying for him on a full-time basis. He was the hardest guy I ever caddied for and was unbelievably demanding on the golf course, and I actually liked my part-time arrangement of caddying for him about ten to twelve times a year.'

Williams had regular assignments with Norman, but also worked for Ian and occasionally for Clayton. The enterprising Kiwi would select which tournaments he wished to attend around Europe and then try to match a venue to a specific player who he knew had entered. The current practice of an elite player paying their caddie's airfares and expenses did not generally apply in the 1980s.

Continuing his travels around the different European Tour events over the next four seasons, Williams naturally gravitated towards and socialised with Ian, Jennie, and the other Australian and Kiwi golfers. He caddied regularly for Ian on the European Tour from 1985, which gave him a first-hand opportunity to observe the strengths and weaknesses in Ian's game. 'He was the best putter on the European Tour. He was brilliant, absolutely brilliant. I would put him in the same class with his putter in hand as Bob Charles.

'If he could, he always putted out, because he was just so confident in that part of his game. If he was not likely to be standing on anyone's

One-year-old Ian with his mother, Joan, at the beach in May 1962.

A Queensland holiday: Ian and his siblings Robyn, Lawrie and David stand in front of their father Tony's repurposed VW work combi at Boreen Point in 1965.

Three-year-old Ian on the beach at Coolum, Queensland, in 1964.

The pink family home in Peachester, Queensland, in 1962.

Ian, the New South Wales Junior PGA Champion, at Penrith Golf Club in 1980.

Victorian Open Champion Ian and then girlfriend Jennie at the Yarra Yarra Golf Club in 1985.

Peter Thomson (left) and Ian at the Open, St Andrews, 1984. 'I have great memories of Peter showing me around the Old Course,' says Ian.

Courtesy of the University of St Andrews Libraries and Museums, ID: 2008-1-22121

Ian at the Open in 1984. He was later asked by Catherine Lacoste, 'Where did you get that beautiful pink Lacoste sweater?'

Courtesy of the University of St Andrews Libraries and Museums, ID: 2008-1-96600

'I went with a little nine-iron,' says Ian, remembering his unfortunate approach to the 1st green during the final round of the 1984 Open.

Courtesy of the University of St Andrews Libraries and Museums, ID: 2008-1-96428

Jennie consoles Ian on missing the cut at the Open, Royal Lytham and St Annes Golf Club, 1988.

Courtesy of the University of St Andrews Libraries and Museums, ID: 2008-1-96561

line, he would quickly say, "I'll putt out," and would then knock it in without a moment's hesitation. He used that Ping Anser of his; it was slightly longer than normal, and his stroke was poetry in motion. He did swing the club well, was very straight, but may have lacked some clubhead speed and distance off the tee.'

After the baptism of fire that was his first major, Ian finished midfield in the Dutch Open to win £915 and then went to Ireland for a profitable sojourn in the Emerald Isle, where he was midfield in the Irish Open and tied second at the Celtic International. A decent cheque for £1000 followed in Spain to further offset his and Jennie's travel expenses. The bold prediction he had made in New Zealand at the end of 1983 was proving to be correct: he would not run out of money on his ambitious tour.

After the Open, Grady and Clayton outperformed Ian. Grady won the German Open and £17,000 in fine style in Frankfurt. Clayton and fellow Australian Rodger Davis were there to carry Grady off the 18th green to celebrate his overdue moment of triumph. Six years had passed since his first victory at the West Lakes Classic, with 17 runner-up finishes sandwiched in between.

For the young Australians, the travel involved in competing on the European tour was extensive and costly, with certain parts of Europe being more unaffordable than others. One of the most expensive tournament venues was Sweden. Williams says, 'There were two tournaments in Sweden on tour, one in Malmo and one in Stockholm. Very few of us caddies could even afford to go there. The flights were exorbitant, as were hotels and food. Because of the shortage of caddies in Sweden I would regularly arrange one job in the morning field and then another one in the afternoon field on Thursdays and Fridays.'

Ian and Jennie developed their own routine for travelling between events in Europe. Jennie explains, 'Monday was a travel day for us. On Tuesday Ian would practise on the course at the tournament venue and I would unpack, do the washing and get organised. Wednesday was normally a pro-am for Ian that he would have to play in. For me that was a day where I may get to know some of the other players' wives and possibly go sightseeing, then on Thursday, Friday, and usually Saturday and Sunday I walked the course and followed Ian around every day that he was playing – hopefully four days if he made the cut, not two. That was our life. And on Monday we would start the routine all over again.'

The starstruck young couple took overnight trains, visited palaces and attended functions in wonderful places. Jennie recalls, 'I loved Monte Carlo, which was spectacular, Biarritz was beautiful, and we went through Holland, and then on to Germany and Spain.'

With only modest prize money at stake, they travelled as comfortably as they could. There were language barriers at some of the tournaments with limited assistance provided by the Tour in arranging travel and accommodation. The couple realised that it was generally cheaper for them to return to the Heathrow Airport Hotel at the conclusion of most events rather than travel from venue to venue within Europe, where flights were more expensive. The hotel became their home base for the first two years Ian played on the European Tour. Jennie remembers it having a great buffet breakfast. Dinner could be as simple as fish and chips and the laundry was either done by hand in the room or she would use the nearest laundromat. 'Our hotel bathroom frequently looked like a laundry, with washing hanging over the bathtub and everywhere else.'

Their first trip to Europe lasted seven months and Jennie, previously fiercely independent, recalls fondly how Ian responded. 'Ian was very attuned to my feelings and insecurities. By then I was not working, and when touring I never liked to ask him for money. We could not afford to use the hotel dry-cleaning service, so I was the one having to deal with this and some of the other travel expenses.

He was sensitive to this and, without being asked, would always leave money in the room for me for our day-to-day expenses.'

They travelled together with just one large suitcase and would be gone for six or seven days at a time. Ian and Jennie became friendly with the bell captains who, although they were not supposed to, would allow them to leave their other case in storage at the hotel. 'They were such nice people – always interested in how Ian had played in the tournament that week.'

Daily life on tour looked quite different for many of the single Australian golfers. They often shared rooms with fellow players and if they missed the cut on Friday, they did not have the option of returning to London. Plenty of partying and drinking within the group of single players was also not conducive to performing well on the course the next day.

Jennie and Ian may not have stayed in first-class hotels but their accommodation on tour was usually comfortable. 'We stayed in nice places where we could come home after golf and not, like many of the players, have to go out again to escape the dives in which they were staying. Ian did everything just that little bit better and thought if we were happy and together, he would perform better on the golf course. At his age he was so far ahead of most of the other golfers.'

The Citroen that had been used by the three Australian pros and Williams did not finish the season well. After caddying for Clayton in the Hennessy Cognac Cup in Dorset in mid-September, Williams was last to leave the club with three of his fellow caddies. 'I was driving away at rapid speed and, put it this way, I drove the Citroen through the roundabout and not round the roundabout. Unfortunately, that was the end of the Citroen.'

The 13-tournament odyssey through Europe had taken Ian's golf to another level, as had his performance in the Open Championship at St Andrews.

At season end, Ian finished the 1984 European Tour in twenty-ninth position on the money list with earnings of £38,000. Grady was twenty-first on the list with £47,000 and Clayton secured the eighteenth position with £50,000. Williams says, 'There was just no money at stake on the European Tour in the 1980s. I have no idea how the players made a living, and I certainly have no idea how us caddies even survived.'

By October 1984, the European Tour was winding up and it was time for Ian and Jennie to return to Australia for the second half of the Australasian Tour. Ian recalls, 'Coming back to Australia at the end of 1984 was a huge return home for me. It was clear that everyone now thought of me differently. I had graduated into being one of the stars on my home circuit each week and started getting the good draws.'

His accountant brother, Laurie, may have highlighted his net losses in previous seasons, but by 1984 the financial tide had turned for Ian. He was slowly but surely transforming himself into one of Australia's leading touring professionals.

Jennie also arrived home feeling more confident about the choices she had made during the year. 'I may have been hesitant initially to accompany Ian to Europe, but I arrived home in Australia feeling incredibly positive about him. He had played decently, and I just believed in him, because he believed in himself. He had done everything correctly and was always focused and thinking ahead.'

Ian's run of good form continued into the second half of the split Australasian season. At the Lakes Golf Club in the A$100,000 New South Wales Open, Ian spreadeagled a field that included Norman, Graham and the other top Australian players, all of whom were left foundering in his wake with a 15 under par total of 277, winning by a remarkable 13 shots. Runner-up Peter Senior was the only other player in the field to break par. 'The best I ever saw Finchy play was at the Lakes. He played and putted as well as I have ever seen anyone play.'

Ian's all-round game may have been solid at the Lakes, but his putting had placed him in a class of his own. In 2023 Wayne Grady reflected, 'Finchy showed us in the New South Wales Open that year what he was capable of. His putting was nothing short of unbelievable.'

The season continued with Ian losing a play-off to Wayne Riley at the A$50,000 Victoria PGA Championship, with the field quality and prize money improving for the A$200,000 Australian Open at Royal Melbourne starting on 15 November. Tom Watson opened with 67 and was the only player to break 70 in the first round, his fast start enabling him to hang on to win the Open by one shot from Bob Stanton, with Norman tied for third. Ian was tied fifth, losing a lot of ground in the final round with a 76, after being just one shot off the 54-hole lead.

Ian tied sixth at the Air New Zealand–Shell Open at Titirangi Golf Club in Auckland then mounted a credible defence of his New Zealand Open title at Paraparaumu Beach Golf Club the following week, charging home in the final round with 66 to finish tied fifth behind the American Corey Pavin.

Returning to Queensland, Ian finished the year on a high note as he won the Queensland PGA Championship in mid-December at Royal Queensland. The prize money was again modest and Ian's three under par 285 was good enough to win by one shot from Ossie Moore, who faded to 76 in the last high-scoring round of the event.

The three friends who had toured Europe together all featured in Mark McCormack's world money list of the top 200 players in professional golf at year's end in 1984: Grady at 109, Ian at 119 – with previously undreamed-of earnings of US$94,100 – and Clayton at 121.

It had been a year of real progress.

CHAPTER 10

THE JAPAN AND AUSTRALASIAN TOURS 1985 TO 1987

A world player

IAN BAKER-FINCH WAS able to play regularly on the Japan Tour from 1985 by virtue of his 1983 and 1984 performances in Australia and Europe. He and his Australian contemporaries generally started each calendar year by competing for the balance of Australasian tour events post-Christmas. From there it was a matter of travelling to whichever of the world's tours they could access and afford. Golf on the Asian and Japan tours was in a growth phase throughout the 1980s, and Australians became frequent visitors there. The Japan Tour had started officially in 1973 and a number of the Japanese events fell conveniently for Ian between the end of the Australasian Tour and the beginning of the European Tour. Globe-trotting Peter Thomson had paid the tour frequent visits, winning regularly and claiming his final victory in Japan in 1976.

Venerable British sports manufacturer Dunlop had also seen the potential of the market in Japan. They started producing golf balls there in 1930 and manufacturing golf clubs from 1964 onwards. Many of the Australian players, including Ian, used Dunlop clubs and balls and Thomson particularly favoured the plain soft white leather shoes Dunlop manufactured in Japan. Dunlop DDH and Maxfli balls became the balls of choice for many top international players.

Thomson played a hand in Ian's equipment choices. Ian had played Australian-made PGF equipment until 1982, but it became clear to him better equipment was available. Thomson gave his protégé a set of Japanese-made Honma irons around the time the pair golfed together on the Mornington Peninsula. Ultimately Ian ended up with Dunlop and was comfortable with their clubs and ball from 1983 onwards.

Ian's Australian contemporaries Graham Marsh and Brian Jones regularly prospered in Japan and Asia. The bulk of the top Japanese players remained at home to compete on their strong domestic circuit.

Ian avoided travelling to Europe before the BMW PGA Championship in late April or early May. 'The weather in Europe before May was dreadful, cold and wet, and I loved playing in Japan. The courses were very tight and suited me. It was a similar time zone and was comparatively easy money. Once you were exempt in Japan, with only a few outsiders playing, it was mainly the Japanese players you were competing against. It seemed I hardly missed a fairway when playing in Japan and I was popular there.

'We had lots of Japanese friends and plenty of the locals followed me and I liked the short travel times between events. I was part of a small group of Australians in Japan with Graham Marsh, Brian Jones, Terry Gale, Wayne Smith and Roger Mackay making up a close-knit group that was having a lot of fun.'

Mackay – eight wins – and Jones – 11 wins – would focus their playing careers on Japan. Jones married a Japanese woman, Sachiko, in the early 1980s and based himself full-time in Japan.

Of the group, Graham Marsh most impressed Ian. 'Graham was a role model for me and seemed the most like Peter Thomson in his demeanour, dress and professionalism.' There were similarities between the way Marsh and Thomson took time to set themselves up. 'Graham would stand there and grip the club with his right hand, following the same routine each time and Peter was also meticulous while setting up.'

Caddie and broadcaster Bruce Young observed Marsh closely while caddying for him from 1973. He recalled in 2023, 'Graham took a lot of inspiration from Thomson and was a truly international player. He was technically very correct and an incredibly hard worker. Graham was intelligent, articulate and an immaculate dresser, and also fluent in Japanese. At a presentation after winning, he would give his acceptance speech in Japanese. He was a legend up there.' Marsh won 20 tournaments in Japan and twice won the Asia Golf Circuit Order of Merit, in 1972 and 1973.

Young also observed of Marsh: 'Graham had picked up from Thommo when touring it was necessary to spend money to make money and not try to scrimp and save on accommodation and food. Ian adopted the same philosophy.'

Young remembers the players loved the Roppongi area of Tokyo with its restaurants and nightlife. 'The tournaments in Japan would generally finish around 3 pm on a Sunday and the television coverage would supposedly be played "live" late in the afternoon. We would finish a tournament in, say, Sapporo on a Sunday afternoon but be back in Tokyo by six or seven o'clock that evening.'

TRAVEL – JAPANESE STYLE

Japan was a different proposition from Europe for Ian as he generally travelled alone. He made the most of playing there but missed having Jennie with him. 'I loved playing in Japan; the travel was so easy, and I had a lot of assistance from Dunlop. They helped with hotels, travel and provided us with clothes. Japan was also a learning curve for me in terms of the need to be punctual. For example, taxis were expensive and four of us players would often share one from the hotel to the course for around US$80. If we were leaving a hotel at 8.15 am, and I arrived down in the lobby at 8.16 am, I would find myself alone and having to pay the full taxi fare by myself.

'There were other services available in Japan to make life easier for the players. By mid-afternoon on Sundays, the tournament would be over. We would pay our locker fee, shower, dress and pack a suitcase. We could even send our clubs to the next tournament venue by using a service called *takkyubin* – very Japanese, very efficient. We were given a guarantee our clubs would arrive at their destination within 36 hours of dispatch.

'We would then all catch the bullet train back to Tokyo, have Sunday and Monday night there, and our group would meet again at the train station on Tuesday morning to go to the next tournament. The train travel was also efficient and fast on the Shinkansen [bullet train]. If the train was leaving at 10.21 am it would pull up right on time and you had eighteen seconds to get on, helped by the station staff pushing us on the train with large paddles – an amazing phenomenon.

'Japan ran on time, and I loved it.'

The prize money in Japan was attractive, and from 1973 the circuit had been dominated by Masashi 'Jumbo' Ozaki, who from 1990 became the leading money winner three years in a row. In the process, Ozaki won almost US$1 million – placing him at sixteenth on the world money list. Ozaki was a colourful character and had been a professional baseball player in Japan until the age of 22, before starting competitive golf. He loved bright clothing, collected classic cars and sported a very un-Japanese hairstyle, with a shaggy mane worn long down his neck.

Ozaki's 94 official wins (and at least another 20 unofficial wins) on the Japan Tour is a record unlikely to be eclipsed – the player with the next highest number of wins is Isao Aoki on 51. Ozaki was the Japan money list winner for the first time in 1973, capturing the title 12 times, until his final win in 1998 at the age of 41. Ozaki, like Peter Thomson, seemed to care little for golf in the US, and suffered from some bad press there. There were whispers that he had Yakuza connections and *Sports Illustrated* writer John Garrity reported in 1998 that his reputation was not helped by Greg Norman accusing him of improving his lie in the rough in 1994.

Steve Williams was caddying for Norman on several occasions when drawn with Ozaki. 'There was a lot of controversy when I was working for Greg in the Chunichi Crowns while playing with Jumbo. Greg had an ongoing issue with Jumbo's interpretation of the rules of golf. For one reason or another, things became very heated during the tournament. Greg had played with Jumbo on numerous occasions, and we played on very tight courses in Japan.

'One thing became very apparent when Jumbo selected his driver on every hole. Each time he missed a fairway his ball miraculously came back out on to the fairway. This really tested Greg's patience because he knew the ball was being thrown back on the fairway by the gallery. At the Crowns, Greg became increasingly upset. There were a lot of dog-leg holes, and Jumbo took his driver every time. Finally, Greg boiled over and it became unpleasant. There was another time when Greg initially refused to sign Jumbo's card.'

There were unsubstantiated suggestions Ozaki was using 'hot' golf balls coupled with allegations his equipment may have been non-conforming. Much of this was dismissed as sour grapes by the overseas players who were competing alongside Ozaki on the

Japan circuit. Ozaki and his many admirers seemed unconcerned by any controversy swirling around him, which was principally generated from the press outside Japan.

In Ian's eyes: 'Jumbo Ozaki was Japan's *ichiban* [No 1]. He was by far the best Japanese player even though Aoki had been runner-up to Nicklaus in the 1980 US Open. He was larger than life and he was Bridgestone's best player. He always had the best equipment. At some stage, Norman requested Jumbo's ball be tested, possibly because Jumbo could regularly hit it further than Greg! By the mid-1990s, everyone wanted a J's Professional Weapon driver, named for Jumbo. And the Bridgestone ball he used became extremely popular.'

In the late 1980s the Asian and Japan tours became somewhat blended, and Ian played in events on both. But the Asian Tour was not as enjoyable for him as the Japan Tour. 'The courses were a bit rough. Fifty Americans would turn up from college after missing Q-school and play there with all the Asian players and there were only about ten Australians on the tour. I really did not love playing on the Asian Tour. It was hot, humid and expensive.'

In 1983 Ian played three tournaments in Asia, and a further three in 1984, when he was troubled by gastric problems and illness. He came home to Jennie. He returned to Asia only briefly in 1986 and for a final time in 1987.

Ian experienced first-hand the efficiency of the Japanese tournament organisers in the running of their events. The cost of televising golf in Japan was high, and there was pressure to compact coverage into a two-hour window, usually between 1 pm and 3 pm or between 2 pm and 4 pm. A bad weather forecast was another factor to be dealt with by the event staff and television crews.

Ian remembers one event in Japan in particular. 'We were playing through a typhoon on a Sunday and the weather was only going to worsen later in the day. The "time-buy" of television time was

THE JAPAN AND AUSTRALASIAN TOURS 1985 TO 1987

Ian becomes the 1988 Pocari Sweat Open Champion at Hakuryuko Country Club. 'I loved playing in Japan,' he says.

expensive, so we were directed to play on through torrential rain using preferred lies and were also allowed to tee the ball up in the fairways. We finished the event. I won the 1987 Polaroid Cup–Golf Digest Tournament event in very wet conditions. The organisers dealt with it in typically efficient fashion. It was going to rain all day, so all the pin positions were placed in the back centre of each green. We would play onto the green, pace the distance to the pin from our ball, and find a dry section of green and putt out from the same distance.

'You would never do that for television today, but somehow the Japanese made it work.'

CHAPTER 11

A BREAKTHROUGH IN EUROPE

And first steps on the PGA Tour 1985 to 1988

IAN BAKER-FINCH RECEIVED his first coveted invitation to the Masters tournament in 1985.

Augusta National destroyed him in his first 36-hole outing through the azaleas. After poor rounds of 77 and 79 he missed the cut by the wide margin of seven shots. He recalls, 'I had never putted on such fast greens and had ten three-putts in the two rounds. It took me quite a while to realise I should be leaving my long putts closer to the hole at Augusta – not charging them. I never really figured out how to lag a short putt by hitting it outside the hole. For me, a three-footer was always "aim inside the cup and firm" but this method definitely did not work at Augusta.

'A perfect example was my first time around the course when I almost holed my tee shot on the par-three 6th hole. It finished three feet past the flag. I tried to jam my short birdie putt straight into the hole; it caught the edge and my second putt back for par was from thirty-five feet. The rims of the cups were like plaster of Paris after they had painted the inside of the holes white for television in the morning before each round. I had never three-putted so often and was completely discouraged after hitting the ball perfectly.'

Ian needed to modify his entire approach to putting at Augusta. 'The greens were so fast and undulating that I needed to figure out some way of lagging my putts close to the hole. Tiger Woods and Phil Mickelson have always been the masters of the lag. I was disappointed in my first performance at Augusta but was also grateful to American pro Tom Weiskopf who was particularly encouraging to me, consoling me on the practice fairway.'

Ian played in seven tournaments in total on the US Tour in 1985, including Greensboro before the Masters and Hilton Head the week after. The Colonial, the Memorial and Byron Nelson followed, with the World Series in July completing his short tour of the US. The seven tournaments he competed in, and his lack of success, made him realise there was still a great deal of work to be done on his game if he wished to be competitive in America.

Jennie also found the US Tour an unfamiliar world. She remembers being invited to go on a shopping trip at the Byron Nelson tournament. 'I went shopping with a group of American players' wives and we were looking at Chanel handbags which were retailing for eight hundred US dollars plus tax. Ben Crenshaw's fiancée, Julie, liked the bags and ordered one in each of the five colours – almost five thousand dollars, just like that! I would not think of paying eight hundred dollars for a handbag, but the experience was a wow moment. We had suddenly arrived in a very different world.'

After his largely unsuccessful joust at the PGA Tour, Ian returned to the European Tour, which had become 'all exempt' for the first time in 1985. The dreaded Monday pre-qualifying had been abandoned. There were 26 events on the Order of Merit, and Ian's performance the previous year gave him full status.

Ian consolidated his position in 1985 and performed well in his second major, the Open Championship at Royal St George's Golf Club in England in July. Leading up to the event, Ian received an unsolicited invitation that would never have featured in his wildest dreams growing up in Beerwah. Jack Nicklaus's caddie Jimmy Dickinson approached Ian on the practice putting green at St George's to enquire if Ian would like to play a practice round with Mr Nicklaus.

Ian says, 'Of course, I accepted immediately and asked what time we were off.' Dickinson told him that Nicklaus was going on to the course immediately. Ian recalls, 'So off we went, just the two of us playing together. I could not wait to tell him he was my idol, which he may have already known, based on my interviews since St Andrews in 1984.'

Nicklaus had his own unique way of putting the 24-year-old Ian at ease. 'We were walking up the hill past the big bunker on the right of the 3rd when he let one go! He looked back at me, and said, "Can you believe they have the South African barking spider in this place?" I replied to him, "And I thought you had just cut the cheese." He replied, "No, that was definitely a South African barking spider!" Jack was trying hard to make me relax, and it worked.

'We had a great time; he showed me around the course, and he talked about his years of playing the Open Championship. As a fourteen-year-old I had studied Jack's book to learn the game, and then ten years later here I was playing a full round with him. It was unbelievable.'

Ian played consistently in the 1985 Open to finish tied twentieth with rounds of 71-73-74-70 for 288, six shots behind the Champion Golfer of the Year, Scotland's Sandy Lyle.

Jack Nicklaus, Ian's practice round partner, fared poorly. He started with 77 and was then unlucky with the weather his draw delivered to him, faring only marginally better in the second round with 75 to miss his first cut in an Open since 1962.

Peter Thomson had maintained his interest in Ian's progress and ensured he had a quiet chat with him from time to time. Thomson also had a strong connection with Ian's now more regular caddie Steve Williams, who at the age of 13 had first worked for Thomson in the New Zealand Open at Heretaunga near Wellington. 'Peter knew I was caddying for Ian from 1985 onwards and was still extremely interested in his progress,' says Williams. 'I still clearly remember his words to me around that time: "Son, do not ever let that boy try and hit it further. He hits it so straight, and he is the best wedge player in the world."'

Ian's breakthrough win in Europe came at the Scandinavian Enterprise Open in Sweden in 1985 at the Ullna Golf Club at Akersberga on a course designed by the famous Swedish ice hockey player Sven Tumba. After he retired from ice hockey in 1969, Tumba reinvented himself as a golfer from the age of 30, reaching a scratch handicap. He played in the Eisenhower Trophy for Sweden in 1970 and turned professional in 1974. Tumba then set about almost single-handedly growing the game of golf in Sweden. He attracted Arnold Palmer and Jack Nicklaus to compete in Sweden during the short six-month season there and established the Scandinavian Enterprise Open in 1973.

Ian's landmark win in Europe was the result of his consistent play in the first three rounds, which included two rounds of 68. He compiled a final round of 66 to finish 14 under on 274, two shots ahead of Graham Marsh, with Johnny Miller and Terry Gale one further shot back. The prize money for the event was £130,000 and so in the mid-range for the 1985 tour, but Ian's cheque for £22,000 was the largest of his career to date. Ian's stature in Europe was growing and his win came with a bonus: a Saab 9000 Turbo, which Ian exported back to London and sold for £16,000.

Lyle won the 1985 Order of Merit with winnings of £162,000, well ahead of both Bernhard Langer and Seve Ballesteros. These three stars dominated the tour, with the prize money dropping rapidly to £62,000 for the eighteenth position Ian occupied at season's end.

Ian's decision to travel to Europe and risk A$50,000 on his first campaign had paid off – and Europe was providing much more than just financial returns. Jennie recalls, 'We tried to see just as much as we could, but there was an element of hard work as well in the travel, flights, accommodation and everything else that went with touring life.'

Ian was back briefly in Australia in mid-season in 1986 when an ugly incident unfolded on the Sunshine Coast in June at a restaurant and bar near the Headland Golf Club. Ian and his friends had played 36 holes and were enjoying a quiet dinner together after a long day's golf. Ian remembers, 'It was a small bar, and we were having one last drink at about 9.30 pm. An overserved patron was sitting a few chairs along from us. Apparently he had been attending a conference nearby. He was there with his girlfriend, who said to him, "There is that famous golfer – isn't he cute?" or words to that effect. I did not hear any of this, and only found out about it later. He then moved his chair in behind us, and one of us said, "What's up with you, mate?" I sensed it was time to leave and asked for the bill so we could get out of there.

'The first hit with his right hand came from nowhere and cracked three of my ribs. The second hit with his left hand, on which he wore a big ring, broke my cheekbone, chipped a tooth and shifted my nose under my left eye. I went down and finally made it to the bathroom to assess the damage. My face was unrecognisable. I was stitched up and ended up spending the night in hospital.'

Ian's friend Jeff Woodland was in the group at the bar, and later that night told Ian, 'Don't worry, mate. I got a really good one in.' No one was entirely sure who Woodland had connected with.

Ian suspects it may have been the barman, who had jumped over the bar to try to shut the fight down. The assailant had disappeared, never to be seen again. He was never charged.

Jennie took Ian to a plastic surgeon in Brisbane the next day to repair the damage. 'My nose was still well off to the left. They opened up my eye, packed my nose, and for a year or two you could still see it was on an angle.' The press, particularly in the US, would later portray the incident as the possible cause of Ian's subsequent eyesight problems, but Ian is still not sure how true this is. After the unprovoked assault, Ian had his nose unpacked and went back to Europe to complete what was proving to be an even better year for him than 1985.

However, the assault did affect Ian's performance in the 1986 Open at Turnberry in mid-July. 'I went back to play in the Open, but if you look at any film of me my eye was still red, and I was finding it difficult to play with the effects of my injuries. My ribs were

Troppo Tour graduates Jeff Woodland, Wayne Grady and Ian.

still taped, and it was cold and windy in my first round at Turnberry. I could not swing properly and shot eighty-six in the first round.

'I bounced back the next day with a sixty-nine, seventeen shots better than the first round and only missed the cut by a shot or two. Steve Williams was on my bag, and I hit my second shot on the 18th over the back of the green and could not get up and down to make the cut.'

The Turnberry Open was a milestone event for Queensland and Australian golf: Greg Norman won his first Open by five shots. Norman had been in commanding form during the year, leading both the Masters and the US Open after three rounds but could not convert either into a major win. His major career tally on retirement would show an unflattering two wins and eight runner-up placings in the events that a player is defined by.

In August, an amusing Steve Williams–created crisis unfolded at the PLM Open at Falsterbo Golf Club south of Malmo. Williams was caddying for Ian at the two events in Sweden. 'Ian was playing well in the tournament but after the third round a bunch of us caddies went off to a driving range down the road to keep ourselves amused. I decided to take Finchy's clubs without him knowing. Unfortunately, during our session, the head came off the driver. We all banded together to try and find another driver for Ian to use in the final round, and amazingly enough we found an identical Dunlop driver another player carried with him as a spare. The next day Ian did not even notice the change and he played well with it!'

This story was news to Ian when recounted to him in 2023.

Fellow Queenslander Peter Senior won the event and Ian finished handily placed in a tie for twelfth with a driver that he had never used before.

Ian and Jennie had decided to become engaged in mid-1986 and another good result for Ian in the Ebel European Masters in early September – tied third behind Jose Maria Olazabal – made the purchase of an engagement ring for Jennie in Bond Street relatively painless. 'We settled on the antique ring I still wear today,' she recalls.

IAN LOSES THE BELLS SCOTTISH OPEN – AND FEHERTY LOSES GOLF'S OLDEST TROPHY

In late August 1986 Ian lost a play-off at the Bells Scottish Open in Glasgow against two Irishmen, David Feherty and Christy O'Connor.

Feherty won the three-way play-off for his second European Tour win and is better known nowadays for his quirky television commentary. He celebrated his win by attending an evening Led Zeppelin concert in Glasgow. He took his trophy with him to the concert and celebrated afterwards with the band's road manager.

The Northern Irishman woke up two lost days later, 45 miles away on the 16th tee at Gleneagles, minus the trophy. One of the oldest trophies in golf remains missing to this day.

In 1986 Ian played 17 events in Europe and made 16 cuts, winning £105,000 and climbing into the top ten on the Order of Merit. This allowed Jennie and Ian to buy a home near Heathrow at Shepperton in south-west London to use as their European base for the next two seasons – a home they later sold to fellow Australian pro Craig Parry in 1988.

After their return to Australia and the end of the European season, the couple married on 17 January 1987 at the ANA Hotel on the Gold Coast. Jeff Woodland was Ian's best man and Steve Bann, who had introduced the couple, was the groomsman. Jennie's twin sister, Jackie, and her friend Kerri Bann were bridesmaids. Jennie recalls a fun party atmosphere. 'We had people from Melbourne come up and a lot of other interstate guests. We had drinks in the lobby the night before. The media wanted to attend but we did not allow that. We were married outside by a celebrant and came back inside for the party.'

The newlyweds made quite the couple. Jennie, her blonde hair twisted into a braid, wore a full-length silk dress with three-quarter sleeves and a plunging back, paired with white court shoes. Ian wore a pale grey suit with a black bow tie. A wedding photo shows the tanned young couple gazing into each other's eyes and smiling.

John Farnham had been invited to the wedding but was on tour and unable to attend. As Jennie walked into the ceremony, their chosen wedding song played: Farnham's 'A Touch of Paradise'. These were the days of telegrams being read out at weddings, and Farnham and his wife Jill's message to Ian and Jennie expressed their regrets about not attending, adding rather eerily, 'I just hope today is a special touch of paradise.'

The next day the newlyweds travelled back to Melbourne. Ian drove their new Peter Brock Commodore while Jennie opened the wedding presents. It was an unbroken 16-hour road trip followed by a flight to Canberra for their honeymoon. Jennie remembers, 'The dealer had given us a thousand-dollar radar detector at no charge with the Holden. The detector had plenty of use on the long drive. Ian tends to speed. We stayed in a seedy Canberra motel. Despite being given the honeymoon suite featuring a heart-shaped bed and pink champagne on ice, it was really not very romantic.'

Ian's final full season on the European Tour was 1987. He had hit his peak the previous season. Despite playing a full schedule of 18 events and making the cut in 14, he dropped to No 43 on the Order of Merit, earning £57,000 with no top-three placings, and only four top tens.

During what was only an average season for Ian in Europe in 1987, the Baker-Finch and Williams team conspired to create yet another unfortunate incident of their own making at the Spanish Open in Marbella in mid-May. At the time there were few driving ranges at most European Tour venues, and the players customarily travelled with their own bags of practice balls.

The duo had developed their own risky routine on the practice range where Williams would bind up his right hand with a towel and proceed to catch Ian's practice shots on the fly. Williams's habit was to catch the ball, clean it and then put it back in the 'shag' bag before the next ball arrived. Ian was an accurate iron player and in Marbella he proved it. In a moment's inattention Williams looked away at the wrong time and looked back up just in time to sustain a direct hit to the mouth from Ian's well-struck seven-iron shot. Williams suffered a split lip and two broken front teeth. But Williams was tough; he was carried off the practice fairway and after being stitched up by the tournament doctor, who appeared to be fresh from a liquid lunch, player and caddie went back on the course. Perhaps unsurprisingly, they finished in one hundred and thirtieth place to miss the cut.

Jennie has many happy memories of touring Europe with Ian. 'We had four full seasons of Ian playing in Europe. It was such a whirlwind of travel, and we went to some wonderful places. For the first two or three seasons we did get to know Nick Faldo and his girlfriend at the time, Gill. [The couple would marry in 1986.] The four of us did quite a lot together. Other wives started travelling and eventually we had a great group of girls.' Jennie also observes how tough golf can be on marriages and relationships. 'Over the years there have been a lot of second and third marriages. There are not too many of us who have been together the whole time.'

Steve Williams was still caddying for multiple bosses and remembers working for Ian in the 1987 Singapore Open. Williams, then and now, justifiably prided himself on being the fittest of his peer group of caddies and could not resist using a practice round at the Singapore Island Country Club to rib his boss about his perceived lack of fitness. 'We were on the uphill par-five 18th, and I said to Ian, "Mate, you are so out of shape I can run up this hole with your bag on my shoulder and still beat you to the green." Which I did.'

Ian accepted the challenge but balances the story somewhat by recalling Williams must have felt pressure near the end of the uphill run as he progressively threw Ian's clubs out of his golf bag to lighten the load on the way up and secure his win. The other caddies looked on in amazement at the Kiwi and Aussie's antics and everyone had a laugh about it at the race's conclusion.

Ian and Williams continued with their respective careers over the decades, enjoying their relationship. A recurring theme throughout Ian's career was his lack of deep desire to be the No 1 player in the world; he is still clear he never wanted to be a Greg Norman or a Nick Faldo during his career. In Williams's book *Out of the Rough*, Ian says Williams fulfilled dual roles. 'For me to get a travelling companion and a great friend for company in those early years around Europe was fantastic.' Ian regarded Williams as his 'perfect wing man'. Ian is further quoted in the book as saying Williams 'provided the best support and was the best man on my bag. He gave his player added confidence.'

This was perhaps one factor that strengthened their relationship: while Williams clearly had his sights on being the best caddie in the world, Ian lacked Williams's intensity. It is easy to understand how a full-time relationship on the course between Norman and Williams would fail to endure because of the driven nature of both men's personalities.

By Christmas 1987, Ian and Jennie had moved into their new home, a large villa built on the water overlooking the marina at

Sanctuary Cove on Australia's Gold Coast. 'In 1985 I had been down to Pimpama, sugarcane country on the Gold Coast, and met the developers' representative, Reg Saunders,' recalls Ian. 'The marketing material promised 900 exclusive house sites, branded Sanctuary Cove, overlooking water and would ultimately include an Arnold Palmer–designed golf course by 1988. I left Steve Frazer to deal with Reg to buy us a house on favourable terms. Between the two of them, they produced a deal for me to represent Sanctuary Cove for five years.'

The sponsorship rate was agreed at A$50,000 per year with healthy bonuses payable to Ian for wins.

In 1988 the resort, master-planned and developed by Mike Gore, staged an opening party like no other. In the 'Ultimate Event', Frank Sinatra had top billing along with Whitney Houston and Peter Allen. Clive James was hired to host the lavish event in front of an audience of 40,000. On meeting Gore, James described him as being 'as quiet and sensitive as a wounded water buffalo'. At 72, Ol' Blue Eyes was past his best and required an autocue to guide him through his numbers. He was not interested in staying at the new resort and insisted on being flown by private jet from Sydney to the concert venue and back on the same day.

Ian remembers the opening. 'The weather was horrendous. It had poured with rain all week – the ground was a mess. Mulch, gravel and sawdust had all been mixed together to mop up the rain.' As a result, hordes of flying insects plagued the guests whenever their chair legs penetrated the malodorous top layer of mulch. The Ultimate Event included a golf tournament, also played in dreadful weather, with the best field ever assembled in Australia, including Palmer, Floyd, Ozaki, Norman, Woosnam, Faldo and the eventual winner, Curtis Strange. Shortly after the opening, Gore sold Sanctuary Cove to Japanese real estate company EIE and in 1992 he fled to Canada, leaving behind debts of A$32 million. He died of a heart attack in 1994.

Despite the development's shaky financial beginnings, the Baker-Finch family would call Sanctuary Cove home from 1987 to 2000, as the resort prospered and grew.

By 1988, Ian's thoughts were gradually turning towards the United States and away from Europe and Japan. 'I realised I was never going to reach my full potential by playing in Japan and Europe. I needed to play in the US.' He began his year well on his home circuit in Australia in early January, building momentum by winning the 1988 Australian Masters in February against a top-class field at Huntingdale in Melbourne.

He prevailed in a three-way all-Australian play-off against Craig Parry and Roger Mackay by birdieing the first extra hole – the actual 17th – in fine style with an unerring five-iron to 18 inches off the flag from 195 yards. Underlining the quality of the field, Norman and Faldo finished tied fourth with Woosnam and Langer further back.

At Royal Canberra the next week, Ian was playing a practice round on the Tuesday before the event and was taken to safety 30 yards behind the third green for a brief television interview focused on his win the week before. The playing group behind him included Langer, who had been wrongly handed a six-iron instead of a nine-iron for his approach to the green, and the German's shot struck Ian on the back of the head on the full. 'I went straight down to the ground in mid-interview letting out a loud "Oh fuuuck" on national television, but somehow jumped straight back up, made my hands into a megaphone and yelled "Fore!" at the group behind. Not bad television probably.'

Jennie was unaware of the incident and walked into her hotel room late in the day as the television news broke for a commercial with the teaser 'Baker-Finch down and out'. She waited nervously during the break before discovering on the news Ian had suffered no permanent damage, and he finished tied seventh in the event.

While the Masters was being played without him in early April, Ian travelled to Japan to win back-to-back events: first at the Pocari Sweat Open, where he won by two shots from Marsh, Jones and Parry, and the week following he won the Bridgestone Aso event. His appearances in Europe were limited in 1988, playing only seven events as a part-time player, making five cuts, and dropping down to one hundred and tenth position on the European Order of Merit.

Future full-time entry into the US was then assisted by Ian's play in the World Series of Golf on a brief trip to the States in August 1988. The event at the Firestone Country Club featured an elite field of PGA Tour winners from top-tier events and included certain foreign players who had qualified by virtue of their positions on their own tours. The tour commissioner, Deane Beman, in the middle of his 20-year dynasty, had expanded the field from the four major winners to 47 players in 1985, with the objective of easing access to the PGA Tour for foreign players.

Ian made the select field on merit after winning the Australian Masters and his performances in Japan. He took full advantage of the opportunity and led the rain-soaked event with two holes to go, but bogeyed the 17th with a poor wedge shot, compounding his error by dropping another shot on the 18th. He failed, by a single shot, to make the play-off in the rich event but tied third, earning himself US$52,200.

Ian's World Series earnings together with those from his two other placings – ninth and twelfth – on his short three-event 1988 trip to the US came to more than US$100,000. This gave him enough PGA Tour ranking points to finish one hundred and thirty-third. By finishing inside the top 150 on the US PGA Tour,

Ian became an exempt player, earning himself unlimited starts for the following year.

His fine play in the season saw him finish thirty-eighth on the world money list in 1988 with earnings of US$498,329 – still not good enough to secure a 1989 Masters invitation.

Ian's focus was shifting towards the US PGA Tour.

STEVE WILLIAMS PROSPERS – WITHOUT NORMAN

After Steve Williams secured his US work permit in 1988, he and Ian went their separate ways. Williams was employed by Greg Norman as his full-time caddie. As the 24-year-old New Zealander had suspected, working almost solely for Norman was to prove too challenging, and the job rapidly turned into a poisoned chalice.

The final break came after Williams caddied for Norman in a stressful win in the Chunichi Crowns event in Aichi, Japan, in May 1989, where Norman again clashed with Jumbo Ozaki. The following week Williams was caddying for American Jeff Sluman when he received a call from Norman to his hotel room. 'How Greg got the phone number for my hotel I have no idea,' says Williams. 'He said to me, "After what transpired last week, I think we need to call it quits." It was really no big deal for me as Greg was just too hard to work for. The end was unexpected but came as no real concern to me.'

After being summarily fired by Norman via telephone, Williams had various options available to him. When news of his departure from Norman became known, he immediately received two calls from high-profile American stars, first from Andy Bean and then from Raymond Floyd. He caddied for Bean for two weeks but realised 'the deal Ray Floyd offered me was just too good to turn down'. Williams moved on to enjoy a lengthy, successful and close relationship with Floyd on both the PGA and Senior tours. He finally achieved his goal of becoming golf's most successful caddie in the majors while working for Tiger Woods. He was on the bag for a record 14 major wins: 13 wins with Woods and one with Queenslander Adam Scott.

Down to earth and now fully retired, Williams clearly enjoyed being on Ian's bag and deeply respected him. 'I caddied for Ian often during the mid to late 1980s,' he says. 'Ian would be the best bloke I ever caddied for. He was an absolute gentleman and a completely genuine character.'

CHAPTER 12

JOINING THE PGA TOUR

Instant success on the toughest tour

In 1988 the US PGA Tour may have been the world's most challenging tour, but it was the pinnacle of professional golf for Ian Baker-Finch and his Australian contemporaries. As Peter Thomson and other 'foreign' players had found in the past, the US Tour was a hard nut to crack and had not always welcomed players from overseas.

From 1947 South African Bobby Locke played the PGA Tour and became almost *too* successful, winning 11 events over his first two seasons, and finishing in the top three on 30 occasions. Ian recalls hearing stories about Locke and his becoming so good in the US by 1948 that the Tour tried to neutralise him by placing the pins in the back right corner of the greens; with his habitual looping draw, Locke could not easily hit his irons close to these positions. The press in America mocked Locke, labelling him 'Old Muffin Face'.

The tour took even more drastic action against Locke in 1949 by inexplicably banning him. His crime? As 1948 Masters champion Claude Harmon put it: 'Locke was simply too good. They had to ban him.'

Ballesteros and Norman both experienced their own issues with the US Tour, but several Australians had settled seamlessly into successful playing careers in America. Players such as Bruce Devlin, Bruce Crampton and David Graham had moved there from the 1960s and became permanent residents.

In 1985 Wayne Grady fought doggedly to take his place on tour by qualifying – and he remembers how driven he was. 'From when I was five years old, all I wanted to do was go to America. I hated Europe and only lasted two weeks on my first trip there. When I went through the tour school at Palm Springs it was my twenty-second tournament in a row on four different continents, and I earned my spot the hard way. The American players treated me very well, and I got along great with everyone. We bought a house in 1986 in Orlando because we believed we had to commit to America and had a great bunch of fellow players living in the area.'

Ian may have been an unknown on the PGA Tour at the end of 1988 but, like Grady, he knew this was where he had to play to progress his career. Ian and Jennie decided to move to the United States for the start of the 1989 season. Ian says, 'I was never going to know in my heart whether I could become one of the best players in the world unless I could make it over there.'

While travelling together in Japan during the 1988 season, Ian and Jennie had made the decision to start a family. Jennie became pregnant with Hayley and the couple joked that their daughter was 'made in Japan'. Hayley was born on 7 February 1989 in the blue room of the birthing unit at Pindara Private Hospital on the Gold Coast. America beckoned for the young family and just three weeks later, on 1 March 1989, the Baker-Finch family arrived in the States.

Once in the US, the Baker-Finches had few problems making friends. Any perceived negativity towards foreign players on tour never eventuated and the family established a permanent home there.

Ian recalls, 'We were lucky to have Wayne and his wife, Lyn, already in the US and while waiting for our house to be built, we stayed with them, making it a lot easier to settle in. The Gradys were good friends to us, and our two families eventually lived only a mile apart.'

The house they built was in the Bay Hill Village near Orlando in Florida, costing US$200,000 and financed by the developer at 7 per cent. Bay Hill would be their base for the next two years, and the area suited them for a number of reasons. 'My mate Payne Stewart was living there,' says Ian. 'We had become friends on his trips down to Australia each year. His Australian wife, Tracey, was the sister of touring pro Mike Ferguson. Greg Norman and Nick Price were both close by.'

The Baker-Finches could travel in the US as a family, something impossible in Europe. Ian was determined to travel as comfortably as possible, and he took Jennie and Hayley with him as often as his

Jennie, Hayley and Ian at home in America.

schedule permitted. The US Tour came with benefits, including courtesy cars and creches. 'We would fly to the tournament venue on Delta or American, pick up a cheap rental car at the airport, courtesy of the great deal the PGA Tour had, and then go to the tournament venue or hotel. Once at the course or hotel we would have the use of a courtesy car for tournament week.' Every tournament venue had a creche for the competitors' children, recalls Ian. 'Hayley grew up in the creches with a group of players' children who remain friends today. The Faxon, Love, O'Meara and Tway children were there, and many others.'

THE BABY IN THE DRAWER

Ian and Jennie improvised on occasion. 'It may sound strange but, when Hayley was a baby, we would put her to bed by fluffing up the bedding for her in a hotel-room drawer and then put it next to our bed,' remembers Ian. 'As she got bigger, we sometimes put her in a bathtub, again made up with hotel bedding. We did not have travel cots or anything like that.'

Looking back, Jennie says, 'Hayley was a perfect baby, and she did all the right things, which made our life on tour so much easier. We only needed one hotel room and could watch TV while she slept.'

Ian played Doral and Bay Hill after arriving on tour but again failed to receive an invitation to the Masters in 1989.

Bruce Green, who became an institution as the pro at Royal Melbourne, had been coaching Ian in Australia in preparation for the conditions he was about to encounter in the US. Australian Steve Bann, and occasionally Alex Mercer, the legendary Sydney-based instructor for the likes of Steve Elkington, also assisted Ian in readying himself.

After the move to the US Tour, Ian required a coach in the States – preferably one based in Florida. He had been interested in Englishman David Leadbetter's methods for some time and selected Mitchell Spearman, another Briton, as his coach, overseen by Leadbetter. Both coaches were based at the Leadbetter Golf Academy, which had opened in 1983 in Orlando and operated from a modest building at the end of the practice fairway at Lake Nona.

Ian recalls, 'Leadbetter fascinated me. My friend Robert Ramsey, a talented player and ex-club champion at the Australian Golf Club, owned the post office and news agency at Sanctuary Cove. He would copy and print every article about Leadbetter from the magazines coming into his store. Robert was a serious student of the game and very technical in approach. I read all the Leadbetter articles Robert gave to me. I was always setting goals for myself and within those goals were steps, one of which was going to the US. Another was to improve my golf under Leadbetter to a level where I was capable of winning the Open.'

At this stage of his playing career, Ian made no dramatic changes to his swing. 'David and Mitchell were hesitant to change too much. They noted the changes to my swing and their connection to David's articles. I worked on two changes in particular – Peter Thomson had helped me to get flatter, but I also realised I needed to hit the ball higher to play in the States. I started trying to take the club back squarer and wider. The technique was all about turning my shoulders and taking my hands out of the swing. It all seemed quite simple to me at the time, and it was still my swing. I was playing well with a good understanding of my swing, practising and working out with my coaches, and not really changing anything major.'

While developing his interest in Leadbetter, Ian was also following the teachings of the unconventional American Mac O'Grady, believing around this time the teachers he was following were 'modernising the swing'. He was also interested in *The Golfing Machine* by Homer Kelley. 'I did a lot of work on the swing by myself and tried to figure it out my way.'

O'Grady's colourful career included 17 separate Q-school attempts before he finally obtained his card in America in 1982, but by 1989 back problems forced him off the tour. He was ambidextrous and once tried to enter the two-man Chrysler Team Championship on his own, with the intention of competing left-handed with one ball and right-handed with the other. Unsurprisingly, his entry was declined. He was fined and suspended in 1986 for conduct unbecoming a professional golfer, after engaging in a sustained series of attacks on tour commissioner Deane Beman.

'Mike Clayton and I regularly discussed the swing and how it worked,' Ian recalls. 'I also really enjoyed my time spent with Mac. I remember once we debated the merits of the long thumb and the short thumb in relation to the grip and swing, and we ended up sitting on the floor of the locker room for two hours discussing this one aspect of golf.'

Clayton has his own view of O'Grady's multiple talents. 'Mac was a genius and was the best teacher in the world at the time by a streak. I think Mac has forgotten more about the golf swing than most of his contemporaries knew.' He also recalls, 'In 1982 Mac played the entire European Tour with eight clubs – a driver, a three-wood, three-, five-, seven- and nine-irons, a sand iron and a putter. He came third in the British PGA at Hillside and finished forty-second on the money list – with half a set.'

Ultimately, Ian made the decision to work with Leadbetter.

In April Ian continued his US campaign, playing in the Byron Nelson Golf Classic and then the Memorial Tournament. He made the cut in both events but collected only modest cheques. It was then on to the Southwestern Bell Colonial in Fort Worth at the Colonial

Country Club. Jennie and Hayley were able to attend for the week – another benefit of the family's home base in the US.

Colonial suited Ian, reminding him of some of the better Australian courses. At 7100 yards, the course was long – and playing even longer after 4 inches of rain fell on the Tuesday and Wednesday before the event. Ian's perceived lack of distance off the tee presented no barrier; the course dried out quickly in Texas's typically windy conditions and the greens became firm and crusty.

Tour rookie Ian shot 65-70-65 to lead through 54 holes in only his sixth event on tour, finishing the third round with another of his birdie bursts. He led by four shots, but he had experienced this before in St Andrews in 1984 and he was not entirely sure how he would manage the pressure of the final day.

On Sunday, his final round of 70 did the job, giving him a wire-to-wire four-shot victory over David Edwards with a ten under par total of 270. The first-prize cheque was US$180,000 – out of a total purse of US$1 million – and the amount seemed almost unbelievable to the young couple. The decision to move to America had paid off handsomely. Along with Jack Nicklaus's and Arnold Palmer's events, the Colonial was one of the top three tournaments (excluding the three US majors) on the PGA Tour in that era.

Ian's caddie at the time of his Colonial win was known as Alaskan Dave Patterson. 'I wrote Alaskan Dave a cheque for eighteen thousand dollars for the customary ten per cent of my winning cheque, and he said, "See you, Ian. I am off fishing in Alaska," and with that was gone. He was a great guy, and I knew that it was his habit to head home at some stage during the season. He had already sorted out Larry Nelson's caddie Russell Craver to work for me as his replacement.'

Jennie was there to witness Ian's first win on tour. 'Hayley loved being outside so I could walk the course watching Ian with her in the pram and never making a sound.'

Ian partially credited Jennie for the win, mentioning to the press she was 'making it her mission to make every week feel like home for me'. Theirs was a genuine 50–50 partnership.

Three weeks later, Wayne Grady won the Manufacturers Hanover Westchester Classic and US$180,000. The two Queenslanders from the Nissan bus in 1980 seemed to be feeding off each other with their US Tour successes. Grady further enhanced his reputation as a player by coming agonisingly close to winning the 1989 Open Championship at Royal Troon in July. He led the event for the first three rounds but faltered slightly near the end of the final round of regulation play. Grady joined Norman to lose a four-hole aggregate play-off – the first of its kind in an Open – to fast-finishing American Mark Calcavecchia. Grady remembers with regret, 'The only time I wasn't in the lead in the Open at Troon was when I finished the first hole of the play-off. However, I was determined after losing the Open that it was not going to finish me, so I kept working hard.'

The rest of the 1989 season was not as productive for Ian, but his first season in the US had undeniably been successful. The couple had developed their own routine and system for travelling together and life was good.

Jennie recalls her husband in the role of first-time father. 'He could not be around all the time, but he was very patient and besotted with Hayley and later with Laura [their second child]. There were times when he may not have had a full night's sleep, but he coped with all that really well.'

Later in 1989 Ian made the tough decision to leave his manager, Steve Frazer. 'I had a discussion with Steve, telling him IMG could get me starts in events that he could not. I also told him now that I was in the States, and he was in Australia concentrating most of his time on tennis, it was time for me to make the move. I was allocated David Yates by IMG, and as much as I liked him and his family, with hindsight, the move to IMG was the wrong decision. I should probably have stayed with Steve. I think if I had been given a Hughes Norton as my manager I may have done a lot better with IMG.' Yates had been a college coach but did not have a great deal of experience in the professional game. 'David Yates had been given several college standouts to manage – Billy Ray Brown, Steve Elkington and Willie Wood – but I am not sure he had too much idea about managing an international player like me.'

Ian had met IMG founder Mark McCormack and his wife, Nancy, and liked them. He found it hard not to be impressed by the sports super-agent and everything McCormack and his organisation had to offer. IMG took a commission of 10 per cent on their clients' golf earnings, and further commission at the rate of 20 per cent was deducted from all other commercial income they generated.

Parting ways with Ian hit Steve Frazer hard. Before his untimely passing in 2024, Frazer recalled, 'I was pretty broken when Ian left. For me, it was more than just a management arrangement with him. I was really angry with IMG for the way they did not seem to understand Ian. The well-being of their clients was not their priority, in my opinion, and they put him with the wrong people as far as his golf was concerned. Ian was a little bit vulnerable and may have been too easily influenced by IMG. It was rare air he found himself in. I believe I gave my clients a special relationship and I thought it even more important to be there for them when they were getting their heads smacked in. The IMGs of the world are only there when you are winning.' Despite the end of their business relationship, Ian and Steve Frazer and their wives, Jennie and Vonnie, would all remain friends for life.

During the season Ian started to feel the pressure of his newly elevated status as a tour winner. 'I did not play very well in the US after Colonial and felt, now that I had won, I was required to play well all the time. I placed a great deal of pressure on myself to continue to play like a tour winner. The win did bring benefits. I had become an exempt player and could play the schedule I wanted to.

'Occasionally I would be invited to a high-end pro-am or a corporate day on a Monday where I would be paid ten thousand US dollars to play. As an example, the Canadian Open had a great presidents' day after the event. I was included in the ten or twenty players invited, which was always a favourite day for me. Thanks to IMG I did get a start in the Suntory World Matchplay Championship for the first time but was beaten four holes up with three to play by David Frost in the first round, which was a kick in the guts for me. IMG would put the leading four or five players in the world in the field and make the rest up with IMG clients, so there was definitely some benefit from being with them.'

Ian's US$421,733 earnings in the 1989 season put him in sixty-fourth place on the world money list. The decision to move to the US with Jennie and Hayley had been vindicated.

CHAPTER 13

A RETURN TO THE AULD GREY TOON

Studying Faldo – at close range

IN EARLY APRIL 1990, Ian Baker-Finch missed the cut in his second Masters by two shots with a total of 151. Then, at the end of May, he came agonisingly close to winning a second PGA Tour title at the Kemper Open in Maryland. His final round of 66 was the best of the day, underpinned by his fine iron play. Unfortunately, his dropped shot on the final hole opened the door for Gil Morgan, playing five holes behind Ian. Armed with the knowledge of exactly what was required of him over the final holes (one under), Morgan edged Ian into second place. But Ian took home the substantial consolation of a cheque for US$108,000. He continued to produce solid performances in the States leading up to the Open at St Andrews, including a fifth-place finish in early July at the Anheuser-Busch Classic in Virginia.

When Ian returned to Scotland for the Open, he no longer had to share a small cottage with one bathroom and an ancient washing machine with five others. It had been six years since his debut major at St Andrews in the most exciting of Opens. 'I loved the course and had great memories from 1984. I was playing well on my return to the Old Course and feeling strong, really strong.' A different player arrived in the Auld Grey Toon in 1990; he was now a PGA Tour winner against world-class opposition.

First, there was a barrier to overcome. Despite being in the top 50 of the world rankings, Ian was required to pre-qualify to play in the Open. In the 36-hole qualifying rounds at Scotscraig Golf Club in Tayport he shot nine under par and cruised comfortably into the field for the Open proper. He arrived in St Andrews with a new caddie he had hired mid-season, Pete Bender.

Old Course champion Seve Ballesteros arrived in St Andrews with his older brother Vicente, a professional himself, as his new caddie. He was accompanied by his wife, Carmen, who was expecting their first child. His form during the season had been average at best, but after his emotional 1984 win at St Andrews he still ranked as a favourite.

Ballesteros may have irritated some of his fellow professionals during his career, but Ian never had an issue with him. 'I played a lot with Seve in the six years between the two Opens and liked playing with him. He was always very friendly to me, and we used to practise together, particularly short-game stuff, at which he excelled. Those hours spent with Seve practising our bunker shots have resulted in bunker play remaining one of my strengths today.'

A NIGHT OUT WITH SEVE

'Seve was a terrific guy,' Ian says. 'He did have one amusing quirk when we went out together while he was single: he habitually had one cigarette in either his top pocket or in his sock, and from there he bummed cigarettes from whoever he was able to for the rest of the night!

'He had so much charisma – and because of his fame there were very few places he could go to escape. Then Carmen came along, and she was such a lovely girl – and great for Seve.

'I may have been frequently drawn with him but I never played at his level and was only ever part of his supporting cast.'

The balmy weather during the 1990 Open saw an unusually large number of visitors and locals stroll and swim along the famous West Sands beach adjacent to the courses at St Andrews. The opening scenes of the 1981 film *Chariots of Fire* were filmed on the two miles of uninterrupted sand, and over many decades Old Tom Morris (winner of four Opens in the 1860s) took his daily early-morning swim off the beach.

The fine weather provoked a burst of low scoring at the top of the leaderboard during the first round. Greg Norman led with 66, Nick Faldo was one shot behind on 67 and there were eight players grouped together on 68, including Ian. Before the tournament Ian faced repeated questions from the press about the 1984 event; they made sure to mention his 'fond memories of six years before' and also his 'unkind last round'. He openly discussed his difficulty over the last six years in living with the disappointment of his final round 79.

The Friday of Open week presented yet another day of perfect scoring conditions for the players, but this did not assist some prominent names. The cut was set at 143, which was low for an Open. Sadly, it was a single shot too low for Arnold Palmer, who had hoped to farewell the Open on the 18th fairway on the Sunday of the event. Ballesteros missed the cut by two and the defending champion, Mark Calcavecchia, missed by three.

Faldo took full advantage of the benign conditions in the second round to shoot 65 and Norman compiled his second straight 66 for the joint 36-hole lead at 12 under par. Ian lost considerable ground with his mediocre even-par 72, to be eight shots off the lead. Then in the third round on Saturday, known in professional golf as 'moving day', Ian did just that in dramatic fashion. He stormed through the front nine in 29. He birdied the first two holes, parred the 3rd and followed with birdie, eagle, birdie in another of his characteristic hot patches. His eagle on the 5th was set up with a four-wood second shot to 15 feet.

'I was nine under after twelve holes and I knew, standing on the 17th tee, I had to shoot par, par for sixty-three. It was a realistic prospect,' he remembers. 'I hit a perfect four-wood second shot into the Road hole green, but my ball rolled back down the slope to the front of the green and I three-putted. I followed by missing a short birdie putt on the 18th.' He finished with a round of 64 and a total of 204. He told the press he was gratified by the round and looking forward to making amends for his final-round crash in 1984. When he reflected on that performance, he noted he had been 'twenty-three and totally inexperienced to have played myself into contention'.

He had improved on his 1984 three-round total by one shot, but still found himself five shots in arrears of a dominant Faldo, who had scored 67-65-67. Ian was tied second on 204 with his friend Payne Stewart. When questioned by a journalist about his putting after his 64, Ian talked about having practised his putting for 'hours and hours growing up' and acknowledged putting was his key strength.

Meanwhile, Faldo was staging a masterclass for his fellow competitors and also the galleries. Overseen by David Leadbetter, Faldo had finally locked in place the drastic changes to his swing. He had taken a major risk in completely dismantling and then rebuilding his swing over three years from 1985, but his fierce concentration, drive and work ethic bolstered the hard-won improvements in his technique. Leadbetter said his star pupil's swing may have looked 'beautiful, with marvellous rhythm' when Leadbetter started coaching him, but declared appearances could be deceptive and Faldo's several swing faults needed to be remedied. His struggling pupil did not win a tournament between 1984 and 1987. In the process, he lost sponsors and endured shaking heads from his colleagues and the press, who were in disbelief over what he was doing.

Of this three-year period, Faldo would later comment, 'I do not know how I did it. [I] would get discouraged and want to see some results with David telling me I was getting closer. Fortunately, I believed him.'

By 1990, the swing changes had granted a dominant Faldo the 1987 Open and two green jackets as Masters champion in 1989 and 1990.

David Begg was the R&A press officer in 1990 and vividly remembers the third round. 'All of the chatter in 1990 was about Faldo destroying Norman while playing with him in the third round, with sixty-seven to Norman's seventy-six. Faldo was determined to play with Norman so he could put pressure on him directly.' History would repeat itself years later in the final round of the 1996 Masters.

By Sunday, the media seemed to have adopted a position after three rounds that the 1990 Open was all over bar the shouting. The bookmakers held a similar view and stopped taking bets on Faldo.

For the second time Ian found himself in the final pairing of the Open, this time drawn with Faldo. The round was challenging for Ian as he continually had to ask Faldo to move his shadow. Ian accepted there was no gamesmanship involved on the Englishman's part; Faldo's lapses of etiquette were a result of his total self-absorption. 'I learned a lot from that round with Nick, watching him and how he went about it. He had become a model for Leadbetter and was far from powerful, but golf was more about accuracy and consistency back then. Nick was so zoned in that he was unaware of where he was standing or what he was doing, but I dealt with it, without letting him put me off completely. It was all about him.

'From the 12th hole coming in the run home to the 18th, he would always go to the right side of the tee, where all the pros like to stand. It also meant that, on each hole, his shadow would fall over the area I was trying to tee my ball up in. I would say to him, "Nick, Nick, please," and he would move away. By the 17th it happened again, and he was still oblivious to what he was doing. All he was thinking about was winning. On the last green he still had no clue of the accepted practice, putting up to inches from the hole. He was lining up to putt out when I had to pull him up again, because I still hadn't finished. He apologised, marked his ball and tapped in in the customary fashion after I had putted out. He taught me a great lesson on how to focus that day.'

Ian struggled slightly, finishing with a 73 to Faldo's 71 but the final round of this major had been another step forward in Ian's understanding of what was required to win the Open.

He was disappointed in his putting performance in the final round. 'I putted poorly, taking thirty-seven putts. It seemed to me there were media and people everywhere inside the ropes and I just could not concentrate, but Nick could. I learned from the experience, and it taught me to focus on myself and concentrate much better the following year.'

Faldo's clinical, efficient final round gave him a five-shot win over Payne Stewart and Mark McNulty. Remarkably, Faldo had avoided taking a single three-putt during his 72 holes.

Shav Glick of the *Los Angeles Times* wrote of the 1990 Open, 'Call Nick Faldo bland, as British media do, but also call him efficient. As deadly efficient as an executioner.'

Faldo paid tribute to his Swedish caddie, Fanny Sunesson, kissing her and then his wife, Gill. 'Fanny is part of the team and does not make mistakes,' he said. 'Golf tournaments are won by making the fewest mistakes.'

Ian dropped three places down the leaderboard to tie sixth with Greg Norman, but won £28,500 for his efforts. More importantly he had survived in the crucible of a final pairing in a major.

When Ian returned to the tour, he played poorly in the last two rounds of his second US PGA Championship. It was the final day at Shoal Creek Golf and Country Club, Alabama, and he took advantage of his early tee off to fly home. He was eager to see Jennie and Hayley.

At the same time, Wayne Grady was navigating his way around Shoal Creek trying to capture his first major. Grady remembers playing with his friend Payne Stewart in the final-round showdown. 'On the 1st hole I holed a sixty-footer and on the 4th hole I holed a forty-footer. By then I had got to Payne, and he went on to shoot eighty. I did bogey the 12th and, having lost the Open at Troon at the very end, I momentarily thought, "Here we go again." But at the 13th I thought, "Stuff it, put your head down," and then played really solidly over the last six holes to win by three shots.' Grady was helped by a pine tree that he hit with his three-wood tee shot on the 15th. The ball fortunately bounced back into the fairway, and Grady held his nerve from there to finish with 72 and win the impressive Wanamaker Trophy.

Ian deeply regretted departing for home early. He wanted to be present at Shoal Creek to congratulate Grady in person on his landmark win. Grady recalls, 'The only other Aussie there was our good mate Greg Hohnen, and if it hadn't been for him I would have been entirely on my own. I went back to the hotel with Greg, shared a bottle of Dom Perignon with him over dinner, and went to bed.'

Ian recalls, 'I was feeding off my mates who were doing well. Wayne had been unlucky not to win the Open the year before at

Troon but Shoal Creek was a great course for him – he was not required to be long, but he did need to be straight, which he was. After Wayne's win in the PGA, I thought, "He has done it. He has won a major, and so can I."

In late October Ian finished third equal in the Nabisco Championship at the Champions Golf Club in Houston for another good pay day of US$146,250.

Ian's year had involved a brutal amount of travel. He found himself in Japan in early November at the Yomiuri Country Club, Inagi, for a one-off event called the Asahi Glass Four Tours World Championship. The format of the event was unusual: teams of six were invited from each of the European, United States, Australasian and Japanese tours. Ian and Steve Williams were together again as part of the Australasian team. The tournament purse was a healthy US$1.15 million, which did nothing to prevent the humorous side of the Baker-Finch–Williams relationship re-emerging.

Williams recalls, 'On the driving range at the event there was a high net at the back of the range to stop balls travelling too far – a common feature of the courses on tour in Japan. In front of a large crowd of Japanese spectators, Ian was busting himself unsuccessfully to hit his driver over the top of the net at the end of the range. I couldn't stand it, so I grabbed his driver off him and knocked it over the top of the net on my third attempt. The crowd loved it and all clapped – but I am not sure it was so good for Ian's ego.'

The relationship between the pair remained intact.

Ian's team of six included his two Queensland friends Grady and Senior, who were joined by the Japan Tour specialist Brian Jones along with Harwood and Parry. Ian played well and was undefeated in the first three rounds of the combined strokeplay–matchplay format, thanks to his rounds of 67, 68 (beating Ian Woosnam) and 68. Ian's low scoring was instrumental in his team's win as the final round was washed out by torrential rain, rendering the course unplayable. The Australasian team – who were without their best player, Norman – were declared the winners from the US, on a countback on stroke total. Each team member collected US$80,000.

It was the final time Williams would caddie for Ian, and it was their first win together.

At the end of the year, it was briefly back to the US for a team scramble event hosted by Greg Norman that finished on 18 November. Ian paired up with Mark Calcavecchia to take third-equal place and US$44,000.

Meanwhile, IMG was putting together a deal for Ian with the Japanese fishing equipment manufacturer Daiwa, who were looking to make inroads with the golf market in their area of expertise – graphite shafts.

At the end of November, the Baker-Finch family headed Down Under for the Australian Open at the Australian Golf Club in Sydney. In pursuit of a punishing annual schedule of 40 tournaments, Ian was seemingly unaffected by all his recent travel. He finished tied fifth behind largely unknown American John Morse, and then contended at the Johnnie Walker Classic at Royal Melbourne, shooting a masterful third round of 63, a course record that stood for 20 years. He faded with 76 in the final round while enduring miserable weather and heavy showers to finish behind Greg Turner. The New Zealander was another successful Leadbetter graduate, who, similarly to Faldo, had endured a traumatic swing rebuild.

Not far from his old family home at Beerwah on the Sunshine Coast, Ian ended the year on a high note at the Hyatt Regency Coolum Classic. In 1990 the Classic had been amalgamated with the Queensland Open to create a popular event with a family-friendly feel, based as it was at a resort wedged between Mount Coolum and an idyllic stretch of white sand beach. The venue was enhanced by its

Robert Trent Jones–designed course, a significant step up from the mainly country courses in the area.

The relaxed end-of-year atmosphere was typified by the 'cut party' at Coolum, held after the first 36 holes. 'The Groover' Tim Ireland, the journeyman pro from Ian's Troppo Tour days, remembers, 'With no warning I was called onto the stage with the band at the cut party to perform "Great Balls of Fire", the only song in my repertoire. There was no way for me to avoid performing, with everyone yelling, "We want the Groover!" ABC [Australia] were there filming the party and incredibly they televised my very amateur act the next day on national television.'

Ian was staving off a few late-season back problems but played well in his first three rounds for 66-67-67. Holding a four-shot lead going into the final round, his one under par 71 was good enough for a five-shot win and A$27,000.

Ian had enjoyed playing in front of family and friends. 'I was leading by seven shots coming up the last, but double-bogeyed. I had played great golf and Coolum suited me because you had to hit it where you aimed. One thing I enjoyed about my win was that Dad and my uncle Clem were there watching the event, and we had time to have a few beers afterwards on Sunday night.'

Ian was seventeenth on the world money list in 1990 after the Coolum win – a reflection of his earnings of US$950,988 for the year. It was a testament to the country boy's tiring but exceptional season. Norman was in third position on the money list, Rodger Davis twenty-second, Steve Elkington twenty-third, and Wayne Grady twenty-seventh.

Australia, led by two Queenslanders, had become a force in world golf.

CHAPTER 14

THE 1991 OPEN, ROYAL BIRKDALE

Leading after three rounds – again

BACK HOME IN Australia, Ian started the year slowly in January with a missed cut at the A$1.2 million Palm Meadows Cup. The following week, representing the resort as its touring pro, he shot a closing 67 around the Arnold Palmer–designed Pines course for a tied third finish in the Sanctuary Cove Classic. He had unluckily struck a freak burst of high wind and torrential rain on his last hole after making up most of an eight-shot deficit on the third-round leader, New Zealander Frank Nobilo. Nobilo faded with 75 to hand Rodger Davis victory.

Another solid performance followed in mid-February at the Australian Masters at Huntingdale Golf Club in Melbourne.

Ian and Jennie were back in the United States by late February 1991, and Ian improved steadily on tour. He played well without winning in Miami at the Doral Ryder Open, and again in the USF&G Classic in New Orleans.

He received his third invitation to the Masters in April and played well to tie seventh at eight under par. 'I putted poorly and still did not manage those undulating greens at Augusta well. I was just too aggressive with the putter. The rest of my short game was good.' Ian finished three shots behind the winner, Ian Woosnam from Wales, who had Ian's old 1984 caddie, Wobbly, on his bag. Five of the six players in front of him were major winners, and Ian finished under par in each of his four rounds.

A week later at Harbour Town Golf Links in South Carolina, Ian chased Davis Love III all the way in the MCI Heritage Classic, but when Ian was unable to save par from a bunker on the 17th, he allowed Love to win by two shots. 'I should have won that event,' he says. 'I played the 18th too conservatively to finish bogey, bogey. It was another of my many second places. It was just how I was – I seemed to lack some killer instinct when it was needed, instead of thinking, "What have I got to do here to win?"'

Still, second prize was US$108,000, and he played well in the Memorial Tournament and Southwestern Bell Colonial, picking up another US$80,000. By mid-June, he had secured a place in his first US Open championship at Hazeltine National Golf Club in Minnesota. The layout had been much maligned the previous time the Open had visited in 1970, particularly by runner-up Dave Hill, who commented that all the course lacked was 'eighty acres of corn and a few cows'.

In 1991 the layout was more acceptable to the players but still demanding. Ian finished midfield behind his good friend Payne Stewart. The two families lived 200 yards apart on the same street. Stewart was a popular and colourful player, with his distinctive flat caps and plus-fours, who won his first major, the PGA Championship, in 1989. 'Payne and I were good buddies,' says Ian. 'We would practise together, go out on boats together, and he was a real character.' In June 1999, Stewart went on to win a second US Open at Pinehurst. He tragically died four months later in a plane crash. He was 42 years old.

Ian's second peak of the 1991 season started to build in June. He tied third in the Anheuser-Busch Classic in Georgia and followed it up with a win in late June at the Westinghouse-Family House Invitational at Oakmont Country Club in Pennsylvania, a two-round invitation event. Three weeks later, in the New England Classic, he lost a marathon seven-hole sudden-death play-off against 42-year-old journeyman professional Bruce Fleisher. 'In the play-off Bruce putted unbelievably,' Ian says. 'I putted second on the first six holes for birdies after he had holed par putts from outside me on each of those six holes. On the seventh extra hole he holed a birdie putt from fifty feet, and I missed the twenty-footer I needed to continue the play-off. It was amazing.'

In July, Ian had cause to be quietly confident as he flew over to the British Open at Royal Birkdale Golf Club in England. Birkdale's history can be traced back to 1889 and it is regarded as one of the finest courses on the Open rota. It sits comfortably among the dunes, providing great gallery vantage points. Ian liked what he saw. 'When you first drive up to the clubhouse you arrive on the ugly side of the building with its stark white walls,' he says, 'but the rest of the building is quite unique.' The course had originally been laid out by professional George Lowe, and it was remodelled in the 1930s by Fred Hawtree and J H Taylor. In 1935, noted Southport architect George Tonge won a competition for his then ultra-modern vision for a clubhouse that 'imagined the lines of a liner at sea, the perfect balance of the ship at whichever angle and from whatever side it was seen'.

Ian was arriving at Birkdale in top form. 'I was driving well, my irons were good, and my short game and putting were in great shape. I always thought that to win a major you had to arrive with your A game; you can never find it out there during the week.' He had cause for optimism after his run of fine form in the US – and his second peak was far from over. In the lead-up to Birkdale, Ian's win at Oakmont and his play-off loss to Fleisher put him at odds of 50–1 on the Monday of Open week. The bookies rated Ian and so did the caddies – several, including Nick Price's caddie, placed substantial bets on him. Ian was later quoted as saying, 'A lot of people at the tournament thought I was one of the favourites for the week. I arrived believing in myself and this was my first time coming into a major where I really thought I could win it.'

The family rented a small house near the course. Ian remembers, 'I had Jennie and Hayley with me. We kept everything simple but comfortable when we travelled, and it all felt very normal in that little house.' Completing the Baker-Finch household during Open week was player turned coach Steve Bann, who was at Birkdale to keep an eye on his Australian pupils, including young amateur Robert Allenby, aged 20. Ian was still being coached mainly by Mitchell Spearman at the time, but David Leadbetter was also at Birkdale maintaining an overview of his Leadbetter 'stable' of players, including Ian.

Caddie Pete Bender was staying nearby and by then had been on Ian's bag for two years. He was one of the first non-club caddies to be allowed to work at Augusta and had also caddied for Norman during his 1986 Open win at Turnberry. Bender's relationship with Norman ended abruptly in November 1987 when Norman fired him by car phone from Australia. Bender asked his boss for a reason and Norman replied, 'I don't have an excuse.'

Ian and his ex–Troppo Tour friend Mike Harwood arranged to play two practice rounds on Tuesday and Wednesday with fellow Australian Graham Marsh. Marsh was a veteran of the tournament contesting his twentieth Open. The condition of the greens surprised them during their practice rounds. Harwood remembers, 'The greens at Birkdale were terrible in 1991. It looked like they had been cored and then suffered from severe weather conditions. The core holes never really disappeared out of the greens during the week. The worst green was the 17th, which was in horrendous condition.'

Ian and Harwood held an advantage over the rest of the field – their formative years had given them experience in routinely putting on poor surfaces. Their form clearly impressed Marsh, who at 47 was competing in his final Open. In 2023 Harwood recalled the two warm-up rounds vividly. 'Ian and I were playing so well that when we finished our second round, Graham Marsh walked off and said, "If I can beat either of you guys this week, I'll win the Open."'

Birkdale has a history of producing great champions. Peter Thomson won there in 1954 and again in 1965, Arnold Palmer in 1961, Lee Trevino in 1971, Johnny Miller in 1976 and Tom Watson in 1983. In 1991, the reigning Masters champion, Ian Woosnam, was the favourite, closely followed by Nick Faldo and Seve Ballesteros.

Unlike at the 1984 Open, Ian failed to set the course alight in his first outing. He was in trouble after 15 holes at three over par but restored respectability to his round with birdies on the 17th and 18th, holing out for an undistinguished one over par round of 71. His name was absent from the leaderboard, whereas Ballesteros had an opening round of 66.

Ballesteros had first attracted the golfing public's attention at Birkdale in 1976 as an unknown, swashbuckling 19-year-old. Fifteen years later, a more conservative Ballesteros navigated his way around Birkdale using his driver only sparingly – on four holes – and mainly employing long irons off the tees.

Faldo was on 68 and Harwood started fast on the same score. Also flying the Australian flag, Marsh and Grady had identical scores of 69.

The troublesome greens, with their strange, straw-coloured hue and slow and bumpy surfaces, were the subject of a considerable amount of unfavourable commentary. Any problems with them hardly seemed insurmountable to the Queenslanders in the field, but Jack Nicklaus was joined by several of his fellow US Tour players in criticising the quality of the putting surfaces. He suggested to the press he had given advice on the greens prior to the tournament, which had been ignored by both the greenkeeper and the R&A.

Friday, the second day of the Open, dawned cold, with the wind and driving rain mixing into a challenging weather cocktail. Theoretically, the conditions should not have suited Mike Harwood, who stood at 6 feet 4 inches and possessed an exceptionally light build. He teed off at 8.50 am, ten minutes after Ian, and despite being buffeted by the conditions he scored 70 for a total of 138 and a three-way share of the 36-hole lead. Ballesteros played conservatively again, scoring 73 for a total of 139. Grady was only one shot off the lead after his second-round score of 70. Faldo struggled with a 75 to fall off the pace.

After the first two days, there had only been 36 rounds under Birkdale's par of 70. And what of Ian? Again, he was in trouble early in the round but recovered well on the back nine with a birdie on the 17th for a one over par 71 and a total of 142. His name was still absent from the course leaderboards around Birkdale, but at two over he was only four shots off the lead.

The Americans once again led a chorus of criticism about the putting surfaces. Tom Kite suggested it was like putting on a sponge cake and Payne Stewart proposed the only solution was to dig them up and lay down new surfaces. Ian was more restrained when asked about the greens; he had putted extremely well in poor weather. Ballesteros, meanwhile, brought into play his unique sense of humour, calling the greens 'perfect' and 'fantastic'.

None of the pre-tournament favourites featured at the top of the 36-hole leaderboard. Harwood and two other virtual unknowns, Gary Hallberg and Andrew Oldcorn, were all tied on 138, and congested below the leading trio, a single shot behind, were Grady, Ballesteros and the consistent American Mark O'Meara.

In the third round, Ian cleared away some of this congestion at the top by producing a low round of 64. He birdied three of the first five holes but then three-putted for a bogey on the 7th. The fireworks started again in earnest on the back nine, with birdies on the 10th and 13th – from 2 feet – followed by a frustrating three-putt bogey on the 14th. Ian's finish was electric – he followed a five-iron from 195 yards on the 17th with a 20-foot putt to produce an eagle three. He finished his round on the 18th by hitting his five-iron again – this time from 190 yards out of a divot – to 6 feet for a closing birdie. He had compiled a great round of 64, including two three-putts, for a third-round total of 206.

CALCAVECCHIA GIVES HIS CLUBS AWAY

Mark Calcavecchia, the 1989 Open champion, scored 79 in the second round and set a quirky record after walking off the 18th green. He approached one of the volunteers accompanying his group who was on bunker-raking duties. While chatting to the American on the way round, the volunteer had revealed that he was a golf professional himself and his own clubs had been stolen. After missing the cut, Calcavecchia removed his offending irons from his bag, sought the stunned volunteer out and gifted them to him over his objections.

When a spectator asked the downcast player what he would use the next day, Calcavecchia apparently replied, 'An aeroplane.'

Mark O'Meara had teed off at 2.30 pm, an hour and a half after Ian, nursing the sore back he had been enduring since the US Open in June. He had been thinking of withdrawing from the Open but instead arrived at Birkdale with an armoury of anti-inflammatories.

His third round of 67 for a total of 206 was a testament to his perseverance, and he finished strongly – identically to Ian, he shot an eagle on the 17th and a birdie on the 18th.

Harwood also played well in a round containing six birdies for a 69. After fading in the middle of the round, he had been reminded by his wife, Lynda, to take on board some energy-boosting nutrition. He accepted her advice and found a couple of bananas in his golf bag. After taking on this much-needed fuel, he birdied four of his last six holes for a total of 207 – the same total as Irishman Eamonn Darcy.

Ballesteros was lurking two shots behind the leaders on 208 after his 69.

The leaderboard had seven players within three shots of the lead. The Open title was there for the taking, most likely from inside that group of seven.

Ian Baker-Finch	206
Mark O'Meara	206
Eamonn Darcy	207
Mike Harwood	207
Seve Ballesteros	208
Mike Reid	209
Vijay Singh	209

Ian had been here before in 1984, and he had also featured in the final pair with Faldo in 1990 at St Andrews. However, there had been less pressure on him then because of the size of Faldo's lead and the Englishman's record in majors.

This time the pressure was intense.

'By the time the final round came I had been through this situation twice before,' says Ian. 'I concentrated on trying to make sure I did what I had to do, not get ahead of myself and just concentrate on staying calm.'

CHAPTER 15

THE FINAL ROUND

'I wanted to get my hands on that jug.'

After the third round the state of the greens continued to occupy competitors' minds and was the subject of much media comment. Most of the players had a view. Nick Faldo, the defending champion and a favourite, had seen his title defence fade over the first three days, though he did shoot 68 in his final round – good enough for 281 and seventeenth place. He left Birkdale with a parting shot: 'It will be nice to get back on some good greens.' Jack Nicklaus finished even further back on 285, in forty-fourth position. He had played well during the tournament but had lost his confidence on the greens and was unable to resist commenting he 'couldn't read the break from one green to another'.

R&A press officer David Begg was a first-hand observer. 'By Sunday, the greens had started to come apart and become very difficult, but it didn't seem to affect Ian on the front nine – he holed everything he looked at, whereas the other guys were shaking their heads and hardly believing what they were seeing. It was very sad for the greenkeeper who knew he had got it ever so slightly wrong.'

For Ian and Mike Harwood, inconsistent, poor and bumpy greens were neither a physical nor mental obstacle. Few, if any, complaints were heard from the pair, nor from their fellow Australians, many of whom remained in contention in the 1991 Open. Craig Parry, Greg Norman, Rodger Davis, Peter Senior and Wayne Grady were all happily lining up for places in the top 30. Graham Marsh, Steve Elkington and Peter O'Malley finished not too far behind that group. It was an incredibly consistent performance by the troupe of Australian players who had made the cut.

Not coincidentally Seve Ballesteros and Lee Trevino also performed without complaint and well on the greens of which the bulk of American and English players were so critical. From the time of each player's introduction to the game, the stars had honed their formidable skills on playing greens that were far from perfect – in fact, they were at home on such surfaces.

Mike Harwood was drawn in the penultimate group with Eamonn Darcy – not his preferred choice of playing partner. Harwood recalls, 'I was putting my shoes on in the locker room before teeing off and sitting close to a television. The BBC commentators were talking about my chances of winning the tournament. Seve was sitting next to me also putting his shoes on. He was fresh from a couple of great years in the Open, and he turned around stared directly at me and said, "Mike who?" I came straight back at him and said, "You'll know after today." That was Seve for you. I had played with him plenty of times before. I found him difficult to play with, but he was a fantastic guy off the course.'

The understated Harwood never rated himself as a great player but before the final round he adopted the attitude that, if no one else wanted to win, his goal was to finish at the top. Ballesteros said his fellow competitors were perhaps 'afraid of the trophy more than me'. He added, 'The trophy means so much.'

The night before the final round had been a typically quiet one for Ian, Jennie and Hayley Baker-Finch. 'Fish and chips from the local store and a Foster's beer for me,' says Ian. The following day he selected his wardrobe carefully. The family was unanimous that he should wear pink – Jennie and Hayley liked pink. 'I liked to dress colourfully, and pink was part of that. I was wearing Lyle and Scott at the time, which had been an IMG deal, and I liked their clothes and colour range. Back home, half of Australia probably thought "What a wanker" and wondered what I was wearing pink for, but I liked it and felt good in it.' The combination of grey trousers and pink shirt had a pedigree and was an Arnold Palmer favourite.

'I have always liked to get to the 1st tee in plenty of time,' says Ian. 'One of the good features of Birkdale for me was that the 1st tee was quite a serene place; it was set away from everything else. There was just the starter and a few others and a grandstand on the left. I could get there with no fuss and be in my own space.' He was joined by his playing partner for the final round, Mark O'Meara – a fortunate draw for Ian. The two players were practice buddies from Orlando.

O'Meara may have been having back problems, but he was an affable player with a sound, rhythmic swing. It was soothing for Ian to watch in the cauldron of that final round of the Open. 'Mark was the perfect playing partner for me. We were good mates, and he has that pleasant demeanour. We could walk fast and talk to each other. I felt completely relaxed in his company and hit a three-wood down the right-hand side, exactly as I had done on each of the first three days.' The pair teed off on time at 2.20 pm in perfect harmony; two good friends, pulling for each other.

After a quiet 1st hole – three-wood and four-iron, plus two putts from 30 feet for par – Ian's round came alive in the most dramatic manner from the 2nd hole, after his drive, six-iron approach and a 12-foot birdie putt. The 3rd hole continued in a similar vein:

three-wood, wedge to 10 feet for another birdie. 'It started to rain on the 4th hole,' says Ian. 'The umbrella was up but I did not put any rain gear on and hit a three-iron to ten feet and holing it for my third straight birdie to go to three under.' Ian had rapidly pulled three shots clear of Darcy and four ahead of O'Meara.

It was only just past 3 pm, and the tournament seemed almost over.

After a safe par on the 5th hole, Ian continued his triumphant march down the most difficult hole on the course – the par-four 6th. It may have been a par four on the card but had averaged 4.6 shots across the field during the Open, higher than the 4.2 average score on the par-five 17th hole. 'I chose to be aggressive off the tee, driving to the right of the bunker rather than taking a safe option left. Instead of a three-wood, I picked up extra run by driving down the right side to leave me with only a seven-iron into the green.' Ian holed the resulting 6-foot putt, delivering himself a bonus birdie three. He holed a 15-footer for birdie on the par-three 7th, taking him to five under for the day. 'I looked up at the leaderboard as I walked to the 8th tee and saw I was five shots ahead. I thought, "Bloody hell, do not stuff it up from here. I will not be allowed back home."'

Two regulation pars on the 8th – after hitting the flag with his second and running 30 feet past – and the 9th gave Ian a remarkable outward nine of 29. Ian remembers, 'Halfway through the round I thought, "Here I am in the last group, have just shot twenty-nine on the front nine and I am in pretty good shape."' Ian would later tell Mike Clayton, 'I could see a white line on the ground all the way to the hole and I just hit along it.'

Mark O'Meara had a ringside seat. He recalls, 'Ian hit every drive down the middle of the fairway, he hit every iron at the flag and made every putt. It was the most incredible display I have seen for nine holes.'

In a strong crosswind, he was bunkered off the tee on the 10th, played out safely and then hit a seven-iron onto the green followed by two putts to drop a shot. He steadied the ship from there with six consecutive two-putt pars.

Of those six holes the 16th was the most difficult. It was long – 465 yards – and straight into the wind. He hit a great four-iron onto the green 10 feet behind the flag. The television coverage caught his exchange with his caddie, Pete Bender. 'Do you like that one, Petey? You like that one, bud?'

Bender's response: 'I love it, Finchy, I love it!'

Bender was a great fit for Ian. He would later compare caddying for him at the Open that week to riding Secretariat, the champion American thoroughbred racehorse: 'Stay out of the way, and make sure you stay on.'

Jennie, six months pregnant with Laura, had been following Ian's progress during the earlier part of the round. Hayley was in a creche, but Jennie remembers, 'As Ian was finishing, I was aware he was quite a few ahead and knew he was doing well. I went and picked Hayley up, so for the last few holes she was with me as we watched Ian.'

The 17th hole had treated Ian well all week – he'd had two birdies and an eagle coming into the final day. 'By the 17th I was starting to feel the pressure a bit,' he says. 'I was not long enough to play out to the right but hit it perfectly with a draw down the left side, leaving me a five-iron to the green.'

Two putts from 50 feet for another birdie saw Ian scoring five under on the hole for the week as he opened a comfortable lead of three shots. Darcy had finished with 70 for 277. O'Meara was playing steadily alongside Ian without really threatening him. He would ultimately finish with 69 and 275. Ballesteros had lost ground with his 71 for a total of 279. Fred Couples, another player with a set of back problems, had stormed home with 64 for 275. Couples told reporters after the final round that his back was in such bad shape during the week that he had been sleeping on the floor of his hotel room.

This left Harwood as the only challenger still on the course. He played the last 12 holes in four under to finish his final round in 67 – a total of 274. It was an impressive performance, but not quite a winning one.

Ian stood on the last tee with a three-shot lead and decided he could afford to play the final hole conservatively. The 18th featured a deep bunker within his driving range. 'That bunker sits right in the middle of the fairway and I had to avoid it at all costs,' he recalls. 'It was not easy walking up the narrow path to the 18th tee. The crowds had been pushed up onto the tee and were uncomfortably close to where I was attempting to tee off. I had to back away and then my marshal managed to bring the gallery under some sort of control. Setting up for the second time, I saw a fence down the right-hand side that I had never been conscious of before. I thought, "There is a reason I have just noticed that." I readjusted my line and drove into the left rough pretty much where I wanted to be. I knew I was safe in there; although it was almost three feet long in places, it was wispy, not thick and juicy.'

He faced a second decision on the final hole. There were two bunkers on either side of the fairway about 50 yards out from the green. 'Instead of trying to fly them, I thought I would play a six-iron in between them to finish short right of the green and chip on for a safe [bogey] five and the win.'

The plan was sound, and Ian found himself about 40 yards short of the par four in two.

'"Do not try and be a hero," was my thought. I wanted to get my name on that jug.'

As he walked up the 18th fairway the crowd broke loose to form an unruly circle around the green. O'Meara lost a shoe – and his balance – trying to break through the gallery to reach the 18th green. Ian was luckier, being escorted through the gallery by English bobbies.

'I am lining up my third shot, after taking my glasses off, wiping them and putting them back on, and Pete said, "Are you sure you don't want to just run it up left of the bunker instead of playing a pitch shot over it?" I said, "Mate, if I cannot hit this shot, I do not deserve to win the Open." On reflection, the shot was not that easy, pitching over a bunker off a hard fairway to a firm green, but I almost holed it.'

Jennie had walked beside Ian for a time up the 18th fairway, understandably in tears. 'Hayley and I walked up the last hole. It was amazing and I was so proud of the way he had handled himself during the whole week. He was thirty and in the process of winning the Open Championship.'

Ian Wooldridge from the commentary team called it 'a very emotional moment'. 'He has suffered before,' he intoned. 'It is not the dream finish, but who cares?'

Ian's pitch from in front of the green had finished 10 feet past, and he putted safely from there to less than a foot. O'Meara putted out for his 69 clearing the way for his good friend to enjoy his triumph. Of O'Meara, the commentator said, 'A nice man to spend the most important day of your golf life with on the course.'

Ian safely holed the winning putt as the commentary continued: 'Ian Baker-Finch is the champion. He has dreamed of this moment many times, I am sure. In she goes. Victory for Australia and how proud they will be. Over to the home team.'

Jennie remembers, 'When Ian holed that final putt on the 18th, I remember seeing his tears, his excitement and his sense of relief that "I have finally done this". It brings tears to my eyes even now.'

Jennie and Hayley came onto the green to embrace Ian in his moment of triumph. The R&A official film and the battery of photographers captured a touching family scene as the small, close group hugged. Wayne Grady arrived with two glasses of champagne to celebrate with his old mate: a pair of major winners from similar backgrounds. Ian had dominated the last two days of the championship. With his total of 272, he'd won the Claret Jug and a cheque for £90,000.

At the trophy presentation, Ian hesitated before speaking, his eyes glistening and his voice close to breaking. He looked down, composed himself and spoke sincerely to the huge crowd he had taken with him during those two magnificent closing rounds. His speech was heartfelt, natural and moving – vintage Ian. 'I have dreamed about this for a long time. The pain of the other couple of times when I had a chance to do it gave me the strength to do it today. I will cherish this trophy forever.' He thanked his supporters over the last eight years. 'I have felt like you have got behind me.' He concluded that he hoped now that he was a winner 'not a loser, you will stay behind me'.

Ian holds the Claret Jug surrounded by volunteers at the 1991 Open, Royal Birkdale Golf Club.

The solemnity of the prize-giving and the emotional final scene was broken by Hayley breaking away from Jennie and joyously toppling into a nearby bunker, where she was retrieved by her mother. After the formalities Ian, trophy in hand, proudly waved a large Australian flag that a patriotic spectator had thrust into his hands.

The final scene of the official R&A film shows Ian kneeling with the Claret Jug. He is surrounded by the championship committee. This normally staid group of administrators, in dark jackets, white shirts and ties, are beaming to a man, as they join Ian in yet another chorus of 'Waltzing Matilda'. The film fades to the credits as Ian looks up and smiles broadly. This Open had been a triumph for Australia with Mike Harwood in second place, Craig Parry tied for eighth and Greg Norman tied ninth – four Australians in the top ten.

In 2023, runner-up Harwood reflected on that final round and Ian's Open win. He had played a great deal of golf with Ian over the years and they shared aspirations to make their mark on the game. Harwood summed it up: 'I travelled with Ian regularly and I am sure I understood him well. Ian's whole goal in his life was to win the British Open. He used to talk about it all the time. He had his chances in two British Opens before 1991. When he did finally win the Open, it seemed to me he had reached his pinnacle and achieved his goal.'

WAYNE GRADY'S AND IAN'S RENOVATIONS

Wayne Grady had a unique take on the financial benefits of his and Ian's major wins.

'When I won my major, I made an addition to my house. Finchy did the same when he won his. The difference between me and Finchy was that my addition was a pool table and a bar; Finchy's was a sauna and a gym.'

The Baker-Finches returned to the house hey had been staying in. Ian supplied Australian beers – Victoria Bitter and Foster's – and a party ensued. 'Steve Bann was there with us, and I gave the Australian boys two hundred pounds to go and buy as much Australian beer and wine as they could find. It was a good night, not a riotous one. Jennie put Hayley to bed and made a big pot of spaghetti bolognese to feed everyone, and a few of the Australian press turned up as well.

'At midnight we put a nice bottle of Aussie shiraz in the jug and went back to the club – Jennie and Steve Bann and me. The security guard let us in after I showed the jug to him. Jennie stayed at the

An Australian victory party with Foster's. Back row (from left): Steve Bann, John Wade, Paul Moloney, Ian and Robert Allenby. Front: Glenn Joyner.

green while Steve and I walked back up the last hole in the dark and I showed him where I had hit my second shot from.'

Ian Baker-Finch, 1991 Open Champion, reflects, 'Growing up in Beerwah, my goal early on was to become a club pro and perhaps one day become a good-enough player that I could play in tournaments – and maybe even one day be fortunate to *play* in a British Open.'

CHAPTER 16

AFTER THE OPEN

Equipment changes and a new ball

Ian Baker-Finch woke up on Monday 22 July 1991 as the Open Champion.

With the Claret Jug came the lifetime label of 'major winner'. Looking back, he says, 'Words cannot describe how I felt the next day. A lot of people called by the house we were renting near Birkdale while we were packing and preparing to fly back to the US. We said goodbye to everyone, and then a bunch of local schoolchildren turned up to the house to have their photos taken with me and the Claret Jug. All I could think was "I have done it".'

As Mark McCormack says, 'It could not happen to a nicer guy.' The nice guy had not come last. Despite his Open win, Ian never visualised himself as a Nick Faldo or a Greg Norman. Nor did he believe he was one of the greats. The Birkdale Open champions preceding Ian were all multiple major winners: Thomson (five), Palmer (seven), Trevino (six), Miller (two) and Watson (eight).

In 2017, the often contentious 88-year-old American journalist Dan Jenkins belittled Ian's Birkdale performance on Twitter:

'How can a course that has provided us with such winners as Palmer, Trevino, Miller and Watson also have given us Ian Baker-Finch?' Jenkins clearly did not rate Peter Thomson, who had won the Open at Birkdale twice. The golfing world swiftly formed ranks behind Ian, with others suggesting Jenkins should know better. Tiger Woods had already tangled with Jenkins in 2014, labelling a piece of his work as character assassination.

THE BAKER-FINCH OPEN STATISTICS

- In 1991 his 272 total was the lowest winning Open score at Royal Birkdale. (Jordan Spieth would score 268 in 2017.)
- In 1991 only Watson and Faldo had posted lower 72-hole Open scores.
- Only one player has posted a lower nine-hole score than Ian's 29 at Birkdale: Englishman Denis Durnian with 28 in the second round of the 1993 Open, also at Birkdale.
- At the time of writing, Ian remains the only golfer to achieve two nine-hole scores of 29 in the Open.
- Ian and Watson are tied record holders for the lowest final 36 holes at 130.

Ian may never have believed he was one of the greats, but in 1991 he undoubtedly put on one of the great performances in golf's oldest major. He had observed first-hand many of the multiple-major champions of his era when playing with them – the laser-like focus of players like Faldo and Norman as they applied themselves to the mental and physical sides of the game. These players were a different breed. Their personal lives often reflected driven, self-centred personalities that may not have been easy to live with.

The boy from rural Queensland was not like that, and it is unlikely he ever wanted to be Norman's successor. He had nagging doubts about his inability to convert winning opportunities into first-place finishes. After the Open, Ian still did not see himself as being any different from his peer group of players like Mike Harwood, Craig Parry and Peter Senior.

But he was mistaken. Now Ian *was* different, and he had just won the Open in commanding fashion to prove it. David Leadbetter would later comment, 'Ian did not have a lot of self-esteem. Even though he had won the Open there was always something in Ian's make-up; he was never the cocky Australian.' Ian, too, has reflected he may have lacked the killer instinct required to be either the No 1 player in the world or the sport's leading money winner. His less lofty ambition was to be the best that he could, and to provide well for his family, which he was doing.

The family flew back to the US the day after his win. 'Hayley was carrying the blue box with the Claret Jug in it and after we boarded we passed the jug around the other passengers, which was fun.'

The next week Ian telephoned his last-round playing partner from Birkdale, Mark O'Meara, who recalled in 2023, 'We were both living in Orlando at the time, and I came over to Ian and Jennie's house. He toasted me and I toasted him out of the Claret Jug he had just won, and he said to me, "M O, I am so pleased I was paired with you in that final round, because that helped me win."'

Ian did not take a break after Birkdale. 'I had entered the Greater Hartford Open, which was only a small tournament then. The organisers were expecting me to pull out after having won the Open; every other Open winner from the week before their event had done that to them in the past. I played, perhaps setting the tone for myself of how well I was to deal with my Open win.

'After the Open, I was immediately invited to play in the next six tournaments in Europe with appearance money on offer of £100,000 per event. I did not take the money and stuck to my commitments back in the US. A couple of months later I came second in the International, losing to Olazabal by one shot, but hardly excelled for the rest of the season in the US.'

After the Open, Ian deservedly climbed into the world top ten, but he did not play particularly well for the rest of the 1991 season. He again received an invitation to play in the rarefied air of the World Matchplay Championship, starting on 17 October. In the Toyota-sponsored, IMG-run event at Wentworth, he was drawn to play against Nick Price in the second round. Ian was never really in the game, losing three down with two to play to the Zimbabwean. Price went on to lose to Ballesteros in the final.

There were other distractions. 'We wanted our second daughter, Laura, to be born in Australia. We saw our doctor in Orlando and Jennie was cleared to fly to Australia while seven and a half months pregnant. I flew home in September to have a month off golf and Laura arrived on the seventh of October.' The family's homecoming to Sanctuary Cove was memorable for Jennie. 'As we drove in there was a huge banner saying, *Congratulations, Ian Baker-Finch – Open Champion.*'

Australia then hosted the Four Tours World Championship at Royal Adelaide. 'I was the team captain – Greg [Norman] did not play that year because he did not get the appearance fee he requested.' Ian and his team were keen to defend the title they had won in Tokyo the previous season, but Europe won the event and Australia came in second. The format and lack of direct payment to the players meant the event was never played again after 1991.

The following week the first PGA Grand Slam of Golf was played in Lihue, Hawaii, for two days starting on 13 November. Jennie,

Hayley and six-week-old Laura travelled along with Ian, who was playing against the year's three other major champions: Ian Woosnam, Payne Stewart and John Daly. They played for what Ian describes as 'an unheard of' US$1 million. Ian finished second behind Woosnam and won US$250,000, the largest cheque of his career.

But there were already worrying signs, as Ian recalls. 'The US Tour wound up in November, and from there I went back and played a few of the Australian tournaments. I did not play well, was worn out, and was the type of person who would go to an award night, a tournament or a sponsor's dinner every night, intending to just visit briefly, but as Open Champion I would invariably end up staying for the whole thing. By the end of the year, I was completely exhausted. In retrospect, IMG was not really looking after me properly and managing my time commitments as well as they could have, but part of that was my own fault.

'It was a disastrous time in my life. I never really had good advice after the Open win on how to manage the pressures of being a major winner, but a couple of my advisers outside IMG did look after me very well. My accountant Drew Robinson and a businessman, Kevin Cross, did all they could for me.'

Despite Ian's lack of self-belief, he finished his stunning year at fifth on the world money list with US$1,495,550. Norman was in a distant twenty-ninth position.

Ominously, and almost undetected, golf was beginning to change. By 1991, new technology was being introduced to the game at a rapid rate, and not all the clubs and balls suited every player. Though radar tracking systems like Trackman (available from 2003 onwards) would not appear on the scene for more than a decade, Ian had started selecting experimental equipment for himself in 1990.

Ian had been contracted to Dunlop for clubs and his ball until the end of 1990. His mentor, Peter Thomson, played Dunlop.

'Along with most of the Australian guys – Graham Marsh, Terry Gale and Brian Jones – the Japanese connection was important to me until I started playing the US Tour full-time. Dunlop gained us entry into the upper-tier events in Japan.' By 1990, he was receiving about US$100,000 per year in sponsorship across all of his equipment.

At Birkdale, Ian was pleased with the Dunlop ball. 'Dunlop Japan was a big company, and they manufactured the ball preferred by most of the players around the world at the time. Peter [Thomson] was one of the first to properly understand the ball. He used the Royal Maxfli or the HT and played well with both balls until the mid-1980s. The Japanese ball he used was better than any of the competition.'

Then, with chequebook in hand, along came Titleist, a brand that had been in the American market since 1935. Its enduring logo was scribed by Acushnet office secretary Helen Robinson as she handwrote the name 'Titleist' on a sheet of paper just once. The branding has never changed. The company may have had a long history, but their ball was quite different from the Dunlop ball.

A top golfer's choice of golf ball involves a strong element of personal preference. The great Ben Hogan famously left MacGregor Golf in 1953 after refusing point blank to use their newly developed, and inferior, golf ball. He liked the Titleist ball he adopted prior to winning both the US Open and the Open Championship. Jack Nicklaus used the MacGregor ball to capture his 18 majors – a decision that fuelled speculation as to how many more majors he could have won by using a better-quality ball.

Titleist made a softer balata ball, which clearly suited some players but did not completely suit Ian. He recalls, 'Titleist went on a mission at the end of 1991 to sign as many of the top players as they could to use their ball.' They approached Ian through IMG and offered him US$200,000 per season to play the ball from 1992 onwards. Ian reflects, 'The Titleist Tour 100 ball spun more and was not as good in the wind as the Dunlop Maxfli ball. My swing produced a lot of spin anyway, and I found it difficult to hit the new ball as far as the Maxfli and be competitive. However, I took a supply of the Titleist balls home to Australia at the end of the year and practised with them before the start of the 1992 season. I did not anticipate a major problem with the change of ball brand coming into the new season.'

Also in the mix was a lucrative new club contract Ian had recently committed to. 'In 1990, again through IMG, I was offered a club contract with Daiwa. Dunlop was naturally disappointed about my leaving them, and I continued to use their ball. The Daiwa contract obliged me to use the Daiwa visor, Daiwa bag and Daiwa clubs. It was a difficult decision and they sold me on it because it was only an eleven-club deal – a ten-club deal, really, as I only had to use a Daiwa driver if they made one I could use, which they never managed to do. I kept my wedges, my driver and my Ping Anser two-putter.'

Ian was paid a healthy and enticing US$250,000 for the first year by the emerging Japanese club manufacturer. It was a five-year contract with US$50,000 increments for three years, and a 'balloon payment' of US$500,000 to be paid to Ian at the end. In total the contract was worth US$1.5 million.

Daiwa was naturally delighted when, almost immediately after signing with them, Ian won a major with their equipment at Birkdale.

But warning bells should have been sounding for Ian and IMG: Daiwa's background was not in golf. It was principally a fishing-rod manufacturer, its expertise confined to graphite. Dunlop, on the other hand, had an excellent pedigree in golf that reached as far back as 1922. Ian recalls, 'There was no money in actually playing the game back then. Now I tell younger players, "You should use whichever clubs you want to use," and they can go and earn ten million US dollars by playing the game with their equipment of choice.'

Kevin Cross (left) and Ian (centre) join the Daiwa team.

The driver Ian favoured at the time of his Open win was not exactly mainstream either; his Founders Club nine-degree driver featured two rails on the sole and was fitted with an HM40 graphite shaft. But there was nothing wrong with the Daiwa iron heads. 'I loved those irons. The pitching wedge was called a ten, and the gap wedge an eleven and I kept mixing other wedges in with them during this time. I used a fifty-six-degree and sixty-degree pair of Hogan wedges that I liked. I often added a Ping L Wedge to my bag, which had virtually no bounce on it; it had a sharp leading edge and was great for use in the British Open and the Masters.'

Ian was not the only player who liked the irons' design. A promising junior also admired the Daiwa iron heads. 'After I won the Open,

I was asked to go and play with fifteen-year-old Tiger Woods at Isleworth. He had just won the first of his three US Junior Amateurs in a row and went on from there to win three US Amateurs in 1994, 1995 and 1996. Tiger played with me for three days at Isleworth. He played well, we became friends and I have known him ever since.'

Tiger admired Ian's Daiwa DG 273 irons, which featured slightly longer blades and a thin top line. Like Ian, Woods felt that the Japanese manufacturers made the best irons. Early in his career, Tiger would use Mizuno blades – MP 29 (two- to four-iron) and MP14s (five to pitching wedge). David Graham was travelling regularly to Japan to complete design work for Daiwa on their irons. Ian recalls, 'I was partly sold on Daiwa because Graham was involved in their design. Everyone used to think the DG brand was David Graham, but DG actually stood for Daiwa Grind – but the "273" did represent David's winning score at the US Open at Merion in 1981.'

Looking back on his equipment choices from 1991, Ian says, 'After the Open win, I seemed to be constantly trying different shafts, but no one knew a great deal about graphite. New technology was making its appearance regularly. By 1993 the shafts I was using became a real struggle for me, so we had them assessed on a new machine. They were 8.5 on the frequency matching equipment, which showed they were far too strong for me. I was used to irons measuring 6.5. The shafts were banded with a pattern around the graphite, and were way too stiff for me. It had all turned into a shitshow.'

Over the next two seasons Ian experimented with cavity backs, metal heads and different driver-head materials combined with graphite shafts. By 1993 his Japanese Daiwa irons were a cavity back design, fitted with graphite shafts. 'Every now and then I would hit a 240-yard four-iron, and I would be left thinking, "What the hell happened there?"'

While Ian was experimenting with new shaft materials, Tiger Woods was using a True Temper Dynamic steel shaft, which had been introduced back in 1941.

A similar scenario played out for Ian Woosnam, formerly a Dunlop player, when IMG signed him with another niche Japanese manufacturer, Maruman, in the late 1980s. Mike Clayton recalls a trip to the Australian Open at Royal Sydney in 1994, when Woosnam visited the pro shop and purchased a set of Dunlop irons to use in the tournament. 'It was just insanity some of these club deals that the top players were signed up to for money.'

Driver heads also started to enlarge and manufacturers were introducing a range of different head materials. Ian recalls, 'When I look at the Founders Club driver I used to win the Open … until about 1994 it was tiny – about the size of a five-hybrid today. The driver was the hardest club to use back then. Now it is the easiest.'

During Ian's playing career there was little or no science involved in his equipment and ball choices. It was mainly done on the feel and look of the clubs. To Ian, the evaluation of new equipment and ball selection 'was literally hit and miss'. He recalls, 'The whole period from 1990 to 1995 was one of radical and constant change. With the benefit of hindsight, I would also never advise a player to consider changing his ball and clubs at the same time – but I did.'

Without the benefit of technology, even golf's greatest player, Jack Nicklaus, made his own instinctive equipment choices during his unmatched career. During his heyday, Nicklaus customarily used a driver that was more like a three-wood; it had a short 42.75-inch shaft and 11 degrees of loft. When playing at windy venues like the Old Course (where he won two of his three Opens) his highly developed tactical brain would see him change to a driver with 9.5 degrees of loft and a longer 43.5-inch shaft.

Ian and Jennie's wedding day on the Gold Coast, Queensland,
17 January 1987.

Caddie Pete Bender helps Ian with the line at the Open,
St Andrews, 1990.

Courtesy of the University of St Andrews Libraries and Museums, ID: 2008-1-96412

A happy family: Jennie, Hayley and Ian with the Claret Jug, Royal Birkdale, 1991.

Courtesy of the University of St Andrews Libraries and Museums, ID: 2008-1-96080

Pink on pink: Ian at the Masters, Augusta, 1992.

Courtesy of the University of St Andrews Libraries and Museums, ID: 2008-1-96688

International Team captain Gary Player (left) and assistant captain Ian at the Presidents Cup, 2005.

Chris Condon / Getty Images

Ian congratulates Tiger Woods (left) on winning the World Golf Championship, Harding Park, 2005.

Stan Badz / Getty Images

Ian (left), wearing the Colonial winner's jacket, with CBS anchor Jim Nantz.

The ABC broadcasting team on Swilcan Bridge at the Open, St Andrews, 2000.

Ian and Jennie at home in Florida with daughters Hayley (left) and Laura (right).

The Australian golf team at the Olympic Games in Rio de Janeiro, Brazil, 2016.

Jennie and Ian at the Australian Masters Gala Dinner in 2009.

Quinn Rooney / Getty Images

It was not until several years after the end of Nicklaus's and Baker-Finch's playing careers that equipment trailers, club fitters and radar ball-tracking would make their appearance on the various golf tours, dramatically reducing the guesswork in equipment and ball selection.

Adding to Ian's downward spiral were changes to his eyesight. By 1990 he could not see the flags on the greens clearly. He borrowed his caddie's glasses and, as he says, 'could suddenly see the flags crystal clear'. He went to an optometrist and discovered he was 20/30 in one eye and 20/40 in the other. Contact lenses did not feel comfortable, so he experimented with larger-than-normal glasses that were rimless so he could read the greens – he wore them to win the Open. His vision was restored to 20/10 in 1994 by refractive surgery.

Ian's profile grew with his Open win; he was a photogenic and marketable commodity. He and Jennie developed their own good-natured strategy to counter the inevitable attention Ian was now attracting – particularly from women within his galleries. Jennie trusted Ian and enjoyed walking with him on the course as often as possible. She remembers, 'He was incredibly good at managing the attention paid to him and I would say to him, "Do not walk up and talk to me when you are playing. Just let me do my own thing." I would walk ahead, to where he drove, and then be ready to watch the next shot.' If it became known in the gallery that Jennie was with him, she would be irked by inane questions, such as 'Do you know him?' or 'Are you his wife or girlfriend?'. She steadfastly maintained her position with Ian: 'Don't come up to me!'

It was a tactical error on her part. 'I made a bad, bad mistake by telling him not to come up to me on the course,' she says, laughing. 'What does he do? He comes up to me! It became a joke between us. There were times when I was standing there and girls in his gallery would give him their phone numbers. Ian was really good in those situations. He would reply, "Just let me ask my wife over there to see if it's okay!"'

Golf, at the elite professional level, inflicts a higher-than-normal casualty rate upon marriages, particularly among some of the more recent multiple-major champions. The Baker-Finches – with Ian's single major and their 40-year relationship – seem to have dealt successfully with the challenges arising from the travel and enforced absences that are part of the touring professional's life.

Jennie sums it up: 'From the time we started to travel together Ian always wanted to do it the right way. He was never one to love going out with the boys by himself. I told him I understood golf has to be No 1 in his life, but I needed to be No 2!'

CHAPTER 17

CAUSE FOR OPTIMISM

Contending in the majors

As 1992 dawned the Baker-Finch family were in Sanctuary Cove at their family home. 'Each season Jennie was at Sanctuary Cove from October to the end of February,' says Ian. 'Typically, I would not return there until the end of October – depending on my tournament schedule. I would then start my playing year in the States at Doral in late February or early March.'

By the end of January Ian was feeling optimistic about his 1992 campaign after a win in the Heineken Vines Classic in Perth, Western Australia. He scored 276 to win by one shot from New Zealander Frank Nobilo. (Nobilo would later become Ian's broadcasting colleague.) It was an emphatic victory; under pressure coming to the final hole, Ian drove well, following with a fine three-wood onto the green for a two-putt birdie and the win. Ian mentioned to the press the toll off-course commitments were taking, saying, 'It has been a wonderful but mad world since [the Open], but now I'm back on track and I intend to stay that way.'

Ian's solid form continued into late March. After three rounds of the 1992 Players Championship at TPC Sawgrass, the tour's first US$2 million tournament, he was third with 70-67-68. In the final round playing together in the last group, Ian shot a lacklustre 72 to Davis Love III's 67. 'Davis chipped in twice in his last round for birdies, both from places where he would normally have been lucky to make a bogey. He beat me comfortably.' Ian tied for second place and prize money of US$118,800.

Ian's positive start to the season continued through to the 1992 Masters in April with scores of 70 and 69 in the first two rounds. He teed off late in the third round on Saturday, in the company of American Jeff Sluman. On reaching the 16th hole the pair was starting to run out of daylight and produced an inventive solution – speed golf. With his partner's full agreement, Ian raced to the 17th tee to drive while Sluman was still putting out on the 16th green. The pair managed to finish the round without the inconvenience of having to return early the next morning to finish the last hole or two. Ian's 68 left him alone in fourth place overnight.

Ian commented, 'I can sleep in tomorrow and take my time to get to the course.' He was in the second-to-last pairing on the final day with Raymond Floyd, but Augusta's fast greens were still presenting problems for him. 'I putted terribly. I had still not learned to lag my putts properly. Compared to the great Masters lag putters, like Tiger, [Ben] Crenshaw and [Phil] Mickelson, I was just a basher on those Augusta greens. I would stand up and bang them in. I tried hard to get better at Augusta, and each time in practice before the event I would try to hit as many long breaking putts as I could from the edge of those undulating lightning-fast greens.'

Ian's mediocre 74 in the final round dropped him back to tied sixth with Greg Norman on seven under for a decent US$43,000 payday.

Ian's perceived lack of length did not seem to be a problem. 'Maybe if I had been longer off the tee, I would not have had to hit a five-wood into the 13th and three-wood into the 15th, and additionally, I was not good enough at Augusta around the greens. If you look back at all the winners at the Masters, many of them were incredibly good chippers, and may not necessarily have always been good putters. Bernhard Langer won there twice for instance. Tiger was the best putter from long distance on Augusta greens; Jack Nicklaus was another great lag putter.'

Ian was feeling unusually confident heading into the US Open at Pebble Beach in June. 'It may sound strange, but at the beginning of the week I thought I could win. I was the best prepared for any major since Birkdale and the course suited me.' But he battled in tough conditions in the final round with a 76 and ended up thirteenth. High winds and burned-out greens challenged most of the field, with 20 players scoring 80 or worse.

It was off to Muirfield in Scotland in mid-July to defend his Open title, but Nick Faldo was dominant in winning his third Claret Jug. Ian was solid, if unspectacular, in his title defence, with rounds of 71-71-72-68 leaving him tied nineteenth, despite a disappointing double bogey six on the last hole. He had been drawn with a future Open winner, 23-year-old Paul Lawrie from Scotland, in the third round. In his 2012 autobiography, *An Open Book*, Lawrie described playing with Ian as a thrill.

> He was awesome to play with and such a nice guy ... He hit one shot I will never forget. It was at the 14th, long par four, playing into the wind. He hit a driver off the deck right onto the green. I can still see the ball now, boring through the breeze.

Ian's season had been solid so far, but the PGA Championship ended this run of impressive performances in majors as he limped into sixty-ninth place at Bellerive. He finished the year in sixty-sixth position on the world money list, earning US$519,311. It had been Faldo's year; he led the list with US$2,748,248.

For no good reason, Ian was feeling low by the end of the season. 'I felt I could have performed better in the majors. Looking back, I think I may have been far too tough on myself. I really needed someone to help me put my year in perspective. To make it worse, I returned to Australia and played very badly there.'

Clayton recalls, 'Ian came back from America and thought his result in the 1992 season was a disaster – which of course it wasn't.'

Ian says, 'The start of my not playing well was due to my strange lack of self-confidence at the end of 1992. I should have come back to Australia and talked to Thommo about it. It was the second year of the World Golf Championship in Jamaica and I was invited because I was in the world's top twenty-five. For some reason, I did not play in the two-million-dollar tournament, saying I wouldn't go because I did not believe I was good enough.'

On his friend's lack of self-belief, Clayton comments, 'I wonder if the seeds of his destruction were sown when Ian tried to change what Peter had done with his swing, which was really simple. If you look at his swing in the mid-1980s, it was pretty darn good. But by 1992 he had gone so far away from what Peter had told him. Peter told me once a swing is like a finely tuned car engine and tweaking a nut here and a bolt there was unnecessary. In Ian's case, Peter didn't understand what Ian was doing it for.'

Jennie was doing all she could to help. 'He was one of the straightest drivers on tour,' she says, 'but he thought he needed more distance. Well, he really didn't. Back then there was not the access to all the information and golf technology there is now. He didn't have *that* person to help him through it.'

Ian started 1993 believing his game was in poor shape. He travelled to Japan to visit Daiwa, who had produced a new graphite shaft they wanted him to use. 'The players, particularly the older ones, were all looking into graphite shafts. It was experimentation time and Daiwa were putting a lot of pressure on me to use their new shaft.'

In addition to the trip to Japan, Ian played in an event in Brunei at the invitation of the Sultan of Brunei. 'It paid a guaranteed hundred thousand dollars for a two-day event. I had turned down the invitation the previous year because it was Hayley's third birthday, but in 1993 I played as one of the world's top ten players. We received the payment and a beautiful gold watch. The sultan's nephew kept a garage with three hundred and sixty-five luxury cars, one for each day of the year. Back then, I was a big car buff and loved looking at all the Rolls-Royce and Bentley cars. When we arrived, there were seven 959 Porsches lined up outside the garage. I was impressed but was told they were on the way out – the sultan would buy the first-release cars and ship the year-old ones out.'

Ian's nagging doubts about his form led him to a two-month break from tournament play at the beginning of 1993. He practised every day while setting himself one of his customary goals: the top ten in each of the four majors. It seemed an achievable goal after his 1992 results but it wasn't to be.

'I made the cut comfortably in all four majors but in each one I had a dreadful last day,' Ian says. At the Masters he shot 80 in the final round and tumbled to fifty-fourth, at the US Open he finished with a pair of sixes to drop to nineteenth. 'I needed to birdie the last two holes to finish third. At the time, I was putting far too much pressure on myself.'

The Open Championship at Royal St George's was no better. After 69-67 to start, he crashed with a final-round 80. It was the worst round in the field on the last day and he dropped down to seventieth place behind Greg Norman, who won his second and final major championship that week.

He wouldn't have dreamed it at the time, but Ian would never make another cut in his beloved Open.

Ian's old Troppo Tour friend Peter Senior finished, in typically unobtrusive fashion, tied fourth.

It turned into a miserable year for Ian, with a sixty-sixth at the PGA Championship to conclude the major season. He was so disappointed in his performance, particularly in the States, that he came back to Australia earlier than usual. 'Before the big tournaments in Japan in 1993 I took a month off, I went to the gym every day, hired a trainer. I was determined to find out what was going wrong. I finished in the top ten in two of the three events on the Japan Tour and felt better about myself again after my disappointment at dropping out of the top hundred in the States.'

Then, a glimmer of hope. Ian finished the year with a victory at the Australian PGA Championship at Concord in Sydney, storming home with a final round 64 to tie with Peter Fowler and the New Zealander Grant Waite, then taking the title on the second extra hole of the play-off.

Ian thought of it as a good way to finish the year, but Mike Clayton was not so sure. 'Ian came out of nowhere and shot sixty-four in the last round to win at Concord, but I believed his game was gone by then. At the time I thought, "What is going on here?" He never recovered and started hitting it either high right or low left. The club was coming too much from the inside.'

The 1993 Australian PGA Championship was to be the last of Ian's 17 title wins as a professional golfer.

As a father, Ian remained in the top echelon. Jennie says, 'He was besotted with the girls. If we wanted to do something or be with him and he had other plans, he always put family first.' His golf was another matter.

At the end of the season Ian was still tinkering with his swing. 'I started talking to my friend and coach Steve Bann about trying to get *deeper* in my swing. Two weeks after the PGA I was playing in the Australian Open at Metropolitan. I remember hitting my second shot into the par-five 8th hole. I always used to aim down the left and just let it drift back with a little fade. Instead, the shot went about ten feet right to left in a little draw. I thought, "Hell, what just happened there?" It was an alarming feeling, and that was the first moment in which I thought, "The ball is not going where I used to hit it."'

All-pervasive doubts were starting to creep into Ian's mind. As his shots started to go to the left and the right, it was clear he had serious swing issues to resolve.

Despite the success and the Open win his method had produced in 1991, Ian had never really liked his own golf swing. On the surface, it is difficult to comprehend why he felt that way. In a 27-minute edited version of the Open film *Every Shot: Ian Baker-Finch the 120th Open*, Ian produces shot after perfect shot from an upright, elegant action, delivered with perfect tempo. The Baker-Finch swing in 1991 appeared to be a thing of beauty, sending his tee shots to the centre of the fairway and his iron shots closer to the hole than his fellow competitors. Despite this, Ian believed major changes were necessary to progress his playing career. His high hand action and his 'reverse C' were swing characteristics he may have shared with Faldo in the early part of his career, but by 1987 Faldo had successfully shed his 1970s swing.

Ian's desire to make swing changes was also motivated by his view that he needed to drive the ball further to be competitive for his return to the US Tour in 1994, and to achieve his goal of winning more majors. He had never been long off the tee but was more than adequate in length, and there was little wrong with the rest of his game. Mike Clayton wrote, 'His irons were both pretty and reliable.' Pete Bender, his caddie, gave his impression: 'He will kill you from eighty yards in.'

Ian's final-round partner at Birkdale in 1991, Mark O'Meara, was an early example of a player adopting radical swing changes and winning. Starting in 1982, O'Meara went through a swing transformation under a young assistant pro on the teaching staff at Pinehurst, Hank Haney. O'Meara recalls Haney saying, 'Mark, your swing is very upright with a lot of hands in there. You need to get your swing on plane, round it out and take your hands out.' The changes took O'Meara two years to implement. In golf writer John Huggan's words, O'Meara and Haney had been 'Faldo and Leadbetter before Faldo and Leadbetter'.

From 1984 Leadbetter had guided Nick Faldo through a long and disruptive period of swing change. During the period of rebuilding with Leadbetter, Faldo almost disappeared off the golfing map. Leadbetter prescribed six changes for Faldo's backswing alone, having concluded that Faldo swung the club on too upright a plane. As a result of these radical swing changes, the poster boy of British golf spent two years in golfing oblivion. The press were mystified, and the time became known as Faldo's 'wilderness years'.

Leadbetter estimated that when Faldo was working with him on his swing changes he was hitting between 500 and 800 balls a day in the Florida heat. Faldo was able to bear down and overcome the challenge of a complete swing rebuild. His new method subsequently returned him three Opens (1987, 1990 and 1992) and three Masters (1989, 1990 and 1996).

The New Zealand golfer Greg Turner – who, like Clayton, would later develop into a successful golf architect – went through his own swing rebuild in Europe, guided by Denis Pugh of the Leadbetter school. In 2024, Turner said, 'Teaching up until the late 1980s boiled down to swing path. Leadbetter and Pugh concluded that the clubface was the most important part, and the object was to try and keep the face square to the target for as long as possible. A whole different set of rules came into play, so the swing had to work much more rotationally than laterally, which was a significant discovery. Faldo was Leadbetter's most visible and notable early success, and the first to get everyone's attention. I suspect that rotational movement wouldn't have worked well with the equipment of the 1970s and 1980s. Still, the new equipment and the change to a rotational movement during Ian's and my era happened in concert over about a decade from the late 1980s.'

Turner struggled to implement the swing changes. As to how long it took him to make the transition? 'It was brutal, and my game was really limited for a while; I am not sure I ever got there!'

Turner went on to win three more European Tour events after his swing changes and also added the 1997 New Zealand Open and the Australian PGA in 1999. He stayed working with Pugh until the end of his playing career in 2003.

Faldo and Turner are two examples of Leadbetter's and Pugh's success, but Turner concludes, 'Ian was the most striking of Leadbetter's failures, but it is very, very complicated, and with him it was not just any one thing.'

Wayne Grady summed it up rather less technically: 'We all used to say, "Finchy caught lead poisoning."'

Leadbetter may have been partially blamed for Ian losing his game, but it had been Ian who initiated the search for additional length off the tee, and he had already sought advice from Leadbetter prior to his Open win. In 2004, Leadbetter commented to *The Guardian* that Ian:

> was not ultra-long but had a beautiful short game and was a great, great putter. But he was never content. To get longer, that was his downfall. He kept saying, 'I've got to get longer, longer.' But he was long enough, and, with his other attributes, he was fine.

But Ian Baker-Finch was not going to be fine. His own wilderness years were looming.

CHAPTER 18

THE NIGHTMARE BEGINS ... AND ENDS

'It was not my swing anymore.'

In 1994 Ian headed back to the US Tour confused about his swing and concerned about the way he was missing shots to both the left and the right. His work ethic was unchanged. 'I was hitting so many balls while searching for answers, practising and testing, striving to hit it further. I was changing my swing. I wish I had Trackman in those days – science may have been able to tell me where I was going, because I had no idea.'

Jennie was also struggling to deal with Ian's loss of form. 'When he played and did not have a great round, we would not say anything. I learned not to ask too many questions, especially if he was away on tour by himself. If he was at home, we would just let him mope, and do whatever he needed to do. Then he would flick out of it, become the dad and part of the family again.'

The previous year Ian tried to work through his problems with Leadbetter's assistant Mitchell Spearman, but the coaching had produced no results. He then sought out his friend Steve Bann, who tried his best to help Ian out of his slump. 'Every time I went to Steve, we tried new things. His advice was I needed to try and flatten my swing like I had done with Thommo's help. By 1994 and 1995 I was working on things I had never tried before. It was like we were trying to fix problems rather than practise my swing.'

He sought help with his mental approach from Dr Dick Coop, a psychologist, who worked along similar lines to the renowned mind coach Bob Rotella. 'I spent a week with Dick Coop, a lovely man, then there was Deb Graham, who was a psychologist on the tour. I had great relationships with them both. They were helpful, but no one could give me the magic pill that I needed!'

The 1994 Masters provided Ian with one ray of hope in a dark season. In fourth place after three identical scores of 71, Ian fell away with two balls in the water in his final round of 74, dropping down into a tie for tenth. Spain's Jose Maria Olazabal won by two shots, continuing the inspired scrambling tradition of his countryman Ballesteros. The Masters that year was notable for being the first time since 1954 neither Nicklaus nor Palmer made the cut. Their long era was over, but so was Ian's tragically short career in the majors. He would never make a cut in any major again and was losing his game with alarming speed.

He played poorly at Hilton Head the week after the Masters, and it only got worse from there; he missed the next ten cuts in a row as a worrying pattern developed for Jennie and the children. The family was living in Orlando and their plan was for the two girls to attend school during the week, then for Jennie to join Ian at the weekend. 'It became dispiriting for all of us, as I was always home by Friday night after missing every single cut.'

Ian's loss of form became equally tough on Jennie and the girls. Jennie says, 'I would just leave Ian alone and avoid asking, "How do you feel?" He would disappear into his room and was obviously upset with himself. Two or three hours later we could talk about it, but I wouldn't try to make him feel better – that didn't work. Ian tried extremely hard not to bring it home but became a little depressed. One thing about having little children was they did not really know about the issues. All they cared about was the fact their dad was home. He was with a beautiful family which helped put it into perspective.'

A cruel joke circulated among the caddies: 'Whose is the best bag to have on tour?'

Answer: 'Finchy's because you get every weekend off.'

It looked briefly as if Ian was emerging from his slump in August at the World Series in Ohio, when he shot 67 in the first round to sit just two shots behind the leader. But his second round was the stuff of golfing nightmares. 'That year the World Series was played on Firestone's North Course – they were rebuilding the greens on the South Course. There was water on every hole of the North Course, and what I feared most on some of the holes – a combination of both out of bounds and water. If it was there, that is where I hit it.

'I shot eighty-two, which included ten penalty shots and twenty-one putts. The rest of my game, apart from my driving, was fairly good. With three holes left to play, I only had one ball left in my bag. The 16th had water, the 17th was a long par three over water, and the 18th also brought water into play. I survived the first two of the final three holes with what I thought was my last ball. On the 18th, I hit my drive over the water and thought I was going to be fine, then I shanked my second shot into the water.

'Walking down the last hole I said to my caddie, Pete, "Hey, mate, we must be out of balls." Luckily, Pete had saved one used ball we had rotated out on one of the par threes – we never used a new ball on a par three in those days. So, I used this final recycled ball, making a bogey five on the last hole and was able to at least finish the round – with eighty-two.'

Ian's crash had become so dramatic he was starting to receive a torrent of unwanted advice from the public. 'During this time, I had 4000 letters. I had so many flaming rocks sent to me and suggestions like, "Come with me to the mud baths in southern Italy and you are sure to be cured."'

A letter to Ian from Carol in New South Wales was typical.

Dear Mr Ian Baker-Finch,

Sleep with this Indian stone under your pillow. It resonates with your spirit. You have given away your own power. You have forgotten the beauty of your own soul.

Carol

Looking back on this traumatic period in their lives, Jennie says, 'The unsolicited advice overwhelmed Ian. Sending a rock to him? Ridiculous. These days he would have one person to listen to, but he never really had a coach and he had learned golf from a book. Even when he was feeling like crap, if someone approached him, Ian would be nice and friendly while a total stranger tried to give him advice. He would just sit there and nod when anyone else would have said, "Off you go." Ian was far too nice. A lot of people told him he needed to be more like a Greg Norman or a Nick Faldo but that was not his personality, and he was never going to change.'

Ian and Jennie have since disposed of the mountain of well-meaning correspondence – and those magical rocks.

Ian took further advice from Bob Rotella. 'Bob and I played golf one day together during my lost years and he said, "I can tell you one thing, Ian. When you learn how to try harder at trying less, you will figure it all out." He was telling me that, basically, when golf finally did not matter to me anymore, I would recover. His words proved to be true.'

But in the short term, Rotella's advice did not help Ian to make cuts. 'I was still searching for my swing and everything felt so different out on the course. I did not have *my* swing anymore. I had someone else's swing. I started trying to pretend I was another player. I thought, "Today I am going to swing like Davis Love III, today I am going swing like Freddie Couples, today I am going to pause at the top like Mark O'Meara."'

Ian shot 66 in the pro-am at the Hyundai Masters in Korea for a new course record, then an 81 when the tournament proper began. By this time, he was practising far too hard, hitting at least 100 drives a day, every day. His body was not enjoying the workload. 'I have never blamed my loss of form on injury, but possibly it contributed to my decline. I was starting to develop serious issues with both my shoulders.'

By 1995, the state of Ian's game was dire. He played in 15 straight tournaments on the US Tour, missing every single cut. He was shooting 80, or worse, in every fourth round he played and was averaging a near-fatal four penalty shots per round. It was not getting any better.

'By 1995 I was in a terrible state. I started working with David Leadbetter and his fitness guy. In April and May I decided to get fit and took six weeks off golf. I became fit and strong, but my golf did not improve as a result. I was hitting double the number of balls I normally would, and only served to wear myself out. We all have days when we may be feeling a bit flat, but in my case I felt like that every day. It had become very depressing.'

He saw more coaches – Jim Flick, Hank Haney, Rick Smith and Chuck Cook, among others – but he still felt terrible. 'I had become almost an object of pity, and a potential case study for every coach. I would exhaust three or four coaches at a time. There was always someone coming along and saying, "I have the answer for you."

I was always searching for something without really knowing what it was. I was looking for a needle in a haystack.'

Clayton has his own opinion on the cause of Ian's problems. 'Ian had reached the top ten in the world but from 1992 started looking around him at his contemporaries on his level. I think he thought Greg and Woosie [Woosnam] were better drivers, Seve was a better long iron player, Faldo, Stewart and Langer were better middle iron players. He thought of all the things they did better than him and that he had to change somehow. He gave himself no credit and should have been thinking, "I can out-pitch and -putt them. I can drive it straighter than Seve and Woosie." He also didn't need to be any longer and with a wooden driver he was perfectly long enough. Peter [Thomson] had changed his swing effectively, but Ian kept fiddling with it to try to get better. There was a time where he should have left it alone, but he went past that point and it got to where he couldn't play anymore.'

Jennie found it heartbreaking to watch her husband's torment at close quarters. 'He felt he had to do something about his game but just could not work out why it was happening. It just got worse and worse with the pressure of competition, not knowing why he was hitting those bad drives. It wasn't all the time, but it was enough to make him miss cuts. The girls were a little older, and they became sorry when he came home early. They knew the reason was he hadn't played well.'

Family life continued as best it could under huge strain. Jennie recalls, 'I used to call him Mr Disney and I was the Gestapo. If he hadn't seen Hayley and Laura for ages, he tried to make sure he was the fun parent. Ian tried never to be away for more than two weeks.'

The elder statesmen of the game, Nicklaus and Palmer, were sympathetic to Ian. He had played with Nicklaus in the US Open in the process of another missed cut. Nicklaus kindly offered Ian the opportunity to stay with him for a week or two to try to sort out his problems. Ian did not take advantage of the invitation.

Then, at the 1995 Open Championship, Ian was drawn with Palmer for the first two rounds at St Andrews. It was Palmer's last Open and huge galleries followed them on the first two days. Ian's opening tee shot, hit out of bounds left, has been unkindly described by media as 'the worst tee shot ever seen at the Open' because players have a double fairway – the 1st and 18th – to aim for. Ian avoids recrimination and blame when looking back, but he bristles at the portrayal of his infamous tee shot, feeling it should be put into proper context. 'Commentators and spectators say the 1st fairway on the Old Course is one hundred and sixteen yards wide from one side to the other – but it is not. During the Open, the stands encroach on the right-hand side of the fairway by about fifty yards.

'The best play is to the left with the drive, aimed at the Swilcan Bridge, to give you a better angle into the green. The day of that tee shot with Arnie, we had a thirty-mile-per-hour wind into us. My hat came off on the downswing and I hit a hook out of the toe, which landed on Grannie Clark's Wynd [the road running across both fairways]. The ball shot left and under the fence – out of bounds. People have harassed me since the day I hit that drive, but it was not really that bad, and was barely a twenty-five-yard hook.' In the inaugural four-hole event for past champions in 2000, four previous champions, including Bill Rogers, hit their drives out of bounds down the left side of the same shared fairway.

By 1996 Ian's playing days were swiftly coming to an end. 'It had become impossible for me to keep playing, particularly with the press continually crowding in on me. It was so very embarrassing. It was like, "Finch is coming and he's going to miss another cut. Let's go and watch him and harass him." After the first two rounds of the British Open at Lytham in 1996 I had scored 78-81 and was surrounded by the media. It was like they had put me on some form of death watch. So, I said to them, "I have finished. I am done. I am going home to Australia, to rest and try and figure this out." But ultimately I could not figure it out.'

Jennie was frustrated and felt helpless. 'I would say "It's okay" when I knew it really wasn't okay.'

The late Bruce Edwards, Tom Watson's caddie, caddied for Ian during the Open in 1996 and Ian recalls, 'Apart from the penalty shots I incurred, Bruce could not believe how well I played from all the impossible places I managed to hit it into – including several drives out of bounds. I could still chip and putt with the best in the world, but I had totally lost confidence in my long game.'

There is a strange, rather ghoulish symmetry in the timing of Ian's demise as 1991 Open Champion. Ten years before Ian's win at Birkdale, Bill Rogers won the 1981 Open at Royal St George's, became one of the world's leading players, then completely lost his game. Within three years of his only major win, Rogers's career was over. His game deserted him during the same Open in which Ian debuted at St Andrews in 1984. Rogers never made the cut in a major again and later talked about living in fear of the game from the moment he woke up.

Rogers's problems were compounded by IMG sending him all over the world chasing appearance fees and deals. He told Rick Thomas of the *Texarkana Gazette* in 2023, 'To make money then you had to travel. I liked that money. I was in pursuit of the almighty dollar and IMG could open the doors.' By the mid-1980s he was 'totally burnt out' and shellshocked. He turned to coaching in 1985 and became the director of golf at the San Antonio Country Club for 11 years after the premature end of his playing career.

Ten years after Ian's 1991 win, the 2001 Open Champion, David Duval, suffered an almost identical fate to Rogers and Ian.

Duval's win in the Open at Royal Lytham was his only major championship, and after 13 wins on the PGA Tour he never won there again and his playing career went into freefall.

So the careers of the 1981, 1991 and 2001 Open winners followed an eerily similar, and almost identical, downward path.

At this point Ian had not entirely given up. He went through a period near the end of his playing career when he was trying almost every available top-level coach. 'It started in 1996 when I had played so badly in the US Open. Butch Harmon came up to me and offered to try to help me. I was going to see him but never made it, which was probably a mistake in hindsight. He left his offer open to me, but it was a tricky situation because he was Greg Norman's coach by then. So, I stayed away.'

By 1996 Ian and Jennie decided to quit the US Tour and move back to Australia. 'I was not quitting golf, but I wanted to get back to Australia, take a six-month break and fix my injuries. I was still exempt on the US Tour for the rest of 1996 and for five years after that. I had played eleven events in 1996 and then the Tour banned me in 1997 as I had not played the required fifteen events. In hindsight I should have taken a major medical exemption at this stage of my career to leave my playing options open.'

Jennie remembers their painful departure. 'We left Orlando in mid-1996 and it was sad. We left behind lots of weeks without making money and Ian wondering why this was happening to him. Each week he would go out and it was there in his mind: "Am I going to play well this week? Or am I not going to play well?" It was very tough so we went back to Australia to have his shoulder injuries treated, and his feet also needed to be repaired.'

Ian recalls, 'All of my friends had been trying to help me over the last two or three years. Grades had tried hard, and some of the better players who were my friends would get to interviews and loyally refuse to discuss my golf with the press when asked about me. We did stop by to say goodbye to Payne Stewart and his family when we left for Australia. They had been good friends to us, and Payne and I had known each other since the early 1980s from the Australasian Tour days.

'Our children were friends, but the Stewarts understood the reason for our selling up and moving back to Australia. I wondered during the dark times from 1994 to 1996 whether I would be able to play well if no one knew who I was. It was a fantasy, but the media scrutiny in the States was intense, and in Australia it was unbearable. I would hit a drive into the trees and there would be six cameramen there.'

Back in Australia, Ian did not play for six months. Even if he had wanted to, his body needed time to heal. 'I had my shoulders rehabilitated, and they taped up my feet and separated my toes. I could not wear shoes for three months.' The years of cramming his feet into shoes far too small for him as a boy had taken their toll.

Jennie recalls, 'When we went back to Australia, we thought it was only likely to be for a short time. I told Ian that if he wanted to stick to playing and get through the problems with his golf, I would be with him, and we would do it together. I also told him if he wanted to try something else, we would do it. In the end, I told him I could not make the decision for him. I knew he really wanted to stay as a golfer, and if he was honest with himself he probably thinks now he should have given it another go.'

The lack of income would have stressed many marriages, but Jennie adopted a typically pragmatic approach. 'We were fine. We lived within our means and had never been extravagant spenders.'

During Ian's time out of the game an opportunity presented itself: television commentary. He covered 12 events as lead analyst on the Australian Tour for all the networks – ABC in Australia and channels Seven, Nine and Ten – from October 1996 to the end of February

1997. He was paid A$10,000 per week during the few weeks of the season, and he recalls, 'At least it was an income; I had nothing else coming in.'

Before 1996 Ian had tried his hand at broadcasting on weekends for ABC in the US at the 1994 and 1995 Opens, and he worked in tandem with the great BBC commentator Peter Alliss. 'I had plenty of fun with Peter on the BBC. Peter said he loved working with me and reassured me I would be good on the microphone if ever I had to be. In 1996 Jack Graham was the producer for ESPN and ABC in the US, and he said, "We would love you to come in on the weekend at the British Open if you do not make the cut," which I agreed to do.'

In July 1997, Ian had the option to do some commentary work on Open weekend at Royal Troon but had entered to play in the tournament (past Open winners were then exempt until they turned 65). He was in two minds as to whether or not he should play. In the week before the Open, Ian had been on a golf tour in Ireland, driving everywhere accompanied by his coach at the time, Gary Edwin, and some friends, including Kevin Cross and fellow professional Grant Dodd. 'I had sent my caddie home and was talked into playing at Troon.'

Ian's back was aching from all the golf and driving, but Cross was in the minority in trying to dissuade his friend from playing, pointing out, 'You are taking ten Advil per day and would be stupid to play with your sore back.'

Ian reflects, 'Most of the Aussie boys were saying, "Finchy, you have played every Open since 1984, why would you not play in this one?" So, I did.'

It would prove to be the worst decision he ever made.

Todd Woodbridge, an Australian tennis pro and a friend of Ian and Jennie's, was staying in the same hotel during the Open and volunteered to caddie for Ian for the first two rounds.

Ian says, 'It was just a nightmare. I hit every drive in the left rough. It was one of those Troon days with the wind howling at forty miles an hour and I think the average score for the field in the first round on the back nine was forty. It was a tough day. My back was hurting, and I ground it out and shot ninety-two.' Ian signed his card and walked off the last green thinking, 'I just can't do this anymore.'

'It was not that I couldn't play,' he says. 'I just couldn't play under pressure. My tee shots were the problem and I kept hitting these terrible low hooks. Once I had hit one, it was hard to stop hitting them for the rest of the day.'

The end of the road. Ian with Todd Woodbridge (left) 'on the bag' at the 1997 Open, Royal Troon Golf Club.

THE NIGHTMARE BEGINS... AND ENDS

Ian went into the clubhouse and collapsed in the locker room with Gary Edwin and Todd Woodbridge there in support. R&A media officer David Begg recalls, 'Jennie faced the press with Ian, who was absolutely broken.'

Reliving the nightmare, Ian says, 'I then stupidly faced the media and followed by working on the TV coverage in the afternoon for ABC, which was equally stupid, but I had committed to it. I finished the Thursday afternoon coverage and told ABC I was going home. They never paid me, but I was kind of glad they had not. Jack Graham said to me, "Hopefully you can sort it out and get back to playing, but if you don't you have a job with ABC in America next year."'

Ian reflects, 'If I had not played that first round in the 1997 Open, I believe I may have figured it out, come back and played again. My score of ninety-two left me with so much baggage. The fear of going out and doing it again became an insurmountable barrier for me.'

Ian and Jennie had been staying in the Old Course Hotel in St Andrews and taking a helicopter to Troon each day. The night of Ian's final round in a major, his fellow players sent beer, champagne and flowers to their room. On the scoreboard at Royal Troon the next day, '92 WD' appeared beside Ian's name.

At the age of 36, six years after he had become the Champion Golfer of the Year, Ian Baker-Finch's playing career was over.

CHAPTER 19

A CAREER CHANGE

'That is where you sit; there is the microphone.'

After the Troon debacle in July 1997, Ian retreated to Sanctuary Cove. He had the prospect of some broadcasting work to bring in income but found it difficult to face the mental hurdle of giving competitive golf up completely. The sport had been the sole meaningful component of his working life for the last 20 years. He was receiving intensive coaching from Gary Edwin at his base at Hope Island Golf Club, across the road from Sanctuary Cove.

Peter Senior was living at Hope Island at the time. He was, and still is, a fervent admirer of Edwin's method. Edwin's pupils are sometimes thought to employ a technique popularised in the US in the 2010s known as 'stack and tilt', but Senior says this is incorrect. 'Gary teaches a different method. You leave your body where it is at set up, concentrate on swinging your arms during the swing, and return the clubhead to square at impact. It is a remarkably simple method, and Gary has turned a lot of ordinary players into great players.'

Ian started working with Edwin in the first half of the year, but the change of coach brought challenges. 'Gary changed my swing completely and it was not *my* swing anymore. Gary converted me to his method – but it was not mine. The Edwin method allowed me to hit the ball straight, but it was quite different. He taught his pupils a right-sided swing. He got my left side up against a wall which was the opposite of what I had been doing. Gary helped Peter Senior to extend his career and did great work with both Rod Pampling and Peter Lonard.'

During this period Ian and Senior would often play a quick nine holes together around Hope Island. Senior remembers, 'When Ian and I played these casual morning games around Hope Island together, he would absolutely crush it. He was back hitting the ball well again, using Gary Edwin's method.'

The method Edwin was teaching is called the 'one-sided swing'. To Ian, most of Edwin's pupils appeared to be 'hitters' not 'swingers' of the club. 'Gary became an incredibly good friend, and I was at the stage where I would try anything. He never charged me anything and we are still good mates. The major problem with my swing, looking back, was the fear of hitting it left. My body stopped, straightened, and then my hands would flip over.'

The 1981 Open Champion Bill Rogers had experienced his own dramatic loss of form ten years before Ian. When he was contacted by a reporter to comment on Ian's problems, he passed on the advice that Ian needed to face his fear and beat it. He also suggested the dreaded duck hook would be best combated by lining up down the left side of the fairway and cutting it.

In December 1997, Ian made another bad decision: a tentative comeback appearance on the Australian Tour. Troon the year before should have been the end of his struggles as a player, but his choice of event seemed sound; he would play in the Coolum Classic starting on 21 December. The event was family friendly and played in a relaxed atmosphere, and Ian had won well there in 1990 while at the height of his powers.

A CAREER CHANGE

Peter Senior also played at Coolum in 1997. He remembers, 'Ian and I went up to play at Coolum and practised together in front of Gary so he could watch both of us at the same time. Ian turned to Gary and said, "Gary, I think I'll just play normally today." I am not sure why he suddenly dropped Gary's method, because it had been working so well for him. All I could think was Ian possibly thought his new method looked strange and he has always been worried about what people think. So he went out and played terribly with what was left of his old swing.'

Ian's first nine holes were disastrous. He was four over par after seven, and then double-bogeyed the 8th hole, one of the easiest par fives on the course. The 9th hole plays back towards the clubhouse with water on the right and trees on the left – not ideal for Ian in his state of mind at the time. After two drives into the lake, he flung his driver at a tree in an uncharacteristic fit of rage. 'It was a difficult time and I had just had enough of it all,' he says. 'The media were all over me and I think I may even have called them a bunch of sadists.'

Golf had become impossible for Ian. He would arrive well before his tee time and hit the ball perfectly on the practice fairway, lacing 50 perfect drives straight down the middle. 'Then I would arrive on the 1st tee and snap hook my first drive; I was also starting to bottle up all my problems.'

A line had been drawn in the sand. Ian's playing career was finally over.

After Ian won the Open in 1991, he was presented with various business opportunities. 'A lot of people came to me with so-called deals, but nothing eventuated,' says Ian. 'There was a lot of travel involved in pitching for [golf course] design work, but I am not sure IMG was approaching possible opportunities for me in the right manner. Greg [Norman] was the guy everyone really wanted. IMG did arrange appearance fees for me but nothing outlandish in terms of money. I already had the Daiwa deal, which was to balloon in the last year, but they went broke before I could get the last balloon payment.

'A similar thing happened to my Titleist deal. I was due US$200,000 per year but had not played well in 1994 so as a favour to Titleist I suggested they may prefer to spread the 1995 payment over two years at US$100,000 each. The result was that they never paid me in 1996. I went to see them to remind them I had suggested the split as a favour to them, but still they would not pay me. It should have been up to IMG to sort this out, but they failed to go into bat for me, possibly because of the importance to them of their overall relationship with Titleist. They had too large a stable of other Titleist players to rock the boat on my behalf, and I ended up the loser.'

By the time Ian and his family left the US in 1996, his relationship with IMG was scaling down. He appointed his brother-in-law, Lindsay Bullen, as his business manager and still had the benefit of sound advice from his long-term accountant Drew Robinson. However, he lacked a dealmaker or rainmaker capable of maximising sustainable business opportunities and was spending a lot of time attending meetings that never seemed to produce concrete returns.

His investment company in Australia was, and still is, IBF Enterprises. The company invested in commercial property, and with others it invested in a property development on land around the Willows Golf Club in Townsville. There was yet another balloon payment due to Ian at the end of the Willows project, this time A$750,000. 'We were all angel investors in Willows and, stupidly, I bought out all my partners to keep them happy and enable a sale of the development to take place. A sale would have seen me recover my investment. The owner went broke before the sale and my investment, which was mezzanine finance, was never repaid.'

Then there was IBF Originals, a hat business based in Beenleigh, near Brisbane. The enterprise manufactured and exported Aussie-style hats made from synthetic suede. 'It was a good hat with a special band that kept it on in the wind; unfortunately, it lasted forever! Embroidery on the hat was also tricky and was not always possible to get right. Essentially, I sold two hundred and fifty thousand hats, and the venture ended up costing me two hundred and fifty thousand dollars.'

Ian invested in two Cash Converters stores in Mackay and Cairns with his old friend Peter Senior. 'Wayne Grady was in this one with us for a while. We owned the businesses and the buildings. The investment was fine, but I probably exited too early. I trusted Peter and he proved to be an exceptionally good businessman.' Senior has stayed in the business.

Closer to Ian's skill set was the Pure Golf Academy at Albert Park driving range in Melbourne. 'Setting up this business took a lot of time. We virtually wrote all the systems and training packages, which ended up being used by the Victorian Institute of Sport. Steve Bann and Dale Lynch were also involved with me. We did such a good job of setting it up that the owner of the head lease of the golf course saw the potential and took our lease back to run the business himself. Once again, a lot of intellectual property, a lot of effort, all for no financial return.'

There were projects Ian participated in that had a more positive outcome, including the Bintan and Kennedy Bay golf course design projects. Together with Jack Nicklaus, Ian completed a successful new and popular course on Bintan Island, close to Singapore. He also co-designed the Links Kennedy Bay near Perth, this time collaborating with Roger Mackay and Michael Coate. Ian says, 'It was a great site. The year it opened it was included in a list of the top ten Australian courses. Unfortunately, the Singaporean developer reneged on a deal to build townhouses around the course. We did everything we could to get Kennedy Bay off the ground, but it was never developed to its full potential.'

Ian put time and effort into several other projects at Narangba, north of Brisbane; Kingscliff, south of the Gold Coast; and St Andrews Beach near Melbourne. None of the considerable amount of time and effort from Ian and his partners invested in these ventures bore fruit. He concluded it was too difficult to compete against the established design and construction brands of Norman and Nicklaus. Ian did put his name on one course in Japan but was not deeply involved in the actual design.

Together with three friends, Ian bought the Norman-designed Glades Golf Club on the Gold Coast in 1997 and then sold the course in 2004. Asked whether this venture was successful, Ian said, 'That was one of the few.' Overall Ian's business ventures were not providing him and his family with a living.

There was a light at the end of the tunnel: television. In 1997 Ian was interviewed by the *Financial Review* in Australia. The newspaper listed Ian's business ventures and his aspirations for them, and also made passing mention of his first steps as an analyst for the Australian TV networks.

While considering this possible career change, Ian, as always, talked to Jennie. She remembers, 'Ian discussed his options with me, thinking, "Should I accept the prospect of starting a new career, or fight on and keep going with my golf?" I remember saying to him, "Talk to me about it, but it's not my decision." He thought television could be an easy way out, but we had no real idea of how a television career would go back then. There was no guarantee it would be a twenty-year career and any decision had to be his.'

Ian has thought long and hard about his early exit from the playing ranks into a full-time television career. He still regrets not taking a longer break from golf to heal from his injuries. 'I had to rehabilitate my shoulders and tape my feet up for three months. As if that was not enough, I also had severe lower back issues, caused by my right leg being shorter than my left, and was constantly visiting chiropractors at every tour stop.

'After those injuries, I should have come back the next year, fixed and ready to play. I had really beaten myself up with all the practice and mental anguish and carried so much baggage. My fear of hitting certain bad shots at the wrong time was difficult to conquer and trying to hit it further in 1994 made everything even worse. All I had succeeded in doing was to wear myself out. I should have given it another go, but the worst decision I ever made was to play in that first round in the 1997 British Open. Why would I go and tee it up in a major after not having played in a tournament for a year?'

Ian moved in the direction of a full-time broadcasting career. During his playing days, he had frequently been asked to come into the booth to add comments and analysis to Channel Seven's Australian broadcasts by head producer Graeme 'Rocky' Rowland. Ian remembers, 'In fact, he started asking me every week. I did not always feel like it, depending on how I had played, and may have annoyed him some days by failing to show up.'

Years later, when Ian was broadcasting regularly, Rowland told him, 'I always knew you would be good at this – really good. You are a natural. You have the knack of being able to listen to me, talk and feel comfortable in front of the camera. You are a good-looking turkey, and people like looking at you.'

Jack Graham of ABC had also been paying attention to Ian's performance in the booth. ABC had been through a difficult period – at one time it had televised three of the four majors each season and the Ryder Cup, but it had lost both the PGA Championship and the Ryder Cup in 1991. The network was rebuilding its team after

Brent Musburger, an unpopular replacement for anchor Dave Marr, was moved out of televised golf in 1997. Curtis Strange and Mike Tirico had already come on board and Graham clearly envisaged a place on the commentary team for Ian. Strange wanted to keep his playing career alive and had only committed to commentating ten events in 1998, seven of which he planned to play in – circumstances that possibly worked in Ian's favour.

Early in the week of the disastrous Troon Open, Graham had asked Ian if he might commentate for ABC as well as playing. 'Jack and I tentatively discussed a broadcasting deal for me,' says Ian. 'He said he had seen me on television at the end of 1996 and told me I was just what ABC needed in the States, while trying to convince me I was exceptionally good! He told me I would be working alongside Curtis Strange, who was their lead analyst. Jack thought I would fit into the team perfectly and was very encouraging about my possible career change. They offered me US$12,500 per week for two tournaments: the 1998 British Open and the Senior Players Championship.'

RETURN TO BIRKDALE

When the 1998 Open returned to Royal Birkdale, Ian didn't attend as a player but as a broadcaster. His playing partner from the last round in 1991, Mark O'Meara, won the Claret Jug.

Ian enjoyed parts of the return. He agreed to appear in a program for a Japanese television channel leading up to the event. As he walked the course with the host of the show, he talked him through his final round in 1991. The host left Ian alone with his memories on the 18th tee. 'As I walked down the fairway, they replayed the crowd noise from my 1991 win over all of the speakers. The clubhouse emptied as I walked down the fairway, and they all came out onto the balcony and clapped me in. It brought tears to my eyes.'

Ian also had a humorous exchange with the club secretary before the 1998 Open started. 'The secretary was keen to show me the locker room, which had been upgraded, and we went together to find my locker from 1991, number nineteen. We located it, and I opened the locker door and said to him, "I just wanted to check; I think I may have left my golf game in there."'

Ian's voice was a major asset in securing the ABC role. Other players-turned-commentators before him made the transition successfully, all with different styles of delivery. Peter Thomson had a Melbourne-British tone. Jack Newton, with his distinctive Australian accent, pitched to his Australian audience. Ian's voice is deep, incisive but calm, and easy to listen to. He needed no training and knew instinctively what was required. 'I never really thought, "This is going to be my career," and never lobbied for a job. I was fortunate to find myself in a role I had not really had to try out for.'

Even without specific tuition, Ian knew from the start of his new career he could rely on the team around him. 'My teammates were a great help and were all fantastic as they welcomed me on to the team. Judy Rankin, Curtis Strange, Steve Melnyk and Mike Tirico could not have been more helpful. I had always wanted to have a long-term career as a player, but by 1997 I accepted this was no longer an option for me. Somehow, I just fell into television and felt comfortable right from the start. For me, the job was about being a pleasant voice, someone who was interesting to listen to and hopefully talking sense – without too much focus on themselves.'

Ian's induction was brief: 'At my first contracted ABC event in 1998, the Senior Players Championship, Jack delivered a short speech to me: "That is where you sit; there is the microphone. Don't fuck up!"'

CHAPTER 20

BROADCASTING – THE BEGINNING

From playing golf to analysing it

RUEFULLY, IAN ACCEPTED he could no longer play golf well enough to make a living. But he saw broadcasting would keep him connected to the game that had been his life and provide for his family. His new career in television gathered momentum in late 1997 and into 1998; he was now covering ten to 12 events for Australian PGA Tour Productions.

Ian set up an office above his Sanctuary Cove garage to deal with his golf business activities. 'It was a great office with a separate entrance, but the golf businesses I ran out of there were not making enough money to cover their annual costs. On the positive side, each event I covered for television at the beginning of my career as a commentator paid A$10,000. I could see the possibility of making a good living from television broadcasting in Australia. I was not contracted exclusively to any one network, and it was part of the deal that I could work for all four networks. It gave me some real money, which was a relief. It felt like a baptism of fire, working for four different producers in four different teams, with their four different ways of doing it.'

Despite its complexity, Ian found the television work relatively easy. 'I loved doing TV in Australia. I seemed to be highly regarded and had a good profile. For some reason, everyone thought, "Whatever Finchy says must be right!" Everyone seemed to fit in with my way of thinking, and I felt good about that, but it was clearly going to be different for me if I was to break into the far larger broadcasting scene over in the US.'

Graham Marsh's former caddie Bruce Young had started his own early steps in a broadcasting career in 1995. 'I remember working with Finchy at the Johnnie Walker Classic in 1997 and recall the great depth of his technical knowledge. We were both starting out in television at the time and Ian was supportive and friendly. As a recent player, he was careful in his commentary to be generally positive about the players he had just finished competing against.'

Ian was also making progress with Jack Graham of ABC. 'After those first two "probationary" tournaments Jack said to me, "There is a contract for you in 1999 in the States, but I think you can still live in Australia while working for ABC." He floated the concept of an initial two-year contract with unlimited two-yearly rolling renewal rights.'

Ian immediately called in a favour from his old friend and co-manager Glenn Wheatley. 'I spoke to Glenn and said, "Would you mind tying the contract up for me?" Glenn had an office in Marina del Rey in California and, while I stayed in Australia, Glenn sat down with ABC over in the States and negotiated a salary of US$300,000 per year for me. I was contracted to ABC for sixteen events per season, which involved four days per event. Typically, the first two days of each tournament were on ESPN, and ABC would cover the two days of golf on the weekend.'

The 16 events for ABC per year turned into 23 when cable network ESPN invited Ian to join their team for seven events. The first two days were shown on ESPN, with Ian working as the lead analyst, and then Curtis Strange would move into the lead analyst role for ABC's weekend coverage. At some of the more significant events, Strange would frequently fill the lead role on all four days and Ian would happily move to covering either the 15th or 16th hole.

Ian explains, 'I had shown in Australia I was capable of being a lead analyst. Typically, most golfers moving into broadcasting would start on the ground at the beginning of their careers. Still, I had won a major, which was in my favour, and I figured I could fill most of the available roles. In cricketing terms, I was a broadcasting all-rounder. Dad used to say to me, "You have to pick a perfect all-rounder," and point out that Dougie Walters was always the first guy on the plane with everyone else having to earn their seat through the season. Whichever network I was working for knew that I was thrilled to be part of their team. I did not need to be the lead, and this has continued as the theme of my more than twenty-five years in television.'

In 1999 Ian, Strange and the ABC team participated in televising one of the saddest and most dramatic finishes seen in major-championship golf. In the Open at Carnoustie, Frenchman Jean van de Velde, leading by three shots, imploded on the 72nd hole, needlessly selecting his driver off the tee. Bob Rosburg for ABC set the scene with 'he's gotta play an iron'.

Strange chimed in: 'Rossie, just as you said that the driver headcover came off.'

In the extended tragicomic scene following, van de Velde scored a triple-bogey seven and slipped into a three-way play-off, which he lost.

Strange famously described the Gallic meltdown as 'the stupidest thing in sports', and Ian added his own take as it unfolded: 'This is making me physically ill.'

As Ian's career progressed, the travel became too much. 'In 1999 I still believed we could live in Australia, covering my ten to twelve contracted events there, and then travel to the US for sixteen events working for ABC. In reality, it was far more difficult than that. In my first full year I had nine overseas trips to the tournaments I was contracted to cover, and Jennie and the two girls travelled to meet me two or three times a year during school holidays. The time away from home was just too hard on the family.'

Ian developed a routine to make the best of his punishing travel schedule. Typically, he'd make the one-hour drive from Sanctuary Cove to Brisbane Airport then fly to Los Angeles on a 14-hour flight, stay for a day or so, and then fly out to the next event venue on the tour. His home golf club in the US was the Los Angeles Country Club, where he would often take a break and play on Mondays and Tuesdays with his friend Lee (Leon) Davis. They were part of a diverse golf group known as 'the Good Ole Boys' that included legendary golf writer Tom Ramsey. Ian also had a base in Atlanta, a convenient travel hub.

By 2000, as Bob Rotella had forecast, Ian had largely rehabilitated his golf. 'I had not completely lost my game, but I had lost my ability to stand on the 1st tee at, say, the British Open and drive it in the fairway. In the back of my mind, I still thought that maybe I could get back out there one day and play occasionally. But I was earning a good living in television, providing for my family and believed I was doing a good job in America.'

The travel finally took its toll. 'I said to Jennie and the girls, "We have to move back to the States." At the British Open in July 2000, Jennie and I were at one of the functions organised for past Open Champions and we spoke to Jack and Barbara Nicklaus. They were both amazingly helpful. Barbara then had a separate conversation with Jennie, saying, "If you do decide to come back and look for a home in America, please come and stay with us and we'll show you around where we live."' Jack and Barbara had lived at Lost Tree,

Palm Beach Gardens, Florida, since 1966, and Jack a member at nearby Lost Tree Golf Club for more than 50 years.

Ian, Jennie and the girls gratefully accepted the offer. They stayed with the Nicklaus family for two weeks and had a good look around the Palm Beach Gardens area. The couple also considered Scottsdale, Arizona, as a possible future home, but the schools there tended not to have pools and both Hayley and Laura were good swimmers.

The Baker-Finch family made a decision on 24 October 2000, the day of Ian's fortieth birthday, when they purchased lot 40, Harbour Isles, Palm Beach Gardens. By Christmas, the construction of their home was underway. 'We enrolled the girls at a local private school, the Benjamin School, which was a top coeducational day school. Hayley started in grade seven and Laura in grade five, and they prospered there.' The exclusive Benjamin school had educated the Nicklaus and Norman children before Hayley and Laura.

Ian and Jack Nicklaus in 2001. 'Jack and Barbara are truly kind people,' says Ian.

'We rented a house for ten months locally while we finished our home and decided we had selected a lovely place to live,' says Ian. 'The beaches may not have been as good as some in Queensland, but there were waterways, harbours and bays – it was rather like the Gold Coast, and not unlike Sanctuary Cove.'

The Nicklaus family's kindness towards the Baker-Finches continued. Ian remembers, 'Jack and Barbara became surrogate grandparents to the girls and happily attended school on days like Grandparents' Day. They are such truly kind people.'

Orlando, Ian and Jennie's old neighbourhood, was only a two-hour drive from their new home and the couple could still catch up with friends from Ian's playing days, such as the Stewarts and the families of Stuart Appleby, Craig Parry, Robert Allenby and Brad Faxon.

'Our new life really started in 2001 when we moved to the States, dramatically reducing our travel from Australia,' says Ian. 'I was still covering thirty tournaments per year with ABC and ESPN until 2007.'

Commentating on golf is not the most straight-forward exercise. One of the obvious challenges is the sheer size of the stage on which the game is played. Sports like tennis, cricket, ice hockey and all codes of football are played within relatively confined areas, and for the most part they have far fewer contestants. A Wimbledon singles final, for example, only involves two players with a single ball in play at any one time. Golf, however, is spread across 120 to 150 acres. The first two days of a PGA Tour event feature a field averaging 150 players. By the final two days, the field is typically down to 60 or so. Multiple players are frequently in contention on different holes and at different times of the day.

But the size and scale of a golf telecast has never concerned Ian. He's learned to concentrate solely on what is in front of him. 'I just sit in my booth watching my little computer screen, calling the golf from a twenty-inch screen when most of the viewers at home are watching the action on their eighty-inch screens. What I have found difficult to manage at times is the frequency and speed of directions from the producer coming into my ears. There is a lot more going on in our headsets than viewers at home may appreciate.'

Ian's start at ABC was not all plain sailing. 'I had loved doing TV in Australia but did not believe I was particularly good at the new job for those first couple of years in America. I tried not to listen to myself when I started working for ABC. I had to fit in, talk at the right time and often temper my remarks on air. In the US there were a lot more voices involved than in Australia. The pace of television commentary is also very different on US television than it is in the UK.'

Peter Alliss in his BBC and ABC roles became a favourite of Ian's. 'Peter was loved by his audiences on both sides of the Atlantic. At ABC Peter was a colourful addition to the team and was very different from the rest of us. He was given room by ABC to be like he was in the UK. To Peter the picture told a story and so did he. Also, he thought there was nothing wrong with periods of silence during the commentary. The UK style involves more storytelling and less time pressure, and I believe his slower style with fewer voices struck a chord with many viewers in the States. He persevered with his style of commentary all his working life behind the microphone.'

Alliss's meandering, entertaining style endured until he died in 2020 at the age of 88.

Ian says, 'The US quick-fire style of "You've got five seconds, Ian" involves more voices at a faster pace. When I was broadcasting in the States, I quickly discovered that I needed to check my ego at the door. We have to accommodate sixteen minutes of commercials every hour and try not to miss an important shot. I would like to have been able to be more like Peter, tell the story and weave it into the telecast.

I have reached a stage now where I do not critique anything we have done and just do my best until the end of the day.'

As for the components making up the job, each analyst is required to complete their own research on the players. Ian leans heavily on different sources of information and social media available to him. 'For my study, I rely to a large extent on sources like the PGA Tour website, the *No Laying Up* podcast, Geoff Shackelford's newsletter *The Quadrilateral*, and the CBS Sports website. I constantly make notes and have built up my bank of golf and player knowledge over the years.

'Each year out on tour there are at least ten to twenty new players to research and become familiar with. Our team members all have their own distinct research methods and there is a wealth of knowledge within the team itself. I keep my own "book" of players on my iPad. There is generally a researcher, Rick Folio, sitting in the booth with Frank Nobilo and me who will pass over a note relevant to the context of the coverage. It may be a light-hearted piece of information about a certain player that may become relevant if the opportunity arises – these snippets of information may not even be golf-related but add to the fun and broaden the appeal of the coverage.'

The analysts' research styles can differ. 'Trevor [Immelman] has an extensive handwritten list of everyone playing on the weekend. He wants to be as good as possible and is happy to work hard. Trevor has great close-range vision, but his handwritten notes would not work for me as I would need my glasses to read them. We typically don't have a lot of time to tell stories. We might only have about seven seconds on each piece before the producer moves onto the next shot.

'[Anchor] Jim Nantz is more of a storyteller on the broadcasts and always has abundant information on the players as they come off the final green. He is a genius and weaves his story into the show with a perfect rhythm. Frank Nobilo has an amazing knowledge of swing mechanics and uses a different research method again, usually studying the event itself, and he has a one- or two-page summary that he updates each day.'

Habitually, Ian will wander around the driving range wherever possible, talking to players, caddies and coaches. However, a fine line exists between gathering information for the broadcast and being too intrusive. 'Most of the guys playing in the events are a bit precious about their last hour before they go to the 1st tee. Only the players I know are chatty, and I try not to ask too many questions. Golf is vastly different from motor racing, for instance, where the drivers may be strapped to a bomb but will still willingly do an interview from the car right before they go to the start line. In a similar situation, golfers do not always want to know you, but we are gradually gaining better access to the players. The smart ones realise the value of face time on television with our CBS "walk-and-talks" on the weekends.'

When Ian started broadcasting at the age of 36 he found it easier to talk to the players who had been his contemporaries. 'Most of the younger players when I started knew I had been a player. I now go to the range before play to observe quietly; I like to use my eyes to gauge how they hit.' The caddies can be a valuable source of background information. 'I can ask the caddies I know questions like, "Hey, mate, is that the shot he prefers as his go-to shot? Anything new in the bag? What is working particularly well this week?"

'I am also interested in how a player shapes certain shots. Take Jon Rahm, for instance. He drills that favourite fade of his off the tee but has struggled to hit a draw at times. In observing him closely, I have noticed how he puts the ball about an inch further forward in his stance when he wants to hit a draw, but then holds the club back about six to eight inches behind the ball. When I see him bouncing his club back there, I know he will hit a draw.'

As Ian became more senior in the team his work hours improved. 'In the old days I had to be at the event from Tuesday night. There was no need for me to be there for the pro-am day on the Wednesday and I was not too fond of it – I was away from home for five days. Our ABC producer Jack Graham wanted us in by Tuesday night, mainly for meetings, which I thought at the time were useless. On the current team, it is more about Jim, Trevor, Frank and me all being on the same page, along with Dottie Pepper, Colt Knost, Mark Immelman and Amanda Balionis. We will all have been following social media and accessing many of the same stories. I usually get into the venue on Thursday night or Friday morning, go out on the course and then we will often get together for dinner on Friday night or Saturday night.'

As part of his preparation Ian often takes his putter and a ball or two out onto the green on the holes he is covering. He will then hit putts at the hole position cut on the day, so he knows which way the putts break when play begins in earnest. 'At CBS I cover holes two, five, eight, eleven, fourteen and seventeen every weekend, but I would generally only come on to the broadcast at hole number five.' Golf Channel covers the first two hours of play and the technical crew prepare to switch the graphics to CBS at 3 pm Eastern time. 'The changeover is quite an exercise in logistics: the Golf Channel announcers all leave, and the two different crews only have fifteen minutes for what needs to be a smooth transition. It is a very demanding time.'

After play is complete the team wraps up the coverage with no rehearsals required. Ian says, 'If we are any good as a team it just flows. You learn quickly to fit in and become a team player.'

The existing CBS team will often take some time over the selection and addition of any potential new team members. Former US Tour player Colt Knost was trialled by CBS for a year or two before being added permanently. 'Colt was great,' Ian recalls. 'We all realised he would add value because he was younger and knew many of the players of his age group. He is a naturally funny guy, so he brought something new to the team. When he was presented with his first contract, I told him not to take the amount offered and that he was worth more. I had a similar discussion with Amanda about her first contract.

'That is something us older guys can do. Curtis Strange did the same for me about the first contract I was offered, and my contract payment improved because of his advice. He told me not to take less than twenty thousand dollars per week, which is how I achieved three hundred thousand dollars for sixteen events. The lead analyst is typically paid twice as much as the rest of us. All of us on the team seem to know our respective places. For instance, Dottie comes into the tower when I go to lead analyst, but Dottie is simply the best on-course reporter, a role she has filled so well over the last fifteen to twenty years.'

Ian's two-year contract in 1999 was extended after his first term in the role with ABC, and after the move to CBS, and has continued to be extended two-yearly or four-yearly until the present day.

Over the last 60 years, the number of producers and directors at CBS has been very stable. The role of the director is to select who is taking which pictures, but the producer controls the show, deciding which of the pictures to broadcast and when. The network has had only three co-ordinating golf producers since 1959. The first of these was the 'father of televised golf', Frank Chirkinian, followed in 1997 for 23 years by Lance Barrow. Ian says, 'Lance was my producer from 2007 to 2019 and was tough on me at first. At times I disliked his style, but he made me better and we remain friends today.'

The producer of each broadcast is a significant contributor to the quality of the coverage. At the time of writing, lead golf producer

Sellers Shy is only the third to hold the position at CBS Sports. He understands golf, and he's a scratch player who still loves to play the game. He constantly discusses his putting stroke with Ian. Since Shy has been in the role, he has introduced updated graphics, refreshed the music and established a constant mini scoreboard in the lower right-hand corner of the screen.

Some of the interplay between the director and producer, and also the analysts, can become tense from time to time. Ian explains, 'The truck can get a little boisterous at times, and there will be a lot of yelling and screaming bleeding through the headphones. It can be quite disconcerting, but you learn how to deal with it. Sitting at home, you might wonder why I suddenly stop talking and it's usually because I've been told to lay out [shut up] – they're moving on to the next shot.'

Another feature of CBS coverage is the lack of significant discussion during the broadcast on any controversial subjects circulating in the game. For example, it is improbable that the subject of LIV Golf will be raised directly or discussed in any depth during a broadcast, as CBS is in a quasi-partnership with the PGA Tour.

Ian enjoys the added intensity and pressure that comes with network television coverage of the majors. 'At CBS we have covered the Masters for the last sixty-five years, ever since TV coverage started, and for me there have been so many highlights.'

'The 2019 Masters was the tournament that provided me with the most memorable event I have worked on,' says Ian. 'My calling Tiger Woods up the 17th was a special event I will never forget; his win was so emotional and the most unbelievable comeback in sport – not just in golf.'

At Augusta in 2019 Woods ended an 11-year drought in the majors, coming back from a fourth, and potentially career-ending, back surgery to win by two shots. He donned his original 1997 green jacket for the fifth time. As the CBS team applauded Woods's unlikely victory, Jim Nantz commented, 'I never thought we'd see anything that could rival the hug with his father in 1997, but we just did – the hug with his children. If that doesn't bring a tear to your eye, and you're a parent … you are not human.'

Faldo called it 'the greatest scene in golf forever'.

IAN CALLS ADAM SCOTT'S 2013 MASTERS WIN

Adam Scott's Masters win in 2013 was a landmark moment for the Queensland golfer – Scott became the first Australian to don the green jacket. Recognising the significance of the win, Jim Nantz passed over the commentary.

Jim: 'And, Ian, it's your turn for the narrative for this special moment.'

Ian: 'From Down Under to on top of the world, Jim.'

Ian assesses the other majors. 'We also cover the PGA Championship. NBC and ESPN cover the US Open, and ESPN covers the British Open. The US Open is my least favourite major to watch and, in my view, it can become monotonous. The USGA [the United States Golf Association] always seems to trick up the course by growing long, thick, rough, fertilised and watered, also producing extremely hard, fast greens that are incessantly rolled. I'm not too fond of it.

'These tricked-up courses can make the best players in the world look silly, with extreme course-conditioning, green speeds and hole locations. I like birdies and want excitement when I watch an event, particularly one of the majors. The current players are so long and accurate that par on most courses is reduced to 68 – let them play and produce low scores.

'I no longer do any fringe work at the Open Championship. I enjoy going back, watching the event, attending meetings for the Australian PGA and being part of it all.

'The Masters is the highlight of my year, as they set the course up in such a way to ensure we will see birdies and eagles.'

CHAPTER 21

BROADCASTING – THE LATER YEARS

Welcoming – and farewelling – Sir Nick

During his 25-plus-year broadcasting career Ian has worked with a variety of analysts, hosts and on-course commentators, all with their own styles.

Jim Nantz is universally regarded as the best in the business and has worked as an anchor and sportscaster for over 40 years. Ian agrees. 'Jim is the simply best and the glue in our team. He is *the guy*. No one on American television is regarded more highly than Jim.'

The anchor and the lead analyst operate at a level above the rest of the team. 'CBS is sensitive when required and takes the high ground when it comes to the players,' Ian says. 'Greg Norman fell to pieces in the final round of the Masters in 1996, but Jim and the team studiously avoided the word "choke". We maintain a player's dignity and the commentary team never puts the boot into a player. Nor are we there to explain the obvious. We operate in a visual medium and should add to what the viewer can see.'

During his broadcasting career, two-time major champion Johnny Miller upset some players with commentary perceived as overly critical. 'Johnny was not immensely popular with certain players,' Ian says. 'I thought he was a good commentator and he enjoyed twenty-five years at NBC as an analyst beside Dan Hicks. He was down to earth, had a good heart and was never nasty. His problem was he had been a slightly negative thinker as a player who focused too closely on what could go wrong; at times, his negativity may have carried over into his commentary style.

'When Johnny was on his game, he was almost unbeatable. He would knock it close to the flag all day – which is why he won both a US Open and a British Open. He strayed into controversy on occasion, when his commentary could appear to be overcritical. He said things like "I think Tiger should be doing this …" which in my view was ridiculous because Johnny came from a different era.'

The golf networks can be brutal to some of their announcers and analysts. At the direction of the Augusta National Tournament Committee, Gary McCord was famously removed by the CBS director over his Masters coverage in 1994. He had made an indelicate remark about the greens at Augusta National: 'I think they bikini wax them.'

Peter Kostis was dispensed with by CBS in 2019. Kostis lamented later he would have appreciated an opportunity to say goodbye to his fans. 'Peter may have annoyed a lot of players with his swing analysis and calling them out during play,' says Ian, 'but I believe he would have been good in a lead role as a swing guru. He was the best on-course analyst, and it was a big loss to golf when Peter finished.'

During the 2023 season, NBC's Paul Azinger came in for considerable criticism on social media for the quality of his analysis in both the Open Championship and the Ryder Cup. Azinger refused to take a pay cut during negotiations for his 2024 contract. It was announced in November 2023 that he would no longer be NBC's lead analyst for the new season. Ian's view? 'Paul made two or three stupid mistakes at the Ryder Cup in Rome. They were not major, but you cannot present a fact on a broadcast without checking it for correctness. He arrived at the desk unprepared, got caught out, and lo and behold he was gone. All he had wanted to do was renew his contract for the previous amount of one million per season. NBC said no, which I thought was brutal because he did a good job. He knew what he was talking about, was easy to listen to and I enjoyed Paul as an analyst.'

Ian's strategy is to get things right or correct them quickly if he does make a mistake. 'If I make an error and it's a big-enough deal, I try to fix it as soon as possible. It is a lot easier when we are all together – I can give a signal to, say, Trevor, and chip in with a correction after he has finished.'

From time to time, Ian has drawn his share of hurtful criticism. 'Last year, on the *No Laying Up* podcast, I heard someone say, "I know he's a nice guy and everyone says he's great, but it's time he moved on." I talked to the producer and Trevor, who knows the *No Laying Up* guys, and they told me my critics don't like my old style of commentary – they want criticism. But that's never been me. I'm not the lead analyst – it's up to Trevor to analyse critically. I'm there as the hole announcer, I blend into the show, and I don't generally read social media during the week. It only takes one person to say I'm not doing a good job and my day is ruined.'

Some of the older commentators and analysts become vulnerable later in their careers. The network practice of offering one- or two-year contract renewals is hardly conducive to job security – as Azinger, McCord and Kostis have discovered. Cable also tends to refresh teams regularly from the bottom up.

Colt Knost and Smylie Kaufman are examples of a younger breed of broadcaster.

'I see Smylie out there frequently,' says Ian. 'The good thing about these young guys coming through is their familiarity with current players. His is a different level of connection to the players than Frank's or mine. He is popular with the players and has first-hand insight by travelling with the likes of Rickie Fowler and Justin Thomas. There is a place for younger commentators like Smylie and Colt, both of whom will have long broadcasting careers. To the current generation of players, I must seem like a grandfather!'

Ian's style on television is quite different from Gary McCord's or David Feherty's. But he believes the more colourful commentators have their place. 'Gary was great. He livened up the show. David was irreverent, funny and, like Gary, had a place on the team to add variety. David looked lost at NBC and now works for LIV, which nobody watches, and I am sure he wishes he was back having fun with us at CBS!'

Golf Channel and Golf Central lead studio analyst Brandel Chamblee has provoked negative comments from viewers – and from the occasional player. But, at the time of writing, Golf Channel's ratings have not suffered from any controversy generated by Chamblee. His ongoing feud with Ian Poulter generated social media heat in 2017, when Chamblee suggested Poulter had not played for a win down the stretch in the Players Championship that year. Poulter fired back, 'Sorry to disappoint. I can only dream of being as good as Brandel. It's very easy sitting on your arse!'

With his modest playing record, including a single PGA Tour win, Chamblee incited Lee Westwood and Poulter (again) in 2023 by saying LIV golfers were 'sadly playing for a murderer' in reference to the competition's Saudi Arabian backer.

Ian says, 'Chamblee has a completely different role to play. He is a studio announcer who is brought in to talk before or after the show to give his opinion. He has the pulpit to himself for five minutes and knows how to use it. He is well prepared with his script in front of him. The host throws the "ball" to him perfectly, he catches it, runs with it, then passes it off to the next guy. He is great in his role, well rehearsed and on a particularly good team with Paul McGinley, who is a thoughtful and strong partner. If I am walking past a TV set and I hear Brandel talking, I stop and listen because he is interesting.'

Chamblee is provocative and Ian disagrees with some of his views. 'He is strongly against the ball roll-back, which I am equally strongly in favour of. It is far too little too late in my view from a golf course perspective. But, if we see each other, Brandel and I will both sit down, have a beer and talk about it.'

When Ian's old playing rival Nick Faldo joined ABC in 2004, along with Paul Azinger, it heralded a new chapter in Ian's career. Ian welcomed Faldo to the team. 'Back in our early days in Europe, Jennie and I travelled with Nick and his wife Gill. Nick may have been a trifle difficult to play with at times, but we had been friends since 1984.

'Nick was never a fellow player you would arrive on the range and chat with, because you never chat with Nick. He was there to do his job. Norman was the same and would always go down to the end of the range so he did not have to talk to anyone. It's probably a good trait for a superstar golfer to have – the ability to cut yourself off from the rest of the world!'

Ian encountered Faldo as a player in final pairings in the Opens of 1984 and 1990. He observed and learned from Faldo's total focus on his game and how little consideration he gave to his playing partners. Faldo was extraordinarily successful and clinical, but perhaps lacking charisma when at the top. He never enjoyed a wonderful relationship with either the golf press – particularly the tabloids – or television crews. After his victory in the 1992 Open he famously thanked the assembled press corps 'from the heart of my bottom' in his victory speech.

All of this was forgotten as the pair of ex-players were reunited in the commentary booth in 2004. Ian assured the Englishman he 'had his back'.

'I always said to Nick, "I do not want your job. I am here on the 17th to make you better at your job at CBS." We had a great team – McCord on sixteen, me on seventeen, Nick at eighteen and Nantz in the lead seat, complemented by Kostis and Feherty on the course.'

Faldo developed into an accomplished lead analyst on the CBS team. Early in his television career some viewers noted Faldo may have been prone to mention his past performances too frequently, but the trend faded as he developed into a popular broadcaster with a surprisingly dry sense of humour and rare insight into the game.

The team at ABC in 2005 and 2006 was one of the strongest Ian has been part of. 'Nick and I shared the front desk with Paul, Mike Tirico and Terry Gannon, and we all became great friends.' In 2007, CBS took over the broadcasting rights for the PGA Tour under a long-term contract. 'Nick and I went across to CBS and, for me, nothing much changed. It was the same job and I continued doing the same things.'

Faldo finally retired from broadcasting after 16 years. On 22 June 2022 he disclosed that the Wyndham Championship in Greensboro, North Carolina, would be the scene of his final event in the booth. He had made his PGA Tour debut 43 years earlier as a player there during the 1979 Greater Greensboro Open. He cited travel fatigue as the main reason for his retirement, saying he wished to spend more time with his wife, Lindsay, on their farm in Montana.

Ian believes Faldo became better the further he went into his career. An emotional farewell to Faldo from the CBS team took place on 7 August 2023. During the afternoon, Ian, voice breaking, acknowledged that Faldo had 'taught me so much, and for that I am grateful'. He continued, 'I am honoured to have my name sandwiched between yours on the Claret Jug – 1990, 1991, 1992 – I look at that all the time with great pleasure.'

In tears, Faldo struggled to respond, barely managing to say, 'Cheers, mate.'

It fell to Jim Nantz to close the broadcast by saying, 'Congratulations, Sir Nick, let's bring it home.'

Faldo, still battling his emotions, said, 'Thank you all. I am a single child, and at sixty-five I have found these three brothers. Thank you. I am ready.'

Ian summed up the day. 'I knew it would be a tough goodbye when it came. I am sure Nick didn't realise how sad it would be.'

Ian and Faldo have stayed connected. They lunched together at the 2023 Open and walked around the course talking about old times. 'I miss collaborating with him; we share a great forty-year history.'

At the time of Faldo's retirement, long-time CBS Sports chairman Sean McManus announced that Faldo would be replaced as lead analyst by Trevor Immelman, a South African who had won the Masters in 2008. At 42, Immelman was 20 years younger than Ian. The network must have considered Ian as a possible replacement for Faldo but presumably wanted a longer-term solution.

Immelman had an interesting background and playing record that wasn't dissimilar to Ian's. He had won twice on the PGA Tour before securing his sole major at Augusta National in 2008, shortly before he turned 30. After winning the Masters, he tried to practise through injury and a slump. He was a left-hand dominant player, and a diligent practiser, both key strengths.

After sustaining injuries to his left wrist and hand, he continued with a full playing schedule, which resulted in more severe damage. After surgery, Immelman regained neither the former strength in his hand nor his previous form and became a shadow of his former self as a player. Immelman battled on through a winless streak of five years. He lost his tour card before regaining it briefly in 2014 after being forced down to the second-tier Web.com Tour. He continued to struggle as a player, shifting his focus to the European Tour in 2018 with limited success.

That same year, he received an unexpected phone call from Golf Channel producer Mark Summer, who asked the struggling player if he had thought about television. Immelman had lunch with Summer in Orlando and was persuaded to audition for a role with the network. He was initially trialled on a casual basis, but his role soon widened. He enjoyed the work, removed as it was from the day-to-day grind of playing. He joined the CBS golf team in 2019.

Ian is unfailingly positive and complimentary about Immelman and his CBS colleagues. He has a lot of fun with New Zealander Frank Nobilo, whom he first met in 1979 during their playing days. Working together has rekindled their wonderful relationship. Ian is equally appreciative of Amanda Balionis's skill in conducting many of the after-round interviews. 'She is bright, bubbly and does a great job. She is always well rehearsed, with a pleasant smile and engaging personality; the players always say yes to a post-round interview with Amanda. Dottie is the best prepared on-course commentator and a future hall-of-famer for sure! Colt adds the humour and Mark Immelman [Trevor's older brother] brings an intelligent coaching style of analysis to his on-course role.'

Ian compares his CBS team to a rock band or ensemble. 'Jim Nantz is the lead singer, Trevor Immelman is lead guitar, I call myself the drummer, and Frankie is the bass guitarist. Then we have the three out on the course who provide the backing and the harmony. Jim Nantz often tells me, "Ian, don't you leave. You must stay here. We are the last two of this old CBS family."'

But clouds are gathering on the horizon for televised golf. In 2012 40 per cent of golf participants in the US watched the Masters on television: 13.5 million viewers out of 30 million participants.

By 2022 the number of Masters viewers had dropped to 25 per cent of US golfers: 10.2 million of 40 million golf participants.

Equipment and ball technology present televised golf with a new set of challenges. Most notably, they have an impact on the pace of play. Six-hour rounds have become common in the majors and tour events. Most of the par fives on championship courses have become reachable in two shots, and the proliferation of driveable par fours has resulted in long waits for players before the greens ahead are cleared. Players now often wait for the wind conditions to suit them before selecting their clubs and this degrades the viewing experience as the pace of play is snail-like. Officials at many events seem unwilling to impose penalties or even issue warnings to habitual pace of play offenders.

Even the ultimate broadcasting diplomat, Jim Nantz, was recently critical of innovations like Aimpoint, which many players have employed to stand astride the line of their putts. 'The Aimpoint mania that we see today truly drives me crazy. Where is the feel in it? I can't stand looking at it.'

Television networks also face stiff competition from streaming services. The Netflix series *Full Swing* reached 53.1 million viewer hours. At the time of writing, CBS is holding steady with a 1 per cent increase in viewers in 2023, but the 2024 Masters saw a 20 per cent decrease in viewers on the final day. The network has taken a proactive approach to these challenges: at the 2024 US PGA, for instance, the broadcaster had 125 cameras and 150 microphones. Technology is a key ally. There are fly cams, bunker cameras, drones and the venerable Goodyear Blimp to assist aerial coverage. During the event, the player 'walk-and-talks' put the viewer up close and personal. If all of that is not enough to completely immerse golf fans in the event, further technology in the form of Toptracer, PinPoint Wind analysis and GOLFTEC swing analysis all add to the viewing experience.

Ian is his honest self in reflecting on the current state of the televised game. 'Commentating has changed over the last twenty-five years, mainly because of social media. In the US there is an overabundance of opinions typified by faceless comments generated from a limited knowledge base. Everyone knows what's happening – it's a 24/7 thing now with golf on all the time. To be honest there is too much golf on TV; it is oversaturated and ratings at some events are dropping. But because of all this, when we do our job on CBS on Saturdays and Sundays in three- to four-hour shows, we try our best to make the show interesting and fun. Our role is to bring the players to life and make each show informative, a good watch and a good listen.'

Golf has given the sport's nicest guy a career mulligan.

CHAPTER 22

THE PRESIDENTS CUP AND THE OLYMPICS

And a gold medal

Ian found himself on the sidelines of a major controversy in 1996.

He inadvertently became embroiled in the sensational dumping of David Graham as the non-playing captain of the International Team for the Presidents Cup. Graham is the only Australian male golfer to have won two different majors, but he became the innocent victim of a player revolt that led to his humiliating and very public removal.

A scant two months before the matches began on 15 September at Robert Trent Jones Golf Club in Gainesville, Virginia, a mutiny over Graham's captaincy came to a head. On 15 July 1996, during Open Championship week, the international players ignored the warnings of three PGA Tour officials of the damage their rebellion could have on Graham, who had no knowledge of it, and the fledgling event.

The background to the International Team member mutiny in 1996 is as interesting as the event itself. Greg Norman has long been implicated in Graham's dismissal, with rumours swirling about his issues with the process for the appointment of the captain and his antipathy for Graham. Norman had asked permission to arrive at the 1996 event two days after the rest of the team – a request declined by Graham. There had also been an incident at the inaugural Presidents Cup in 1994 when Norman, unable to play in the event for medical reasons, appeared on the 1st tee of the last day, requesting permission to take part as a commentator on the CBS broadcast team. Graham refused the request, bluntly letting Norman know the final day was not going to become 'the fucking Greg Norman Show'.

Another Australian, Steve Elkington, had allegedly been unhappy with Graham's handling of a White House visit by the opposing teams in 1994.

This build-up of bad blood between the captain and at least two of his previous team members is said to have sealed Graham's fate. The players voted, and Graham was deposed as non-playing captain – apparently by nine votes to nil (New Zealander Michael Campbell abstained). The media commented on the coup unfavourably, suggesting the players had behaved like sheep in exercising their votes.

Hapless Australian player Craig Parry had the unwelcome task of communicating the news to Graham. It must have been a tough job for Parry; Graham later admitted that he and his wife, Maureen, cried after he put down the phone. It was a deeply personal insult to Graham, and to Maureen, who had already been to New York to buy personalised gifts for the players and their wives. Of the gifts, Graham wondered at the time, 'What do I do with them now?'

The new captain would be Peter Thomson and his assistant would be Ian Baker-Finch.

Ian believes Graham's removal was unfortunate and poorly handled, but the selection process for the captain was partly to blame. 'David Graham had filled the role perfectly adequately in 1994, then two years later came the players' revolt as they asked, "Who the hell picked him as captain?" It was not as though David had done a lousy job. It became clear that Norman, Price and Elkington wanted to have a hand in picking their own International captain.

'Part of the problem was the PGA Tour selected the captains of both teams and continued to do so for over twenty years. The first time we were able to finally select our own captain was in 2017 when Nick Price was selected. David was justifiably pissed off at his dumping, particularly considering the amount of work he had invested in the 1994 event. The tour then asked Peter Thomson, who was unhappy with how David had been treated, to step in to do the job.'

Taking the players' coup as a fait accompli, Peter and Ian accepted their belated appointments by the tour.

Graham was unhappy with the process and was reported as saying Thomson was an excellent choice in normal circumstances but he could have considered his acceptance of the captaincy more carefully.

Thomson insisted that Ian join him as captain's assistant, feeling that at 35 Ian knew the players on the International Team. 'Peter and I did everything together; we got the players together and went back and forth to the course together on the bus. Nick Price, Steve Elkington and Frank Nobilo told jokes, and we all had team dinners, building a perfect team spirit.'

Jumbo Ozaki added another dimension. Ian recalls, 'Jumbo sent his chauffeur to the local wine store with five thousand US dollars. There, he bought six bottles of fine French wine, including Chateau Margaux, Lafite Rothschild and others, and we drank them at the first team dinner. That is how Jumbo was. His length off the tee was also a feature of the event, and he was the only player on both teams who could hit his driver into the trees over the back of the range – he was genuinely long with any ball.

'It was a great team to be involved with, played on a great course. The event was run by the PGA Tour, which was fair enough as they funded it.'

The format was demanding, with four-ball matches on the morning of the first and second days, followed by foursomes in the afternoon of both days. At 67, the non-playing US captain Arnold Palmer deployed a strong line-up. The Americans came out firing and led the morning four-ball on the first day 4–1 with only the South Africans Ernie Els and Mark McNulty winning a point for the Internationals. The afternoon saw little improvement for Ian's team as they lost 3.5–1.5. After the first day the gap looked insurmountable with the US leading by five clear points: 7.5–2.5.

Day two of the match saw an improvement for the visiting Internationals – three wins in the morning followed by four in the afternoon foursomes. Sunday's matches comprised 12 singles and the honours finished even at six games each. Ian recalls, 'The singles were remarkably close – right down to the wire. On the 71st hole Vijay [Singh] missed a putt and Freddie [Couples] holed his birdie putt for a win. One putt was really the difference between the teams.'

The final score was the USA 16.5–International 15.5.

Two years later, the Internationals took their revenge at Royal Melbourne, securing what is still the only victory over the United States in the history of the biennial competition. Jumbo Ozaki, aged 51, easily qualified in fourth place for the team, but then declared himself unavailable, making way for his brother Naomichi 'Joe' Ozaki, who had finished eleventh in the rankings. Ian had no official role as Thomson, in his even-handed fashion, requested Wayne Grady to be his assistant for the home matches in 1998. The result was a resounding win to the Internationals 20.5–11.5.

Ian's connection to the Presidents Cup resumed in 2003, 2005 and 2007, when he served as Gary Player's assistant captain in all three events. Nicklaus and Jeff Sluman were the United States team captain and assistant captain. Ian remembers, 'My role in the Presidents Cup provided Jennie and me with some of the greatest times in our lives.

In the last three contests, Jeff and I did all the fun work with our teams and Jack and Gary made all the speeches!'

The most memorable finish in the event occurred at the 2003 contest at Fancourt Hotel and Country Club in George, South Africa, where the teams were tied 17–17 after regulation play. Tiger Woods and Ernie Els, the two best players in the world at the time, went to sudden death. Els had just lost four and three to Woods in the singles. In fading light, the players parred the first play-off hole (the actual 18th). Moving to the 1st hole, Els kept the play-off alive with a 12-foot par-saving putt. On the par-three 3rd hole, Els was 45 feet away and Woods 90 feet away after the tee shots. Woods two-putted, holing a 15-footer for par and Els holed his 6-footer right on top of him.

Ian recalls, 'It was getting darker, and Jack and Gary had to call the PGA tour commissioner Tim Finchem for guidance. The ruling was: "It is a tie, so the US retain the Cup." I was standing right next to Ernie, who was not happy, and he said, "Bullshit, let's carry on," and started walking to the next tee in the dark, where his caddie was waiting for him. Jack and Gary got together and suggested we share the Cup and hold the trophy for a year each, and the deal was done, right there, in the dark on the green.'

Ian believes in the future of the Presidents Cup. 'At the time of my involvement the contests were close. The Internationals are gradually becoming stronger with players from Korea and South America contending.'

There is a postscript to David Graham's sacking as captain in 1996: in a conciliatory gesture by the PGA Tour, he was appointed to the executive committee of the Presidents Cup in March 2011 and travelled from his home in the US to Royal Melbourne to fulfil the role of an official observer of the event, alongside Peter Thomson, who was in the captain's role again.

In 2011, in between the Presidents Cup and the Olympics, Ian made a few brief appearances on the Senior Tour, now known as PGA Champions. He played in the two-man better-ball Liberty Mutual Insurance Legends of Golf with Joe Ozaki in 2011, with Hale Irwin in 2012 and then won the Raphael Division of the event with the late Bart Bryant in 2013. The Liberty events were televised by the CBS team, and Ian managed to successfully combine work with pleasure while proving he could still play the game.

In 2016 another non-playing role came Ian's way when he was asked to captain the Australian Olympic golf team at Rio de Janeiro, where golf returned as an Olympic sport for the first time in 112 years. Ian was surprised and delighted to be invited; he was the unanimous choice of Australian golf administrators and the Australian Olympic Committee.

The team was made up of Minjee Lee, Su-Hyun Oh, Marcus Fraser and Scott Hend. Rather than stay in the Olympic Village 90 minutes' drive from the course, Ian insisted the team be accommodated in a comfortable house near the venue. He recalls, 'We did it all properly and spent ninety thousand dollars on a house for the team for three weeks. Gil Hanse had built a great golf course down there and it was a memorable event – very successful overall with some great relationships forged.'

Fraser finished just out of the medals in tied fifth as the best of the four Australians.

Ian was a popular captain and agreed to fill the role again in Tokyo in 2020, although because of the Covid-19 pandemic the Games did not start until July 2021. 'Japan is a golf-crazy country but unfortunately because of Covid we couldn't have fans attend,' Ian remembers.

Ian engendered a great team spirit. 'It was an honour to be selected to do the job and be part of the team. I was the architect of the environment to make sure everything possible was done for the players. I was the team leader, the bus driver and the beer cooler – whatever could be done.'

The opening ceremony in Tokyo presented a challenge for Ian and the team. To attend the opening and closing ceremonies, they would need to arrive far too early and leave too late. 'I wanted them to treat the Olympics like a major, to arrive at the right time, try to win it and then leave. With this in mind, we did not attend the opening or closing ceremonies at either Rio or Tokyo.'

The coaches, caddies and players all stayed together in a hotel near the course, creating a great atmosphere. Ian, with assistance from Brad James and Martin Blake, set it up. 'We booked a spare room, removed all the furniture apart from one bed, put in a whole lot of pillows and set the room up with a projector. Each night we played the Australian Olympic telecast from Channel Seven while having a couple of cold beers. It was just the most tremendous fun – very Australian.

'We were there to perform at our best, treat the week like a major, and win a medal if possible. If he had birdied the last, Cam Smith would have won bronze outright, and a par would have got him into the seven-man bronze play-off. Cam went for the pin, finished past the flag and unfortunately three-putted. Hannah Green was in contention for silver, went for a birdie on the last – good on her – and bogeyed, just missing a medal by one shot.'

Smith tied tenth on 270 and Marc Leishman was well down the men's field on 282. Green was tied fifth on 271 while Minjee Lee finished on 280.

Ian strongly supported Karrie Webb, who he calls an icon of Australian golf, to succeed him in 2024 as captain of both teams for the Paris Olympic Games.

In 2018 a new challenge arose for Ian. In a tradition dating back to 1872, Ian had been presented with the winner's gold medal for his 1991 victory in the Open Championship, but the medal had remained un-displayed in a drawer in the Baker-Finch family home for years. With two daughters and only one medal to pass on to them, Ian floated the idea to Jennie, Hayley and Laura of selling the medal and donating the proceeds to charity. His family supported the idea.

'Over the years I have donated a lot of my memorabilia to charity. It was no use to me sitting around the house. I'd used an auction house in London for this in the past and suppose I may have donated about £25,000 to various charities over the years. The Open medal was reasonably valuable, and a collector approached me who had already acquired a number of winners' medals, but the proposed sale to this particular buyer seemed to take on a commercial element that I became uncomfortable with.'

His next move was to speak to Martin Slumbers, the chief executive of the R&A, about an alternative method for selling the medal.

The gold medal goes to a good home. Ian with R&A captain Clive Brown (right).

The R&A arranged for Ian's medal to be permanently displayed in the Royal Birkdale clubhouse.

Ian divided the sale proceeds three ways. First, at the R&A's suggestion, £10,000 went to the Golf Foundation in the UK to support its 'Girls Golf Rocks' participation program. The balance of A$50,000 was then divided equally between two Australian charities, Challenge and Redkite, both children's cancer networks. Australian professional Jarrod Lyle, who passed away from leukaemia in 2018 at just 36, had also supported Challenge's work for many years before his death.

Slumbers issued a statement to announce the initiative: 'One of Ian's most enduring qualities is his unstinting acts of kindness, and we were delighted to support these charitable activities which mean a lot to him.'

ANOTHER SIDE TO TIGER

Ian saw a private side to Tiger Woods in 2021. His broadcasting colleague Dottie Pepper's close friend Kim Galvin had been diagnosed with stage-four cancer in December 2021. Ian recalls, 'Dottie was supporting Kim, a huge Tiger fan, through her illness and treatment, but she was struggling, so Dottie called me to ask for a favour. At Dottie's request I called Tiger and let him know the situation with his "No 1 fan", and to ask him whether he would mind sending her a message.

'He went one step further and called Kim straight away and spoke to her at length, as well as sending her some of his merchandise, signed and personalised. He stayed connected with her, encouraging her to fight, to kick arse and to focus on "fuck cancer" while suggesting she should concentrate on what she could do better each day.

'Two years on, Kim is still struggling with her illness but is much better. The words of support from Tiger were a godsend for her at that time.'

Over almost 50 years, golf has provided Ian and his family with a great life, at a level unimaginable for him growing up in South East Queensland as a trainee professional. Ian and Jennie travel the world, playing golf together and enjoying close relationships and good times with friends, old and new. Jennie has become an accomplished player herself, with a handicap of eight, but she doesn't take the game too seriously. 'I didn't start playing golf until the girls went to college and I didn't want golf to rule my life,' she says. 'It is not my livelihood and, for me, it needs to be fun. All my life I have been watching Ian and other professionals. I only saw good swings and golf became intuitive for me. If I have a bad hole, I just pick the ball up, put it in my pocket and go to the next hole. As I tell everyone, no one else cares what you are shooting. I only wanted to play well enough to have a game with Ian when we are travelling, and now I really enjoy it.'

Now in their 60s, Ian and Jennie enjoy the rhythm of their lives together. Ian works for CBS each year until the finish of the PGA Tour season at the end of August. Late each year, Ian and Jennie take regular trips back to Australia where, after many years of travelling extensively as a board director of the PGA of Australia, Ian has now been appointed the organisation's chair.

Family plays a big part in their lives. At the time of writing, Hayley lives ten minutes away from Ian and Jennie in Florida and Jennie often picks up Hayley's daughter Eloise from school to put her to bed or to enjoy a sleepover. Ian enjoys taking her to swimming lessons and spending time with granddaughter Lucy, who was born on Anzac Day in 2023.

Laura is married to Spencer and lives in New York working in content strategy for magazine publisher Meredith. Both girls excelled at school; Hayley attended Southern Methodist College in Dallas and Laura New York University.

Ian and Jennie's home today is in Palm Beach Gardens, Florida, at latitude 26.83 north – a mirror to Beerwah, which is at latitude 26.85 south. Even the climates in their lives are aligned. They typically holiday for a few weeks from late October back in Australia, spending as much time as possible with family and friends at Twin Waters on the Sunshine Coast.

While in Australia, Ian is regularly spotted teeing it up in Legends (over-50s) pro-ams, competing against many of his old friends from his playing days, amusing himself and his mates by winning cheques here and there for a few hundred dollars, and winding back the clock to his days as a trainee in 1979.

CHAPTER 23

REFLECTIONS

A life in golf

Success in sport is measured subjectively and golf is no different. There have been 470 majors played in men's golf from 1860 to the end of 2024, and 233 different male players have won majors.

Only 89 players have won two majors or more.

Of the multiple-major winners, Jack Nicklaus is the greatest player the game has seen. His 18 major titles and 19 runner-up finishes may never be eclipsed. Tiger Woods, on 15, has come as close as any player is likely to in the foreseeable future. To quote Shakespeare on Caesar, Nicklaus in golf 'doth bestride the narrow world like a Colossus, and we petty men walk under his huge legs and peep about'.

Growing up in Ohio, Nicklaus was a multi-talented athlete and natural ball player and was raised to be a golf superstar. He was nurtured by his businessman father, Charlie, himself a skilful all-round athlete and scratch golfer. Jack Nicklaus was on a plus-three handicap at the age of 13. He entered the game through a conventional pathway, attending Ohio State University and winning the US Amateur twice.

From the date he turned pro at 21, Nicklaus dominated the game in most areas, particularly with his ability to drive the ball off the tee with the small-headed persimmon drivers of his era. Those 'huge legs' of Nicklaus's generated massive power, propelling the ball high, straight and far, to the extent that he led the PGA Tour's total driving ratings in his early 40s. He had an uncanny ability to hole pressure putts at crucial times, and this underpinned his sublime shot-making and course-management skills.

Tiger Woods had an outstanding junior and college golf career, masterminded by his parents. His father, Earl, introduced him to golf at the age of two. His unmatched junior career culminated in 1994 with the first of his three US Amateur wins, when he became the youngest winner to date. He turned pro at 20, with a five-year US$40 million deal with Nike in his back pocket.

From an early age Nicklaus and Woods were destined for spectacular careers in golf. Their combined total of 33 majors speaks for itself.

Although Ian Baker-Finch's single major win places him in an elite group of golfers, his career record is modest when compared with the two undisputed greats of the sport, Nicklaus and Woods. Ian's career intersected, and at times coincided with, Nicklaus's and Woods's. While he played in their shadows in some respects, his early years in golf could hardly have differed more from theirs.

Nicklaus was coached from the age of ten by ex–PGA Tour player Jack Grout at Scioto Country Club, and Woods was introduced to his first professional coach, Rudy Duran, at the age of four. After six years with Duran, the young Tiger was coached by former PGA Tour player John Anselmo, before Butch Harmon took over in the later part of Woods's amateur career from 1993 through to 2004.

Ian was largely self-taught, and as Jennie puts it he 'learned to play golf from a book'. This education was supplemented by intermittent visits to Beerwah from benevolent pros like Denis Brosnan, Paul King and Charlie Earp. Ian faced obstacles in his obsession with golf. It is easy to visualise the overweight boy wearing hand-me-down shoes that were too small for him, struggling to catch the old 1940s bus to Caboolture High School as he carried his school case and treasured golf clubs in their lime-green golf bag.

On the bus he endured derision and sniggers from his peers because of his devotion to a sport few in the remote area could relate to. He survived by virtue of his good nature and determination, qualities still in evidence today. After school each day he cheerfully returned to Beerwah and walked the half mile from the bus stop to the golf club. Once there he would practise on the rough little country course, hewn out of forest and clay by his father and his friends, until the light failed.

There may not have been an indulgent father on hand to pay for lessons with top coaches, but Ian's parents were as supportive as they possibly could be, considering their lives centred on feeding six children while scraping out a living in tiny Peachester.

Ian had sufficient self-belief to turn pro at 15, starting with menial tasks at two country golf clubs. He turned his hand cheerfully to any task he was asked to perform by his benevolent bosses, including babysitting their children. Perhaps most importantly, he escaped the dreaded schoolwork to play a game he was obsessed with. He was living his own dream, while holding vague ambitions of playing in the few tournaments he could afford to enter during and after his three year traineeship. He then faced a further five years of struggle and grind as a player, when he seriously considered quitting the Australian Tour and taking a club job.

LIV Golf is likely to widen the gap between successful college golfers like Nicklaus and Woods and those golfers like Ian and Wayne Grady who come up through more modest pathways.

TONY AND JOAN

Ian's parents lived long and productive lives. 'Dad died suddenly in 2002 at the age of 80. He was very proud of his role in building the golf course at Beerwah, and I know he was proud of my achievements on the golf course.'

Tony and his friends' backbreaking work has paid off. Today, Beerwah Golf Club is thriving with over 900 members and a reputation for having the best greens on the Sunshine Coast – a far cry from the rough little nine holes of 1970.

'Mum lived until 2018, passing away at the age of 97. She always asked me, "How is Mike Harwood? How is Grades – and Peter Senior?" She remembered all my mates for the rest of her life, and even when I wasn't at home she lived her life with me to the fore. Mum kept a scrapbook and stayed interested right throughout her lifetime.'

Proud parents Tony and Joan Baker-Finch watch Ian's presentation speech at the 1991 Open on television.

The 2006 US Open champion, Geoff Ogilvy, spoke to Colt Knost on the *Subpar* podcast in February 2024 about the yawning chasm between the routes into the professional ranks. 'I feel for the kids coming out of school and being snapped up straight away. It is great for them, and they are going to make a lot of money, but there is a lot of learning, golf experience and a journey they are going to miss. There is something about travelling to a town with a bunch of people, grinding away at a game you are never really going to work out, staying in a crappy hotel, having dinner together and putting that on repeat. There is a really nice cadence in this journey and these college kids just going straight on to private jets are missing out on a bit of golf learning and the fun we all had on the grind in the early days.'

The 1984 Open Championship at St Andrews changed Ian's life and ended his five-year grind as a player. Miraculously, he found himself leading the stars of world golf after three rounds in his first major, and from that point the Baker-Finch story took on an almost fairytale quality. There was a win in Europe in 1985, three wins on the Japan Tour from 1987 and, in 1989, victory on the PGA Tour in his first few months in America. Then there was his dominant win in the Open in 1991. His first major looked like a prelude to future major titles, most likely another of his childhood holy grails – a second Open. Peter Thomson had tutored him like no other Australian golfer in the pursuit of that goal.

Jennie Baker-Finch played a significant role in all of this from 1984. Ian only blossomed as a player after Jennie agreed to join him on their first ambitious adventure to Europe. Their lives were transformed by Ian's success into something unimaginable during their early years growing up in Australia. Jennie has been unflappable, supportive and calm during Ian's career, especially during the dark years. Drew Robinson, Baker-Finch family friend and Ian's long-term accountant, observes, 'Ian and Jennie have had an amazing partnership. If it hadn't been for Jennie, Ian would not be where he is today. She has been his perfect back-up, and she has loved their life all the way through.'

In Ian's formative years, his career was boosted by his golf skills and personality, which attracted the interest of Peter Thomson. Similarly, Jack and Barbara Nicklaus could not have been kinder to the Baker-Finch family when they moved to Florida in 2001. There must have been something about Ian and Jennie to attract such support from two of the sport's greatest players.

It is easy to mock and belittle Baker-Finch the golfer by unfairly fast-forwarding his crash following the 1991 Open Championship win. He was better than that. His decline did not happen overnight, as evidenced by several good performances following Birkdale, including top ten finishes in two Masters and a second place in the Players Championship.

Even the television network Ian now works for, CBS, published a mean-spirited piece on their website, ranking Ian and his Troppo Tour friend Wayne Grady among the ten worst golfers to win a recent major championship. The poorly researched article was particularly brutal to Grady, who had come agonisingly close to an earlier major in 1989 before his PGA win in 1990.

The *Irish Times* wasted no time in responding two days later: 'Who's the muppet who wrote this article? What is the point of an article like this – to belittle those 10 major champions? [...] This kind of gutter golf writing will do him no favours.'

Australian golf writer Martin Blake summed it up in 2020: 'Baker-Finch won 17 times around the world and was inside the world's top-ten players in 1992. He was close to the best putter on the planet. His career stands up.'

When his crash did arrive, there were multiple reasons for it – no single factor was the reason for his loss of form.

IMG was undoubtedly a major factor in improving the financial position of many of its numerous clients, but was IMG a perfect fit for a world player like Ian? Possibly not.

In typical fashion, Ian blames no one but himself for his demise as a player.

Forty years on, Ian's first manager, Steve Frazer, who passed away in March 2024 during the writing of this book, retained a sense of sorrow and loss over Ian's change of management to IMG. Frazer also held a detectable element of anger about the way Ian was represented after his shift to the global giant.

IMG super-agent Hughes Norton was blindingly honest on the subject of player equipment contracts in his 2024 book, *Rainmaker* (co-authored by George Peper). Norton played a leading role in negotiating Greg Norman's contract with Spalding in the mid-1980s. He reflected that an agent's role is to always act in their player's best interest and to do everything possible to advance a client's competitive career. He analyses in some depth the harm that an unsuitable new high-spinning ball, the Tour Edition, did to Norman at his peak – particularly in the majors. He concludes, 'We should have walked away from the Spalding deal […] I failed him.'

As with Ian's Daiwa deal, IMG negotiated Norman's Spalding deal for a term of five years.

Ian shoulders responsibility for any of the decisions he made, including the equipment and ball choices that contributed to his decline. IMG profited from these equipment and endorsement deals, but did they adequately protect their client?

Ian may have loved Daiwa's iron heads but, as he said, 'Daiwa, being a fishing-rod company, were always developing new shafts and I was their test pilot.'

Ian's agents may have served him better by matching him with a Callaway or Titleist. As Ian's playing career declined, did IMG try hard enough to collect the large sums owing to their client at the end of the Titleist and Daiwa contracts?

Mike Clayton expressed his own view on IMG's influence in 2024. 'It is a myth that IMG are working for the player. If you are a player you are working for IMG, not the other way around. If there is a bucketload of money in a deal, they are getting paid twenty per cent of it and they do not care what equipment you end up playing with.'

Did Ian need to make significant changes to his swing at his peak? Top American coach Chris Como, sometime instructor for Tiger Woods, Bryson DeChambeau and Xander Schauffele, discussed this on the *No Laying Up* podcast. Como outlined the pitfalls of a top player making changes at their peak: 'The better the player, the bigger the risk. It is a long way down when you are a top-ten player in the world. Take Tiger in 2000 – in my mind that is the best anyone has ever swung a golf club. Does it make any sense to change that swing? I don't think it does.'

Ian's search for extra length from the tee should serve as a cautionary tale for all levels of golfer. For most golfers, it does not work – ever. Peter Thomson advised Ian against going down that path as did David Leadbetter. The fruitless search for extra length and taking advice from too many fellow players and a phalanx of coaches is on Ian – and no one else. Jennie was there and she reflects, 'He was one of the straightest drivers on the tour, but thought he needed more distance. Well, he really didn't. He was listening to too many people. Everyone gave him advice and he became so mixed up and confused.'

In the end he concluded that 'it wasn't my swing anymore', but he was the one who lost it. His book-learned technique was not too bad, based as it was on the Nicklaus method, and later modified by Thomson. When his swing was deconstructed, there was nothing left to build on. He had no idea where the ball was going, particularly with his driver. Bob Rotella's advice during those dark days was on point: when Ian no longer cared, his golf would return. Ian's game did return, sadly only long after his playing career was over.

Ian's work ethic was another factor contributing to the whole toxic cocktail of his form failure. Tony Baker-Finch had a reputation as the hardest-working man in Peachester, and his diligence and determination were passed down to Ian. But hard work solved nothing for Ian – all it did was place a strain on his body and further degrade his form.

For most major champions, a complete loss of playing ability would have been the end of the road for them in the game. That nightmarish image – 92, WD – on the giant yellow R&A scoreboard after 36 holes at the Open at Troon in 1997 would have broken less resilient men. But when the end came, Ian still had Jennie and his two girls, who meant everything to him. He rebounded immediately and his voice, natural ability, on-screen presence and extraordinary knowledge of golf delivered a lifeline.

Bitterness is not in the Baker-Finch make-up – neither Ian's nor Jennie's. Ian knew nothing else but golf at the time of his form crash and cheerfully worked hard to settle into a new role that he had no training for. Today, Ian has a quiet, barely detectable sense of satisfaction about his transition into a lengthy broadcasting career straight after the shock end to his playing days.

How many golfers achieve their dreams? Jennie sums it up perfectly. 'When I first met Ian, he told me his dream was to win the British Open. He told me that very early in our relationship. Winning the Open drove him from the beginning of our life together.' Ian's single major and single successful marriage have been a good formula for the country boy from a nine-hole course in rural Queensland.

Overall, Ian Baker-Finch, 1991 Champion Golfer of the Year, enjoys a happy and successful career in the sport he loves. Peeking out from under the layers of over-painting from five decades of success and failure, you can still see the boy from Beerwah, smiling at the good fortune of a life in golf.

Q&A: FINCHY ON THE FUTURE OF GOLF

*Compiled with assistance from
Martin Blake and Matthew Lancaster*

When you turned pro, you were a five handicapper. Paul Lawrie and Ian Poulter were similar. Is that pathway still open to young players today?

At 15 I was on a five handicap. There is still a pathway today to be a PGA pro as a trainee or teaching professional, but most good golfers do it differently now. They play amateur golf and, if they're good enough, they enter the Golf Australia program of elite training. They can compete in the Australian Open and state PGA events. Others may attend an American college and do a four-year course there – if they can make it through. No one will ever again do it the way we did.

You, Wayne Grady and others before you – Lee Trevino and Seve Ballesteros, to name two – all started playing on rough courses. How important is course quality to young players looking to play professionally?

Players like Wayne and Pete Senior and Greg Norman grew up on crappy Queensland courses, but we were forced to learn every shot.

We were not spoiled, that is for sure. Many elite American players come through great golf courses and country clubs, superbly conditioned with great driving ranges, but I do not think they are as hard as we were. That tough, earlier generation of Trevino, Ballesteros, Norman and Faldo, who grew up on municipal courses, had to deal with everything golf threw at them.

The ball rollback coming in 2028 – is it too little, too late? You have been vocal on this. Why do you think it is so important? Second, do you think the R&A and the USGA have moved quickly enough?

The ball rollback is far too little, far too late. A 5 per cent rollback will not make an appreciable difference. By the time it happens in 2028, the ball manufacturers will figure the ball out, much like the issue of square grooves on irons. They will find a way around the rollback. So I do not think it will make much difference, and indeed no difference to the average player. You will not see any difference unless you are swinging at over 100 miles an hour. I would have done 5 per cent immediately and then a further 5 per cent in four years.

What effect have the modern ball and the oversized driver had on classic courses like the Old Course at St Andrews and Merion in the US?

Something must be done because the tremendous old courses are being destroyed. For example, Merion was 6600 yards from the tips, but has now been stretched out to 7000 yards. When they play a major championship now on these classic old courses, they are forced to trick the courses up to keep them relevant by fertilising the rough and making it high, wet and juicy. Then they make the greens hard and fast. If they allow players to hit the ball 350 to 400 yards, 350 yards will become the norm, and we will lose all these great old courses. How do you build the same golf course for those who want to play 5000 yards and for those who need 8000 yards to make it relevant?

What about the short hitters who have won major championships, like Bill Rogers and Corey Pavin? Will we see that happen again?

That style of player has become irrelevant – gone completely. We will never see players like Corey Pavin, Jeff Sluman or Bill Rogers win a major again. You cannot survive hitting the ball 275 yards now, which used to be the longest hit 40 years ago. I agree with Geoff Ogilvy in saying that the courses should be firm, and that yardage is just one factor needed to test a player's skill. The longest hitter now hits it 100 yards longer than the average drive – which is ridiculous.

What about the driver head? Nowadays mishits do not seem to matter, so what size should the head be?

The first thing I would change is the driver's head size, which is an easy fix. Pro and elite-level amateurs should be made to use a 300-cubic-centimetre driver, and the other 99.5 per cent of the world's players could continue to use the big 460cc head. They also need to look at having a thicker face that does not have the trampoline effect these modern drivers have. With a smaller driver head and smaller sweet spot, the better players would be measurably better. In days gone by, driving was the most challenging part of the game; now, it is the easiest. In the 1990s the 250cc driver head looked so ridiculously big that I refused to use it for a couple of years.

Do you agree with the 2016 ban on anchoring in the putting stroke? Should it be allowed back at all levels of the amateur game?

This is a difficult one. What could work is if you made a rule that the putter had to be the shortest club in the bag for elite golfers. I certainly would not change it for regular golfers. No one wants to make the game harder than it already is – if you and I get the yips at 70 years of age, why not use the long putter? The arm-lock method that some players are using is controversial, too, and they will eventually ban it.

What about so-called 'rescue' clubs or hybrids as opposed to the old-school long irons?

Rescue clubs have taken over from long irons and changed the game. I know Freddie Couples, who's the same age as me, has a six-hybrid in the bag and a seven-iron is his longest iron. All amateurs should follow suit. Hybrids are far easier to hit in the air and to hit far and straight. You cannot do anything about that for elite golf, but in the old days you never reached the top level if you couldn't hit a one-iron or a two-iron. When the big-headed cavity-back irons came along, many more players became competitive. We used to look at some of the guys in the 1980s who played with shovels and Pings and thought they would never have made it without them. I still retain a traditionalist's image of wanting to hit a long iron properly. However, hybrids are good for the game because they allow everyone to hit the ball in the air.

Do caddies have too much to say and too much influence? Are they slowing play down?

Indeed, in pro golf, caddies are slowing the game down. I would like to see tour pros play in a threesome, and four and a half hours should be plenty of time to finish a round. Five and a half hours is ridiculous. We see it on television all the time – the caddies monotonously drone on over a shot, taking a minute or two to decide what the shot should be. Why is the caddie allowed to talk for a minute before the shot? I am a caddie fan, and they remain an essential part of the game. I have always enjoyed my relationships with my caddies, but caddies need to get out of the way when the time to hit the shot arrives.

Television viewers don't want to watch five- and six-hour rounds of golf. Do you have a solution?

The greens are too fast. They make the greens run at 14 on the stimpmeter. But once again that goes back to the length of the ball. With drivers hitting it so far, they cannot leave the courses defenceless at 6800 yards and with the greens running at ten on the stimpmeter. The pros would all shoot 60 under those conditions. So they trick it up by making the greens so fast that, when the wind blows, the game takes an hour longer than it should. I would have greens running at 12 on the stimpmeter as the fastest speed. The tours have tried to fix the problem of slow play by having fewer players in the field. This approach is wrong, and players need to be fined if they are too slow or, better still, penalised two shots.

Should announcers be allowed more space to tell a story in the style of Peter Alliss? Do viewers need to see every shot?

It would be nice for an announcer to have more time to weave a story like the great Peter Alliss. However, golf viewers are on social media and surveys say they want to see more golf. So our producers show shot, shot, shot all the time, which gives the announcer less time to say anything. We have too many voices on the telecast. We could do it with two or three in the tower and one or two on the ground. Each person would have more time because they wouldn't have to deal with so many voices but, yes, I personally prefer an Australian or European style of commentary, where there's more time to tell a story, like Sam Torrance, Tony Johnstone and others.

Is Greg Norman's 30-year-old version of a world tour realistic?

The PGA Tour will never travel and will always stay American-centric. The money from Saudi Arabia and the Middle East should go to the DP World Tour, which has been the world tour for the last 30 years. This would allow the PGA Tour to become even more US-centric. The US players do not want to travel extensively and, by choice, may travel only once or twice a year. Middle Eastern money has been involved in golf in Europe for over a decade, with tournaments in Dubai and Qatar, so it seems natural that they have aligned with Europe. Additionally, the Saudis should not have taken the PGA Tour on. The main sponsor for the PGA Tour, US television, only wants golf in US time zones.

What are your thoughts on Greg Norman's original concept generally?

The first point to make is that a 'world tour' was not Norman's idea – it was Mark McCormack's back in the 1960s but it was shot down at the time by Arnold Palmer. Greg Norman had a similar concept in 1994. Someone at Fox had said, 'We will fund the concept and get it off the ground. If you get your thirty best mates to play the world tour, we will cover it.' Norman was a long way off signing 30 players and did not even get close to those numbers. It was not like the Saudis were there behind Greg in the 1990s with the US$1 billion they throw into LIV each year now.

Do you see the three tours ever combining?

I do not think LIV, PGA and DP World Tour will ever merge. I believe LIV can be the Formula One, if you will, of golf. The top 50 players, say, go and play team golf for three rounds with shotgun starts and whatever; it is their tour. I am disappointed that the PGA Tour seems to have followed suit with prize money increases, no cuts and shorter fields. Initially the Tour said how stupid and wrong it was, but now they seem to have done the same thing. They pay the best players more, have fewer players and have fewer playing opportunities for young players. It would have been better if they had just stayed with what they had and allowed those players who wanted to leave to go ahead and leave.

What drives Greg Norman? Do you think he is driven by revenge against the US Tour for rejecting his ideas 30 years ago?

Money, plus he wants to be back at the top of the golf world in some form. He should just be happy and proud of what he has already achieved. He was No 1 in the world for half a dozen years and Greg was a great player. He won a couple of majors and close to 100 tournaments worldwide. But he has this revenge or anger within him, whatever it may be.

Having seen golf at the Olympics up close, do you ever see the Olympics becoming equal to the majors?

It has already happened in the women's game. The gold medal is the most prized trophy in women's golf. The status of Olympic gold in the men's game will continue to grow. Scottie Scheffler, with a gold medal and a green jacket in 2024, is as good as it gets. Women's

Olympic golf rates higher on television than any other golf event for women.

What about your golf? Where do you play and what is your handicap nowadays? Did Bob Rotella's comment that you would recapture your game once you stopped caring turn out to be true?

When I am healthy and playing regularly, I am a plus-two handicapper at Jupiter Hills Club. I fly the ball 250 yards, in the fairway every time. On a good day my clubhead speed is around 100 miles per hour. That is not long enough to play the PGA Tour Champions. I still love the game and I played about 200 games last year. Back in the mid-1990s, when I missed every cut on the PGA Tour, I would get home and still turn up to play with my mates on Saturdays. Bob Rotella said to me, 'The only thing you need to try harder at is trying less.' I understand where he was coming from. I also believe I could have solved my problems for myself with aid of the science that is now in the game.

Finally, if you could change one decision in your golf career, what would it be?

Very, very easy. Do not play in the 1997 Open Championship at Troon!

BIBLIOGRAPHY

Clayton, Mike. *Golf from the Inside.* Carlton North: Scribe, 2004.

Concannon, Dale. *Nick Faldo: Driven.* London: Virgin, 2001.

Crockett, Andrew. *Bump and Run: At the feet of the masters.* Andrew Crockett, 2016.

James, Russell. *David Graham: From ridicule to acclaim.* Melbourne: Ryan, 2012.

Lawrie, Paul with John Huggan. *An Open Book: The Paul Lawrie story.* DB, 2012.

Mitchell, Peter. *The Complete Golfer: Peter Thomson.* Melbourne: Lothian, 1991.

Newton, Jack with Peter Stone. *Out of the Rough: The Jack Newton story.* Ringwood: Viking, 2001.

Nicklaus, Jack. *My 55 Ways to Lower Your Golf Score.* New York: Simon & Schuster, 1985.

Nicklaus, Jack with Ken Bowden. *Golf My Way.* New York: Simon & Schuster, 1974.

Norton, Hughes and George Peper. *Rainmaker: Superagent Hughes Norton and the money-grab explosion of golf from Tiger to LIV and beyond.* New York: Atria Books, 2024.

Reid, Kenny. *Seve Ballesteros's Touch of Class: The 1984 Open Championship and the meaning of Europe's greatest golfer.* Chichester: Pitch Publishing, 2024.

Williams, Steve. *Steve Williams: Out of the Rough.* Auckland: Penguin, 2015.

ACKNOWLEDGEMENTS

THIS BOOK OWES its publication in no small measure to the late Peter Thomson. I first met Peter while playing the New Zealand circuit as a young amateur golfer in the mid-1970s.

Our friendship continued over time and in 1997 I was tasked by my club, the Christchurch Golf Club, to work with Thomson Wolveridge Perrett to restore the links character to the course, the Shirley Links.

In February 2015 Peter made his last trip to Christchurch to complete the final design work on Shirley. At the age of 85, despite being in the grip of Parkinson's disease, he was in fine form and remained enthusiastic about the project. Over a glass of wine at home at Clearwater Golf Resort, totally unprompted, Peter ruefully outlined what he termed 'the saddest story in golf' – the sudden decline of Ian Baker-Finch. Before retiring for the night, I jotted down Peter's thoughts about Ian's decline, thinking nothing more of it for five years.

I dropped Peter back to Christchurch Airport the next day and sadly never saw him again before his death in 2018.

I had been fascinated with Ian's career, as my wife, Maree, and I had followed him extensively at the 1984 Open at St Andrews where we both witnessed at close range the young Australian's traumatic last-round collapse. We returned to St Andrews in 1990, observing

Ian's more robust handling of the final-round pressure, in a prelude to his commanding Open win at Royal Birkdale in 1991.

After completing *Sir Bob Charles: The Biography* in 2020, I found my handwritten notes on Ian Baker-Finch. On a rainy winter Sunday in Christchurch, I wrote a magazine-length article on Ian titled 'To Hell and Back' for our New Zealand *The Cut* golf magazine. It was published and then re-printed in the UK. I wrote to Ian about my interest in his story and arranged to meet him at the Old Course Hotel during the 2022 Open. He explained how journalists had been asking him to write his story for years and how he had rebuffed these approaches, possibly finding some of the narrative around his career decline painful. He was pleasant and polite while patiently listening to my 'pitch'.

I persevered and we met again in Queensland at the end of 2022 in Marcoola on the Sunshine Coast for a coffee. Ian was animated and fully engaged in the possible book project. We shook hands after two hours or so and I left with my first interview, which mainly concentrated on his equipment and ball challenges post-1991. His parting shot: 'I have procrastinated too long – let's do it.'

We met regularly at Twin Waters Golf Club in Queensland in late 2023, by which stage Ian had facilitated my interviewing many of his playing contemporaries, friends and his two bosses from his trainee days. By year end we had completed an outline for the book and a number of completed chapters.

Ian's lovely wife, Jennie, became a key part of the book by contributing her own memories to the story. Her astute overview of her husband's career as player and broadcaster is a key ingredient of the story, unlocked by our daughter Anna Saunders, the genuine writer in our family. Thank you, Anna, for your patience, editing and insightful interviews of Jennie.

ACKNOWLEDGEMENTS

To Maree, yet again you have patiently endured my obsessive writing practices while providing your continuous valuable overview of the book, together with the endless proofreading. To Will, I have appreciated your patience in dealing with my technical challenges, and to Dave, thanks for your ongoing, understated support.

A great deal of research on the book content was completed by Matthew Lancaster from Auckland; his contribution to the book has been major in terms of time, research and proofreading. Thank you sincerely for your commitment, Matt.

Des Frith of d.Design was his usual creative and helpful self to me in the early stages of the book and came back into his own at the later stage of photo selection. I greatly appreciate Des's help in sorting and selecting the images for the book, as do Ian and his family.

My hickory golfing companion, Andrew Baker from South Australia, only became involved in the latter stages of the book but his input and guidance were significant. Andrew's writing skills and ordered brain came into their own in his chronological rearrangement of the mid-section of the book. He also assisted with the final photo selections and photo editing.

I enlisted a keen and at times interchangeable group of readers during the writing of Ian's biography. My sincere thanks go to: Bruce Taylor, Geoffrey Shaw, Don Hope, Paul Betar, Robyn Puckett, Simon Robinson, Nicholas Davidson, John Goodwin, Craig Dickinson, Peter Williams, Des Frith, Marion Heller, Kevin Armstrong, Bruce Young, Andrew Baker, Jeff Latch, Greg Ramsay and Brendan Telfer. Our friend from Noosa Springs Graeme Rothwell was part of the informal-reviewing group and, with his wife, Liz, went further in generously allowing me to use their family home as my base to write the book, enabling me to catch up regularly with Ian and Jennie on the Sunshine Coast.

ACKNOWLEDGEMENTS

That 'Senior Pro' of golf writers, Malcolm Campbell from the Kingdom of Fife, was his usual supportive self. Malcolm carried his guidance over from my first book to the second by reading the manuscript through all its tortured stages, providing invaluable advice on editing and publishing.

I am very grateful to the group of Ian's friends and playing contemporaries who provided their time, interviews and insights for the book. My sincere thanks are due to Ian Elks, Denis Brosnan, Garry Wright, Tim and Jenny Bell, John Downs, Charlie Earp, Wayne Grady, Celeste Kutek, Peter Senior, Mike Clayton, John Mellish, Greg Turner, John Lister, Mary Thomson, Peter Williams, Stuart Reese, Steve Williams, Paul Smith, David Begg, Bruce Young, Mike Harwood, Peter Headland, Ian's former manager, the late Steve Frazer, and Ian's close friend and accountant, Drew Robinson.

Thankfully, the team at Hardie Grant in Melbourne were enthusiastic about the project from the outset. Pam Brewster (with Sandy Grant in the background) guided me through the early stages patiently and skilfully, appointing the experienced golf writer Martin Blake as the book's editor. Martin has pruned and enhanced the manuscript. Claire Davis, the project editor for the book, has been a joy to work with. Many thanks Pam, Claire and Martin; we all worked together harmoniously.

Finally, to Ian and Jennie, thank you for the significant leap of faith in my direction in allowing me to record your amazing story – it has been a privilege.

Geoff Saunders 2024